Helion & Company Limited
Unit 8 Amherst Business Centre
Budbrooke Road
Warwick
CV34 5WE
England
Tel. 01926 499 619
Email: info@helion.co.uk
Website: www.helion.co.uk
Twitter: @helionbooks
Visit our blog http://blog.helion.co.uk/

Designed and typeset by Farr out Publications, Wokingham, Berkshire
Cover design by Paul Hewitt, Battlefield Design (www.battlefield-design.co.uk)

ISBN 978-1-804510-18-6

British Library Cataloguing-in-Publication Data
A catalogue record for this book is available from the British Library

CONTENTS

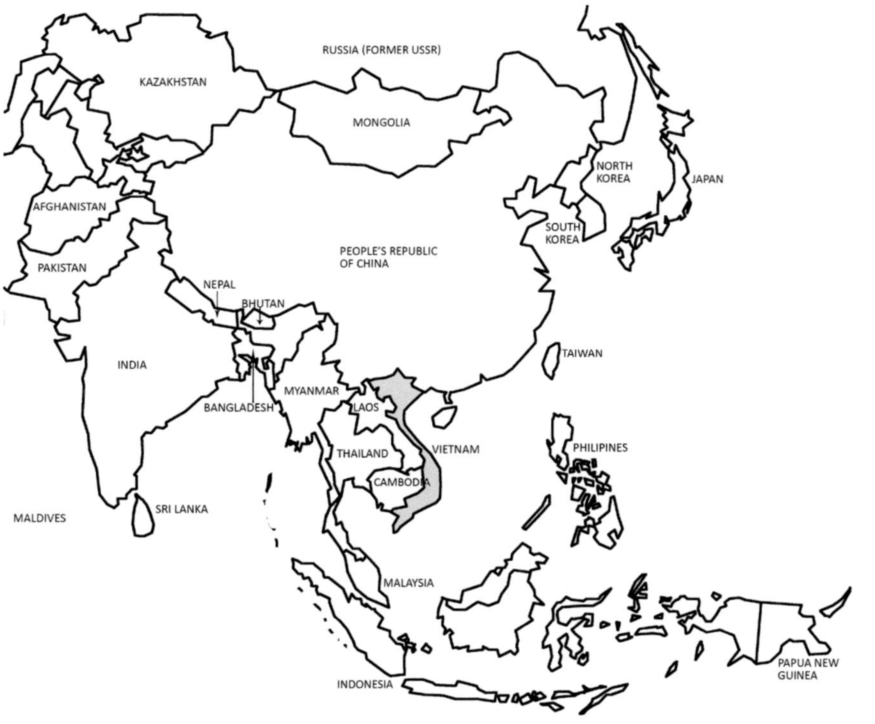

Note: In order to simplify the use of this book, all names, locations and geographic designations are as provided in *The Times World Atlas*, or other traditionally accepted major sources of reference, as of the time of described events.

Dedication

For my family – who have helped me throughout with their love, encouragement, patience and wisdom. Thank You.

The symbol of the Strategic Hamlet Programme – showing the 'Flaming Torch of Freedom'. (Author's collection)

ABBREVIATIONS

ARVN	Army of the Republic of South Vietnam
CIA	Central Intelligence Agency
GVN	Government of (South) Vietnam
NSAM	National Security Action Memorandum
NVA	North Vietnamese Army
PAVN	People's Army of (North) Vietnam
SDC	Self-Defence Corps
US	United States
USOM	United States Operations Mission (local office of United States Agency for International Development)
VC	Viet Cong

Note: Many of the sources used in this research are translated from original Vietnamese documentation. As such, spelling and grammatical errors are left unaltered unless they significantly hinder the reader's understanding. In addition, several captured documents are identified by their date of capture rather than publication.

INTRODUCTION

> Gosh, when they cut off hands, they cut off heads, they put a village chief's head on a pole, not always but very often, and they impressed the kids. They would go in at night, "Join us or else."
>
> Elbridge Durbrow, Oral History Interview, 3 June 1981.[1]

The first volume in this series examined the counterinsurgency plans of the South Vietnamese government and their American allies. It looked at the Strategic Hamlet Programme and the Viet Cong response. This second volume moves on to explain how the insurgents began to gain the upper hand in the conflict and why the best-laid plans of President Diem and his allies failed. In *Hunting the Viet Cong, The Counterinsurgency Campaign in South Vietnam 1961-1963 (Volume 1: The Strategic Hamlet Programme)*, it was revealed that the early American involvement in South Vietnam was based on solid foundations: a detailed counterinsurgency strategy (built around the British policy in Malaya) was in place. There were also experts 'on the ground' advising the South Vietnamese government and American money was aiding the Army of the Republic of Vietnam (ARVN) in their fight against the insurgency. Indeed, the Viet Cong themselves admitted that the strategy was 'cutting them up'. Why did things start to go wrong? This volume tries to answer that question.

The second volume also examines an often-neglected aspect of the study of the Vietnam War: the extent of Viet Cong atrocities and violence and the terror inflicted on civilians by the insurgents. Civilians were beheaded, kidnapped and murdered; children were threatened and disfigured as punishment for attending school and fear of reprisals meant that much of the population in South Vietnam acquiesced to the insurgents' demands.

Using interviews with a variety of South Vietnamese sources (including the Viet Cong themselves) this volume reveals how fear

Viet Cong fighters pose for a photograph as part of their training with old bolt-action rifles. Many VC received covert training from the North Vietnamese Army. (Communist Archive/Albert Grandolini collection)

Viet Cong volunteers mix with NVA (North Vietnamese Army) recruits to undergo jungle weapons training. Notice the rudimentary camouflage on some helmets and weapons: in common with ARVN at this time, there was very little standardisation in this area. (Communist Archive/Albert Grandolini collection)

was a major weapon in the insurgent armoury: people supported the side they thought could protect them from violence. It also examines American measures intended to thwart the insurgents and the overall effectiveness of counterinsurgency policy at this time. Finally, the book presents several theories and concepts to help explain why a well-planned counterinsurgency programme failed. Unfortunately, far too many of the errors committed between 1961 and early 1964 were to be repeated throughout the entire Vietnam War.

Structure

The book opens with a brief recap of events between 1961 and 1963 and then moves on to examine the reasons for the eventual collapse of the Strategic Hamlet Programme and the fall of the Diem regime. The book introduces three themes (on a chapter-by-chapter basis) that help explain why the Viet Cong appeared to gain the upper hand in the conflict. The first theme reveals that terror was a crucial weapon for the insurgency. The Vietnamese population did not have confidence in their government and in its ability to protect them. Many people (particularly in the rural areas) knew that once government forces left their region, they would be easy targets for the Viet Cong. This meant their support was conditional and transitory.

The second theme developed in the book will show that many government initiatives were poorly implemented and actually alienated the very people they were designed to help. For example, farmers had to cut down their bamboo cash crop to build defences to protect their homes. This lost them valuable income and caused resentment against government officials. The final theme will demonstrate that there were recurring problems in the South Vietnamese and Kennedy administrations. Experts and officials 'on the ground' were ignored, successes and failures were difficult to determine and those with a real knowledge and understanding of South Vietnam were marginalised in official planning meetings. All of these factors reduced the effectiveness of the counterinsurgency strategy and led, in part, to the overthrow of President Diem. By early 1964, the Strategic Hamlet Programme was abandoned and South Vietnam began its descent into chaos. The book concludes with an analysis of this failure: what went wrong? How can the mistakes made in South Vietnam be avoided in future campaigns?

There were lots of imaginative uses of animals in the conflict. Here, an ARVN patrol goes into the jungle with elephants acting as logistical support and transportation. (Albert Grandolini collection)

In response, the South Vietnamese government, in a somewhat haphazard coalition with its American allies, developed a counterinsurgency strategy aimed at defeating the insurgents (now renamed as Viet Cong). The focus of this campaign was the Strategic Hamlet Programme. This programme was based on the British counterinsurgency effort used in the Malayan Emergency. It saw the construction of fortified villages aimed at protecting the rural peasants from Viet Cong attack and also aimed to isolate the insurgents from popular support. There were other events worth mentioning too. For example, in 1962 Australia sent its first advisory mission to South Vietnam: The Australian Army Training Team Vietnam (AATTV) initially numbered just 30 advisors. By the end of the war, over 60,000 Australians served in South Vietnam and fought bravely throughout the conflict. There were also increasing numbers of US Marines stationed in air bases around the country protecting US Advisors and American materiel. This second volume will explain why events turned against the South Vietnamese government and led, eventually to the overthrow of the Diem regime and his assassination: it also resulted in the increase in American involvement that triggered the tragedy that was the Vietnam War.

Recap of Key Events

South Vietnam had been plagued by violence since its creation as a nation but after 1960 the insurgency exploded. Between 1961 and 1963 the government of South Vietnam battled against a ruthless, violent insurgency. This insurgency had its roots in the Viet Minh struggle against French colonialism and was seen by many of its supporters to be a continuation of this conflict: with the Americans replacing the French as the targets. In addition, the government of Ngo Dinh Diem was portrayed as being corrupt, out of touch with ordinary people and accused of being a lackey for American colonialism. Many rural communities were attacked and the nation's capital, Saigon, came under assault from bombs and terror campaigns.

1
JUST SHOOT

Why violence was more important than winning 'Hearts and Minds'

> You just shoot. This hearts and minds and this hearts and flowers, do-gooder stuff is beautiful, but when you are in a war, you have got to go in to win.
>
> Elbridge Durbrow, Former Ambassador to South Vietnam, Oral History Interview I, 3 June 1981.[1]

What did Winning 'Hearts and Minds' Really Mean?

How Did the Diem-US Alliance Try to Win Popular Support (1)? 'Hearts and Minds'?

One of the aims of the counterinsurgency strategy implemented in South Vietnam between 1961 and 1963 was to win the support of the local people by implementing social, political and economic change.[2] This was often casually referred to as 'winning hearts and minds.'[3] The idea of 'hearts and minds' was a concept used by the British during the Malayan Emergency and was developed by policy makers such as Sir Robert Thompson.[4] As Thompson was a key advisor to President Diem in the initial stages of the Strategic Hamlet Programme, it was unsurprising that this idea helped lay a foundation for the counterinsurgency strategy in South Vietnam.[5] Unfortunately, whilst the counterinsurgents were trying to win popular support, the insurgents were busy attacking and intimidating the population. As Durbrow noted, a 'hearts and minds' strategy could sometimes preclude or diminish the effectiveness of military action. Durbrow was correct in maintaining that in the context of South Vietnam, 'hearts and minds' may have been misunderstood and actually greater levels of threat and violence were needed to win the war.[6]

However, despite Durbrow's suggestion about levels of violence, winning support would be achieved in less pugnacious ways. Firstly, by increasing the 'degree of physical security' and protecting people from insurgent attack and secondly, by 'enacting social, economic, and political reform meaningful to the peasants in the context of their own traditions and expectations.'[7] A Department of State report, 1 July 1963 described some of these reforms in detail:

Inside the hamlets, the government has taken increasing measures to improve the general lot of the peasant. It has established permanent dispensaries or sent in medical teams, where once modern medical attention was unknown; it has established or rebuilt schools, formerly non-existent or destroyed by the Communists; it has built market places where farmers can bring their produce in order to encourage business; and new roads, wells, and a number of community development projects have been started. Agricultural credit and fertiliser have been provided to the farmer, and agricultural technicians have come to help the farmer improve production.[8]

Female Viet Cong operatives plan a mission whilst hiding in the jungle of South Vietnam. A notable feature of VC activity was the use of women to promote and pursue the insurgents' agenda. Note the rifle grenade. (Communist Archive/Albert Grandolini collection)

Viet Cong volunteers and new NVA recruits take part in a training march through the jungle with a wide mix of attire and field kit. (Communist Archive/Albert Grandolini collection)

Diem called these measures the 'infrastructure of democracy' and stressed that they were – in conjunction with the protection of the people – the 'key to wider public support' for his regime.[9] Harkins agreed and noted in a letter to President Diem, 23 February 1963, that the military effort was 'just half the battle' and alongside military programmes, there had to be other measures enacted 'such as public health, education, agricultural assistance, psychological warfare, etc.'[10] Successful implementation of these reforms, would in his words, be 'necessary to win the hearts and minds of the people.'[11] Whilst 'hearts and minds' may not have been explicitly stressed in every counterinsurgency document, the underlying principles of winning over the local population held true. However, as this chapter will demonstrate, these measures were not always successful in combating the insurgency.

Bicycles and Micro-motors

How Did the Diem-US Alliance Try to Win Popular Support (2)? Improving People's Lives

The reason for wanting to win over the 'hearts and minds' of the rural Vietnamese was that the Diem-American strategists realised – in common with the insurgents – that the Viet Cong's access to rural communities gave them a distinct advantage in the war. In a Memorandum from the Chairman of the Vietnam Task Force

Viet Cong and NVA soldiers photographed whilst attacking a strategic hamlet. (Communist Archive/Albert Grandolini collection)

The Viet Cong recruits here are checking, collecting and organising munitions for future distribution to VC cells around South Vietnam. These include rifle grenades. The VC had numerous ammunition dumps and bases hidden deep within the South Vietnamese jungle. (Communist Archive/Albert Grandolini collection)

(Cottrell) to the President's Military Representative (Taylor), it was noted how the 'Communist operation starts from the lowest social level–the villages' and that the 'battle must be joined and won at this point' or the war would eventually be lost.[12] In order to do this, it was recognised that the lives of the rural population needed to be improved. A paper prepared by the vice president stated that people needed better houses, schools and health services. These would enhance their lives and make support for the government far more likely because they needed 'an understanding government' which was 'close to them and in which they feel a stake.'[13]

Improving the lives of the rural poor could be done in many ways and the strategic hamlet was the focus of this effort. In a Central Intelligence Agency (CIA) telegram entitled simply *Strategic Hamlets*, it was recognised that wealth and modernisation were the keys to defeating communism.[14] It was claimed that the reason for this was that 'the effect of distributing bicycles with micro-motors' would make 'the peasant mobile' and change 'his mode of life' and improve the living standards of rural communities.[15] The telegram went on to claim that the strategic hamlets would 'afford the necessary protection and economic base for such a modernising programme' and that they would enable political reform and institutional capacity to be enhanced.[16] For example, the telegram noted that the hamlets would 'afford a basis for the building of institutions in Vietnam to give additional stability, e.g., co-operatives, medical services, education, women's movements, youth movements, etc.' and all of these initiatives would enhance support for the Diem regime.[17] This optimism was shared by other counterinsurgents and the CIA were not the only ones who were encouraged by the potential for change afforded by the hamlet programme. In a letter to the Joint Chiefs of Staff, General Wheeler claimed that the hamlets were 'the vehicle by which the Government of Vietnam can carry forward a political, economic, and social revolution.'[18] Also, Hilsman noted that many captains and majors on the ground were in favour of a greater emphasis being placed on 'more civil and political action programmes' and a reduction in sweep operations in the countryside to try and win over rural support.[19]

In addition to building institutions, the strategic hamlets were designed to be a focal point for increased economic growth and humanitarian aid. Although it was acknowledged that South Vietnam from 1955 onwards had been 'highly dependent upon the US' for economic and military aid (totalling an estimated \$1.4 billion) it was felt that American aid would bring about favourable economic conditions.[20] Indeed, the CIA believed that because of American backing the Government of (South) Vietnam (GVN) had been 'able to achieve appreciable economic progress' and this would continue with the Strategic Hamlet Programme.[21] This was due to observers being able to clearly see the improvements made in infrastructure in government controlled territories. It was stated that there was a clear distinction to be discerned in terms of economic development between government and insurgent-held areas. For example, a memorandum of 4 April 1963 claimed that it was possible to distinguish between GVN-controlled territories

A well-known feature of the Viet Cong insurgency was the use of home-made booby traps. Here young and old alike construct a punji stake pit – the sharp bamboo was often covered in faeces to infect anyone unlucky enough to fall into the trap. (Communist Archive/Albert Grandolini collection)

'where roads and bridges were repaired and strategic hamlets built' and the less-developed 'VC territory where the bridges were generally down and the roads cut.'[22] This apparent physical manifestation of the counterinsurgency strategy was also leading to 'considerably more optimism among Vietnamese officials' about the progress of the war.[23] Other economic successes were noted by USOM who instigated pig-breeding programmes, helped build schools and brought medical aid out into the countryside. This had a notable effect on the rural Vietnamese. One villager noted that even as early as 1961, the impact of American aid was positive.[24] Other villagers were equally effusive; one claimed that 'as I know now, the Americans came here to help us because we are poor. They bring in money to give us but will not want anything back.'[25] Another talked about how aid was improving the popularity of the Americans amongst the rural poor, claiming that:

> The people began to like the Americans very much. They saw that the Americans gave them all kinds of aid. At Hau Nghia there is an American USOM [United States Operations Mission] captain, he gave us metal sheets and cement. In fact, we would rather ask something from the Americans than from our own people. They just give to us and we do not have to produce any papers. They [the Americans] say give and they give. Now the people here have seen the Americans help them.[26]

All these positive comments helped create an upbeat mood amongst many of those involved in the counterinsurgency operation. Heavner reported that whilst overall progress in the war was not assured, the economic measures aimed at increasing rice production and farmer income could 'work a revolution in rural Vietnam.'[27]

How Did the Diem-US Alliance Try to Win Popular Support (3)? Democratic Reform: 'Rice Roots Democracy'

Economic aid was also to be supported by democratic change. One way in which the hamlets would attempt to win support for the Diem regime was by building institutions aimed at increasing democratic participation and re-designing local democratic processes. Introducing elections was one such way in which a so-called 'rice roots democracy' could be brought to rural areas.[28] This was defined as being 'the application of law and order to rural life' and the residents of each strategic hamlet were to be assured that this law would be applied by the authorities within the hamlet.[29] This was important because these authorities would – in theory – be elected by the residents of the hamlet themselves.[30] This would allow for 'a system of democratisation appropriate to the community' which would remain relatively autonomous even if there were changes of government in Saigon.[31] Increasing local democracy in such a way was considered to have several benefits. Firstly, it enabled the establishment of community administrations that would be more responsive to the village needs. Secondly, although there were doubts cast on the validity of some democratic processes, village chiefs were, as Heavner noted, 'not immune to social pressures. They *live* in the hamlet' and as such they had to respond to the real grievances of the people.[32] Thirdly, this response to peoples' needs would establish a link between the Saigon regime and the villagers on the ground.[33] Therefore, in theory, this increasing democratisation would result in villagers being able to identify the needs of their communities and respond accordingly. On his tours of South Vietnam, Rufus Phillips described how this link between the rural peasantry and the government would result in the needs of the people being met.[34] This would also increase their sense of belonging to the nation and their subsequent support for the government.[35] Phillips went on to say that these reforms would bring rural communities 'into the orbit of the nation' and give them an 'active participation in the reconstruction and defence of the country.'[36] Phillips was not alone in holding this view. Other participants in South Vietnam, such as Ambassador Nolting, believed that these changes within the hamlets would 'significantly' alter the nature of the war in South Vietnam and the CIA claimed that progress towards defeating the insurgency would be seen within 18 months of August 1962.[37] It is interesting to note not only how much faith people in the higher echelons of government placed in the hamlet programme (considering how quickly it was abandoned after Diem's assassination) but the CIA's comments also indicated that the Americans were planning to be in Vietnam past 1964 and offer support as needed. This would seem to suggest a willingness to a longer-term commitment to South Vietnam itself.

However, despite these reforms, the insurgents still held the advantage when it came to winning the support of the people. The rest of this chapter will show that this was due, in part, to their ability to intimidate the local population and the government's inability to protect the people. The Diem regime may have been building schools and hospitals in an attempt to win 'hearts and minds' but

An oft-neglected area of study is the influence of the NVA on the Viet Cong training. Here Viet Cong recruits are being instructed in the use of heavy machine guns at an unnamed Viet Cong jungle base. (Communist Archive/Albert Grandolini collection)

Yet another example of NVA training of Viet Cong recruits – this time in anti-aircraft fire with an American .30-cal machine gun fitted with a water cooling sleeve. (Communist Archive/Albert Grandolini collection)

the people were more scared of reprisals from the Viet Cong. They were making a rational choice to support the insurgency and stay alive. This was because, as yet another unnamed villager noted, the strategic hamlets improved their lifestyle but not their security.[38]

The Terror of the Viet Cong

Using Fear as a Strategy

One of the underlying principles behind the 'Counterinsurgency Plan' and the Strategic Hamlet Programme was a desire to provide security for the general population of South Vietnam. However, any attempts to do so were undermined by the Viet Cong who were more than ready to use terror to further their cause and demonstrate the ineffectiveness of the Diem regime's efforts to protect the people.

In a speech given at Fort Bragg in 1961, Walt Rostow argued that it was essential for the insurgents to gain rural support in order to be successful and that they would do this, not through the promotion of ideology as was often stated, but through fear. Rostow claimed that 'the Viet Cong are not trying to persuade the peasants of Vietnam that communism is good: they are trying to persuade them that their lives are insecure unless they co-operate with them' and as such, terror would become an instrumental method in this process.[39] The Taylor Mission concurred with this and suggested that 'guerrilla forces must rely primarily on terror (and) intimidation' to further their cause.[40] This was important because not only did it demonstrate the insurgents' strength, it also fed into 'the notion that US weakness makes the Viet Cong the local wave of the future' because it showed the inability of the counterinsurgents to protect the people.[41] Furthermore, as the war progressed, it was envisaged that an increase in terrorism 'should be expected' and although this would be the insurgents admitting defeat, it would cause 'unfavourable publicity' in the American press and could undermine the overall counterinsurgency effort.[42]

Establishing a VC Presence

However, violent attacks were not part of the initial tactics used by the insurgents. Violence was often preceded by psychological

One strength of the insurgency was its ability to adapt to the terrain and the environment. Here the VC launch a water-based assault on a strategic hamlet – the defenders were taken by surprise as the river had acted as one of the barriers preventing access to the hamlet itself. (Communist Archive/Albert Grandolini collection)

intimidation. Although the insurgents were happy – as will be demonstrated later in this section – to use physical violence to achieve their goals, they often promoted what they called a 'presence' to intimidate people and gain control of the population.[43] Pearce, in his research report for US think tank RAND, described this 'presence' as being less formal than government structures but instead claimed it was a 'subtle' influencing of people through activities such as tax collection, sniper fire and the distribution of roadside propaganda.[44] This often took place in villages that were not under insurgent control.[45] Pearce went on to claim that occasionally this 'presence' would be backed up by armed force and that by maintaining an informal attachment to a village, the insurgents were able to avoid discovery by the government.[46] They also had a 'psychological' hold over the villagers who were constantly reminded of Viet Cong activity.[47] The result of this was that many villagers were 'clearly afraid' to discuss events for fear of

Another home-made trap awaits unsuspecting ARVN patrols in the jungle. This trap would be attached to a high branch and then swing down to impale an unlucky victim. Edward Lansdale demonstrated this type of trap to Robert McNamara in an attempt to help him understand the insurgency: McNamara was unimpressed and could not understand the point of the demonstration. (Communist Archive/Albert Grandolini collection)

The Viet Cong would often lay traps on key walkways and pathways. The traps could be covered with a bamboo sheet and then mud or soil would be placed on top. The traps were often marked out with a broken branch or collection of stones – indicating their position to friendly units. (Communist Archive/Albert Grandolini collection)

being identified as government sympathisers and as a consequence, did not want to encounter 'violent retribution' from the Viet Cong.[48] What is interesting is that Pearce's study took place in the village of Duc Lap (Hau Nghia Province) which he claimed had never been fully under insurgent jurisdiction and even here would indicate the full extent and reach of the insurgents' 'presence' in South Vietnam.[49] The apparent fear that had manifested itself in the minds of the local Vietnamese was an indication of just how successful the insurgents were in their intimidation of the local population.

A Rational Tool of War?

Establishing a 'presence' was not the only way in which the Viet Cong instilled fear into the people: they also attacked them. This ability to terrorise and intimidate the local population was a deliberate action based around the perceived tactical and strategic advantage that it gave the insurgency. A report on the strategic hamlets in February 1963 noted that the Viet Cong 'always considered the Hamlet as an ideal field for the implementation of their plan of subversion': intimidation was one way to gain control of these areas and further their cause.[50] Douglas Pike agreed with this but also argued – in his overview of how terror was used in the war – that employing violence was seen as a failure of policy and was not something undertaken lightly by the insurgents.[51] Instead, it was simply another tool in their fight against the government and there was an intellectual rationale for its application: terror was part of a logical process that enabled the Viet Cong to wield control over the rural population.[52] In summarising this approach, Pike stated that:

One consequence of Viet Cong terror was the way in which intimidated civilians would turn a blind eye to smuggled goods or (due to threats) allow weapons to find their way into VC hands. Here, shells are hidden inside boxes labelled as banana cargo. (Communist Archive/Albert Grandolini collection)

The scale of goods supplied to the Viet Cong became apparent as ammunition dumps were discovered deep in the jungle, here with anti-tank rockets. Many civilians would lead ARVN to these dumps once they felt safe from VC attack – yet another example of how terror was crucial to the insurgency. (Communist Archive/Albert Grandolini collection)

> Too often communist terror is portrayed in simplistic terms: viciousness for its own sake, terror simply to terrorise, the communists presented as sub-human sadists indifferent to the blood on their hands. Those who paint them thus do a disservice to truth and a greater one to understanding. The average communist in Vietnam thinks of his system not in moral but in utilitarian terms. He finds terror to be the single greatest advantage he has over the government, one which he credits for making possible most of his successes. This being the case, he can intellectualise and semanticise its use and easily come to regard himself as a finer person than those whom he terrorises.[53]

Pike's comment also illustrates the idea of an action that has been justified for a 'utilitarian' greater good.[54] However, even though

Another example of goods smuggled into the country – here it is 7.62mm ammunition for anti-aircraft equipment. (Communist Archive/ Albert Grandolini collection)

there may have been a legitimate (in the eyes of the insurgents) reason for using intimidation, it still meant that for a majority of the rural population, allegiance to the insurgent cause was based 'more on murder than on political or psychological appeal.'[55] This rationalisation of the use of terror and its reduction – in the insurgents' eyes – to an alternative weapon of war, also resulted in the Viet Cong partaking in acts of brutality aimed at punishing enemies and frightening neutrals.

A Threat to the Peace in 1961, claimed that 'while professing sympathy for the needs and hopes of the people,' the Viet Cong had 'resorted to the most brutal forms of force and coercion in carrying out its programme' and were using terror to pursue their political agenda.[56] By mid to late 1961, the State Department believed around 1,500 South Vietnamese civilians were being killed each month by the insurgents.[57] Attacks were stepped up on government bases and buildings too. One RAND interviewee noted that the guard posts in their hamlet were attacked from 1962 onwards.[58] This was when 'the VC started encircling and attacking the posts. These posts were all destroyed and ceased activities in late 1963.'[59] Other RAND interviewees reported that these attacks increased even further in 1963 and noted that 'hardly had we built our houses – the roofs were not completed yet – when the VC, in April 1963, attacked the ARVN company at the top of Nui Mieu mountain, killing the commander, a captain, and 18 of his men' and then proceeded to burn down the strategic hamlet.[60] In addition to targeting the strategic hamlets, training camps were targeted too. After the battle of Ap Bac, a memo from Hilsman to President Kennedy described how the insurgents 'fought their way inside the perimeter of a US Special Forces training camp at Plei Mrong, killing 39 of the trainee defenders and capturing 114 weapons.'[61] These attacks also saw the Viet Cong replenish their own military supplies at the expense of the government.[62]

Insurgents use captured weapons to create a roadside IED. (Communist Archive/Albert Grandolini collection)

As part of the VC terror campaign, civilians would often be forced to construct defences for the insurgents. Here a part of the impressive Viet Cong tunnel system is under construction – all whilst a VC volunteer keeps watch. (Communist Archive/Albert Grandolini collection)

Sometimes the weapons supplied to the VC were shipped in from other South East Asian locations – using the tributaries and access to the Mekong Delta to ship and unload these supplies. In this photo, they are brazenly on display on the deck of a ship. (Communist Archive/Albert Grandolini collection)

Civilian Atrocities and 'War Crimes'?

However, the insurgents did not just attack military bases and strategic hamlets. The general population were also targeted. In October 1961 it was reported that daily 'acts of terror ranging from abductions to murders' were taking place.[63] The figures for these attacks in 1961 alone were '806 deaths and 770 kidnappings, not including cases of serious mutilation committed by the Viet Cong terrorists.'[64] In a detailed analysis of insurgent activity, *A Threat to the Peace* described legitimate targets as being 'any official, worker, or establishment that represents a service to the people by the Government in Saigon is fair game for the Viet Cong.'[65] It is noticeable that the sources then go on to reveal that often it was these public sector workers who bore the real extent of Viet Cong intimidation.[66] This was probably due to the fact that by working as doctors, nurses or teachers they were extending government 'soft' power into rural communities and undermining insurgent claims about the Diem regime and its American allies. Indeed, the full report went on to list a litany of events and assaults on government agencies:

> Hospitals and medical clinics have often been attacked as part of the anti-Government campaign and also because such attacks provide the Viet Cong with needed medical supplies. The Communists have encouraged people in rural areas to oppose the work of the Government's anti-malaria teams, and some of the workers have been killed. Village and town offices, police stations, and agricultural research stations are high on the list of preferred targets for the Viet Cong. In short, anything that spells order or security for the people of the South is anathema to the Viet Cong (VC) unless it be VC "order" or VC "security," anything that represents service or public welfare becomes a target, and a man who serves his Government and his people is likely to have his name inscribed on the Viet Cong's "wanted" list.[67]

This strategy resulted in attacks on young people involved in government organisations and also priests and foreign visitors. For example, on the 23 March 1961 there was an attack on 'a convoy of forty young women belonging to the Republican Youth of Phuoc Tuy, in the course of which two were killed on the spot and nine others seriously wounded.'[68] One of those who escaped the attack was followed home and 'was savagely shot' on 11 April 1961, 'at her dwelling.'[69] Attacks such as this one showed the insurgents were ruthless in their targeting tactics but this also fed into a narrative of intimidation because they followed one unfortunate victim home: the message being that the insurgents knew where she lived and could kill her at will.

Young women were not the only targets of insurgent violence though. In compiling details of these attacks, the United States Mission in Saigon retrospectively published *A Study* (sic) *Viet Cong Use of Terror* which listed more details of the victims and targets of insurgent aggression at this time.[70] This contained examples such as an attack on Father Bonnet, a parish priest visiting parishioners, a Vietnamese labour leader, Le Van Thieu, 63, 'hacked to death by Viet Cong wielding machetes near Bien Hoa' and two French civilians who were 'shot and killed by the Viet Cong whilst boating on the Saigon River.'[71] These were targeted attacks at religious authorities, union power and tourists. All helped develop an impression of a country that was becoming increasingly unstable and unsafe. In addition to these targeted attacks, there were also acts of indiscriminate violence that inflicted mass casualties. For example, in May 1962 a grenade was 'hurled into the Aterbea restaurant in Saigon wounding a Berlin circus manager and the Cultural Attaché from the German Embassy.'[72] In another grenade attack in October 1962, a teenage Viet Cong threw 'a grenade into a holiday crowd in downtown Saigon killing six persons, including two children, and injuring 38 persons.'[73] There were also assaults on a Buddhist temple where a 17 year old trainee monk was stabbed to death, indiscriminate shooting of

Many traps were used to block roads and paralyse the transport network. Ambushes of personnel in cars was common. Here we see a roadside spike trap designed to slow travel and make targets easier to hit. (Communist Archive/Albert Grandolini collection)

Insurgents patiently wait before launching an attack on a strategic hamlet. (Communist Archive/Albert Grandolini collection)

Whilst support for the Viet Cong was often obtained under duress, these three photos appear to show individuals willingly involved in constructing the insurgent tunnel network. Although all three photos could have been staged, there is no evidence that they were falsified. (Communist Archive/Albert Grandolini collection)

Again, we see the Chu Chi tunnels being dug out – the VC used these to ambush ARVN units, hide from patrols and, as the conflict developed, these tunnels even led to underground bases, communication networks and hospitals. (Communist Archive/Albert Grandolini collection)

villagers who tried to protect their own friends and family and the summary execution of school teachers.[74]

Many civilians were also murdered in particularly brutal ways. For example, this description of the murder of Father Hoang Ngoc Minh, highlights the cruelty of the assault:

> A communist road block halts his car. A bullet smashes into him. The guerrillas drive bamboo spears into Father Minh's body, then one fires a submachine gun point blank, killing him. The driver, Huynh Huu, his nephew, is seriously wounded.[75]

The priest was not the only religious figure to be executed by the insurgents. In one instance, 12 Catholic nuns were robbed on their way to Saigon. One unfortunate nun, a Sister Theophile, was summarily executed on the spot when she protested.[76] The nun's vehicle was then sprayed with bullets seriously wounding another nun in the party.[77] Farmers who refused to hand over their land to other peasants or obey Viet Cong orders were also shot dead after a 'people's tribunal' had established their guilt.[78] The long list of attacks on civilian targets also included grenades being thrown into a theatre – one incident killed 24 women and children – victims being hacked to death with machetes and even the murder of train personnel carrying food supplies to other parts of the country.[79] This could have been a case of the insurgents stepping up their attacks on the general population, or as Thompson claimed, a sign of their increasing desperation in the conflict.[80]

When they were not involved in indiscriminate killing, the insurgents concentrated their efforts on attacking rural communities. One of the main targets of Viet Cong terror were the village and hamlets chiefs. They were public servants of high rank who made visible targets and whose absence would be noted by other members of the rural community. This helped project an image of insurgent power and threat. The insurgents tended to intimidate these chiefs through either kidnapping or targeted assassination. Sometimes these kidnappings resulted in the person disappearing completely, at other times they were returned to their villages once a 'sufficient ransom' had been paid.[81] On other occasions the insurgents kidnapped people to threaten them into submission.[82] For example, one hamlet chief described his abduction and claimed that although

Another image of a tunnel being constructed. This required extensive – and exhausting – labour. (Communist Archive/Albert Grandolini collection)

he did not know if the Viet Cong intended to kill him 'they said they would.'[83] Although he continued to work for the government he was so scared that 'for over five months I did not go out of the hamlet. At night I would sleep in the hamlet, but always in a different place so that they did not know where I was.'[84] However, it should also be noted that when it came to abduction and kidnappings, Donnell found a 'significant number of interviews alleging abduction, especially in the pre-1963 period, turn out on close study to reveal a considerable amount of original enthusiasm for the VC.'[85] As a result some claims have to be treated with scepticism.

In addition to the use of abduction, many of the hamlet chiefs were also subject to assassination attempts. It was claimed that the insurgents had 'killed hundreds of village chiefs and other local officials' in their military campaign and that these assassinations had a psychological motivation too.[86] For example, a Special National Intelligence Estimate of 1961 claimed that 'the high rate of assassinations of local officials and retaliatory murders' was a 'continual reminder of the penalty of non-co-operation with the local Viet Cong authorities.'[87] This 'reminder' could also take the form of public execution. One captured interviewee noted how a demonstration against the Viet Cong in their strategic hamlet had taken place successfully but that the bodies of those protesting 'were found the next morning at the gates of the strategic hamlet.'[88] This brutality was not confined to one village. One cadre described an event from August 1963 where a village chief was tortured so badly that the insurgents dared not release him to the villagers and reveal their methods:

> They condemned him to death for spying and exploitation of the poor. At the moment of execution, they gathered about one hundred people from the village to witness it. A few members of Mr. Bat Hanh's family tried to untie him. The cadres opened fire and wounded one of them. After they had beheaded Mr. Bat Hanh, his family asked for his body to bury it. The cadres refused and took the corpse somewhere else. A large number of the people in Phuoc Hai village asserted that Mr. Bat Hanh had been the victim of an injustice.[89]

Murder and Assassination

These were not isolated incidents. In terms of the levels of violence, records are incomplete for the initial stages of the conflict but at least 45,000 'terror acts' occurred during the 1961–63 time period – including at least 5,000 murders and just over 18,000 kidnappings.[90] These figures relate to recorded attacks on government officials; it was estimated that civilian casualties were at least four times higher and that the civilian kidnapping rate was double that recorded here.[91] The overall figures for assassination and kidnapping over the 1960 to 1963 time period were given as shown in Table 1. It should be noted that the figures were considered to be on the low side due to incomplete records.

Table 1: Assassination and Kidnapping in the 1960 to 1963 time period[92]

	Assassinations	Kidnapped
1960	1,500	700
1961	500	1,000
1962	1,700	9,500
1963	2,000	7,000

It is interesting to observe how kidnappings seemed to increase rapidly during this time period. This may have been due to poor record keeping or an increase in Viet Cong activity. However, it may also have shown the relative success of the counterinsurgency strategy. It could have been that people felt safer and so they would report their kidnapping or it may have meant that the insurgents felt the need to intimidate and persuade more people to remain loyal to their cause in the face of government attacks. In either case, it would show growth in trust in the government forces and increasing desperation on the part of the insurgents. It would also fit into Thompson's analysis of the conflict and his predications about the reaction of the Viet Cong to the programme. To add a further level of intimidation, violence was often accompanied by a 'reminder' of the alleged crimes of the victim.

> *For many years, DANG-HANH, the hamlet chief at Hien an, had been an US-Diem lackey. The hamlet inhabitants are extremely angry at him because of his treacherous activities against the country and the people.*
>
> *To fulfil people's aspirations, this man "Hanh" should be severely punished*
>
> ANTI-TREACHERY SQUAD (Security Squad)[93]

These attacks, apart from killing members of the government apparatus, also had a deterrent effect on those still in post. For example, threats of violence meant that previously committed village chiefs 'would refuse to take part in any of the hamlet activities and would even refused to be interviewed' whilst others declined to leave the security of their village office and would not go home at night.[94] This reduced the effectiveness of the government administration and meant that reforms and progress became even harder to achieve and implement in rural Vietnam. In addition, threats of violence could also be used to deter new applicants from continuing in their posts. An account in My Thuan village illustrates this point:

Viet Cong recruits help construct punji stake defences around their jungle hideout. (Communist Archive/Albert Grandolini collection)

> The hamlet chief had recently been killed by the Viet Cong. Shortly after the village chief had appointed an acting hamlet chief to take over for the victim, the new appointee received a threatening letter from the terrorists, instructing him not to take over the duties or they "could not guarantee his life." He fled to the village office, along with another local appointee who had been threatened, to attempt to resign his new position. The village chief begged him not to resign, stating that if the hamlet officials left their hamlets or refused to participate in the administration, there would be no hope for carrying out village affairs.[95]

The families of village officials were also targeted in these attacks. An account of an assassination attempt on a local government official in November 1961 told of how he and his wife were blown up when their car hit a landmine, their children – aged one and three – survived the attack and 'were killed on the spot by the Viet Cong who had prepared the ambush.'[96] These examples all help to illustrate Pike's contention that the violence had a purpose. Not only did violence harm the enemy, it also diminished the effectiveness of government strategy and held up reform that had the potential to win popular support.

Terrorising Teachers. Destroying Schools and Brutalising Children

Although these attacks on government personnel could perhaps be rationalised as an attack on the Diem regime and government apparatus, other areas of Vietnamese society were also targeted. Teachers and schools seemed to be a particular focus of violence. A World Confederation of Organisations of the Teaching Profession report of May 1962 listed some of the challenges faced by education professionals. In a report entitled *Commission of Inquiry Report: Impact on Education of Terrorist Activities in Viet-Nam* the commission revealed the extent of Viet Cong terror against school teachers and school children in South Vietnam:

> Schools have been among their favourite targets. Through harassment, the murder of teachers, and sabotage of buildings the Viet Cong succeeded in closing more than 200 primary schools in South Vietnam in 1960, interrupting the education of more than 25,000 students. The number is reported to have risen to almost 400 in recent months.[97]

The report also disclosed that in the year 1961 to 1962, 150 schools had been closed as a result of terrorist activity (with 22 burnt to the ground), four teachers had been killed and 60 had been kidnapped.[98] Of those kidnapped, three had disappeared and 19 were still in captivity.[99] Attacks on school buildings would often see 'armed gangs attack schools, destroy furniture and books, burn or demolish the school and take away the equipment and school material' which further added to intimidation and undermined government attempts at social reform.[100]

It was not just the school infrastructure that was targeted though. In addition to burning books and buildings, teachers and pupils were threatened and attacked. Teachers were considered legitimate targets. This was because the Viet Cong thought that they were agents of the Diem regime who were essentially abusing their position to indoctrinate and influence young minds against the insurgent movement: many were regarded simply as 'governmental agents in the villages.'[101] Some of the teachers kidnapped were also accused of being spies and informers and were sentenced to 'death in absentia.'[102] The report went on to explain that teachers were particular targets because the insurgents wanted to 'destroy the role played by the school from the national, educational and human points of view' and limit the role that schools played in nation building.[103] Teachers were warned against following government programmes, parents were asked not to send their children to school and if these warning were not heeded, threats were made and kidnappings took place. The general mode of operation was:

> Armed gangs of 30 surround the teacher's house and take him away as prisoner. They rob him of his property, blindfold him, bind his hands behind his back, make him walk long distances and question him on the way. The kidnapped teacher is taken to their camp, kept (hands and feet bound), given little food and beaten. In some cases he is released after a certain time, in other cases he is condemned to death and executed.[104]

Arguably, the most chilling aspect of the insurgents' use of terror was the way in which – if threats failed – school teachers and children were murdered too. One report noted how a Miss Vo Thi Lo, 26, a school teacher in An Phuoc Village, Kien Hoa Province was 'found near the village with her throat cut. She had been kidnaped

Another strength of Viet Cong activity was the way in which women were used to help their insurgent effort. Here we see them constructing a trench line – the location is unknown but it is likely to be on the edges of a jungle base or a pro-Viet Cong village. (Communist Archive/Albert Grandolini collection)

by the Viet Cong three days earlier.'[105] The unfortunate Miss Vo Thi Lo was not the only victim of a terrorist assault on the education establishment. One particularly brutal part of the report described the measures taken against children who continued to attend school against the insurgents' wishes:

> A party of children was stopped while proceeding to school by bus from a neighbouring village. The children were asked to go back to their homes and were told that if they went to the school their lives would be in danger. For a week, the children continued to go to school in the same bus. They were one day waylaid and a little child of six and a half years old was picked out and her fingers were cut off. The children were told: "This is what will happen, and more, if you go to that school." So, naturally, the school closed down.[106]

As a result of these attacks, the report noted that enrolment in schools decreased and many classes were suspended. It estimated that over '1,838 classes (were) suppressed and the enrolment in primary schools was reduced by 78,196 students.'[107] As schools formed part of the government reform programme, a direct attack on them was a sign of apparent insurgent strength and government weakness.

The result of this intimidation was that the general population feared Viet Cong reprisals if they were seen to help the Diem regime. Consequently, they were also more inclined to support the insurgent activity in the villages. Although insurgent terrorism had been a factor in South Vietnam before American involvement, its continuation in the period 1961 to 1963 helped undermine the claims of Diem and his American supporters of an improvement in security. Therefore, the use of terror was a successful tool with which the insurgents could attack government buildings, reduce recruitment to government posts and instil fear in the minds of young and old alike. These tactics of intimidation helped establish a psychological advantage for the Viet Cong: people feared them and as a result would not fight against them. The next section will look at why the 'Counterinsurgency Plan' and the Strategic Hamlet Programme were unable to convince people that they were safe and could not protect them from insurgent attack.

Dien Ben Phu Revisited?

Although the counterinsurgents were trying to win the 'hearts and minds' of the people, this was not only done through economic development and political reform: the security and protection of the people was a vital concern too. The Taylor Mission reported that although the terror of the Viet Cong had 'alienated people deeply' they were too scared to resist the insurgents unless 'given at least the hope of security.'[108] Indeed, Lansdale argued that the Viet Cong were now 'feared and hated' by the rural population and this provided an opportunity for the government to intervene and show it could protect the South Vietnamese from attack.[109] Unfortunately, despite successes the strategic hamlets did not always provide the security that was claimed. Hilsman noted that particularly in the Delta, there was a blanket of 'little Dienbienphus' across the region.[110] Hilsman claimed that many villages and hamlets were simply 'indefensible, inadequately armed hamlets far from reinforcements' and this reduced the ability of the government to protect people and eliminate the Viet Cong.[111]

Attacking Government Bases – a Sign of Desperation?

The first point to note was that the counterinsurgents knew they had to provide protection for the rural population. Increased safety would deliver other benefits and underpin the counterinsurgency campaign. Hilsman again observed that 'no amount of regular troops used offensively will solve the Viet Cong problem' unless the villagers themselves were protected and the Viet Cong were cut off

After the assassination of President Diem, many rural areas rose up and destroyed their strategic hamlets. Here we see a destroyed hamlet in the Mekong Delta – probably in a Viet Cong-supporting area. (Communist Archive/Albert Grandolini collection)

from their sources of 'supplies and recruits.'[112] Hilsman estimated that if this separation was not achieved then 'two or more Viet Cong will be recruited for every one that is killed.'[113] Hilsman went on to claim that intelligence would emerge once people felt secure and that this would result in increased motivation that enabled the 'villagers to pass on information on the Viet Cong to government officials.'[114] It can be seen from this that security was not just an end in itself; providing protection for the rural population would encourage them to resist the Viet Cong, lessen support for the insurgency and increase the effectiveness of the counterinsurgency strategy.

Unfortunately, the insurgents were spurred on to attack the hamlet programme and undermine its claims to provide security. The insurgents stepped up their attacks on the strategic hamlets and they maintained that 'we have been gaining additional victories while the enemy has been suffering heavier losses.'[115] These attacks were characterised by 'destruction of defences, assassination of hamlet officials, kidnapping and theft of foodstuffs' and, in the three month period leading up to November 1962, the strategic hamlets sustained an average of five attacks per week.[116] Sometimes these attacks would even occur immediately after the construction of a strategic hamlet. The results of these attacks were noted when, for example, in 1962 the insurgents attacked and killed a village chief and afterwards 'most of the inhabitants were very leery of serving on the village committee' and this hindered the implementation of government reform.[117] Pearce supported these claims and observed how 'Viet Cong incidents against the population did not diminish' as a result of the strategic hamlets, and, if anything, were stepped up.[118] In addition, the insurgents were also starting to target American bases and larger towns. A rather pessimistic report for the Department of State in October 1963, described the nature of these attacks and the way in which urban areas were also under assault. These attacks were characterised by 'increased daring, planning, and co-ordination' and included an attack against a United States helicopter base and two district capitals.[119]

This information would seem to confirm the claims made in the Vietnam War literature that the hamlets were being overrun by the Viet Cong. However, as Sir Robert Thompson explained, the increased attacks could also have been a sign of insurgent desperation. The problem for the Diem regime was that the former

In response to increased Viet Cong attacks, the government of South Vietnam increased advisory training. Here US advisors join with ARVN instructors to help train recruits on the firing range while a look-out in the tower works to ensure against a surprise attack. (Albert Grandolini collection)

Despite the rapid response units and helicopter transport available (a US Marine Corps H-34 shown) to ARVN, they often arrived after a Viet Cong assault. This undermined trust and increased doubts about the government's ability to protect its own people. (Albert Grandolini collection)

perception rather than the latter analysis was beginning to take hold amongst the rural population. A report on the strategic hamlets for the Department of State, noted how even if the attacks on the hamlets were unsuccessful or did limited damage, they still caused fear amongst the village inhabitants.[120] The report stated that 'armed attacks have risen sharply, but the percentage of their success has been very small' with the result that many peasants were refusing to take part in the hamlet programme.[121] As a consequence, popular support and the ability to implement government reform was being lost. Indeed, Phillips noted that the Viet Cong were engaged in a 'psychological warfare campaign' against the hamlets and that even if the attacks were not completely successful, the incidents demonstrated that 'they were still very much in control' in rural Vietnam and undermined support for the Diem regime.[122] These apparent negative trends were commented upon in October 1963. A Department of State Research Report noted how – after a brief lull:

> Total incidents and armed attacks have increased appreciably. If the present trend continues through the end of this year, total incidents will exceed by more than *ten percent* the level for the period July to December 1962. Large Viet Cong attacks (company-size or larger) have also increased appreciably since July of this year, and, if the trend continues, could exceed by almost thirty percent the level for July to December 1962.[123]

The overall impression created by these attacks was of a government incapable of guarding the people and as a result they were losing popular support.

An 'Inside' Job?

One of the reasons for this loss of faith in the regime was that people simply did not feel protected by the defences in their hamlets. In his research into Duc Lap village, Pearce interviewed the residents and they explained how, from 1961 onwards, the insurgents were able to 'make daylight incursions into the village' without fear of resistance from the Self-Defence Corps (SDC) 'who would retreat to their defence post and wait for the danger to pass.'[124] The inability to stop insurgents infiltrating village and hamlet communities was also commented upon by many of the inhabitants in Duc Lap. For example, one village chief claimed that he 'was aware of the existence of the Viet Cong agents within the strategic hamlets' and the strategic hamlets were failing to 'keep the people and the Viet Cong separated.'[125] The villagers also knew of the insurgent presence within their hamlet because of internal sabotage. This again reinforced the idea of Viet Cong 'presence' in a village and added further to the insecurity that many rural communities felt. One villager commented:

> Those who destroy our hamlet fences are people inside the hamlets. These fences were made very strong, but I have seen evidence of the fence having been broken down from the inside. The Viet Cong demand the people destroy the fence for them and threaten them if they do not comply. The people are afraid because they must go into the fields every day to work and the Viet Cong might kill them.[126]

It is also interesting to note that, in some cases, the insurgents did not have to work very hard in order to gain entrance to the hamlet. For example, the very process of creating a hamlet and the forced relocation that followed gave some insurgents easy access to the hamlets.[127] They simply mingled with the village population and moved into the hamlets at the same time as the legitimate occupants. Again, Pearce noted that:

Dead Viet Cong lie by a river bank after a failed assault on a strategic hamlet, an H-19 helicopter beyond. (Albert Grandolini collection)

Despite the barbed wire and other defensive measures of the strategic hamlets, the Viet Cong agents continued to function in the village. In fact, it can be safely assumed that several of their agents moved into the strategic hamlets along with the other relocated families.[128]

As a result of this infiltration, the people in Duc Lap 'were not certain' that that government could provide security for them from Viet Cong attacks.[129]

Indeed, simply being in a strategic hamlet may have made people more vulnerable. One villager interviewed in Quang Ngai noted how the hamlet defences trapped him within the village when it was attacked. He was, therefore, unable to escape as the insurgents blocked all the entrances and exits and was now in much greater danger. One ARVN officer recalled the interview and how:

> He had asked an old man how he liked the hamlet. The old man replied that he did not like it at all. The officer asked if he was pro-Viet Cong. No, the old man said, he was very much against the Viet Cong. Had he been obliged to work too hard on the hamlet fortifications the officer inquired? No, he said, he had not minded that, what bothered him was that he was now in more danger from the Viet Cong than ever. Before the fences were put up, he could flee the hamlet when the Viet Cong came, now the Viet Cong controlled all the hamlet gates. The officer replied that surely there must be secret exits and the old man said sadly that the Viet Cong controlled those too.[130]

This quote is interesting for several reasons. Firstly, it reveals that the rural villages did not all support the insurgency. Secondly, it shows that the rural peasants did not always object to building their own hamlets and thirdly, it reveals some form of infiltration into this particular hamlet. This would indicate some degree of collusion with the insurgents from others in the village and shows that there was still a struggle taking place for the loyalty of the people even when the hamlets were completed.

Fighting Back Against the Viet Cong

However, not all hamlet residents acquiesced to insurgent demands or wilted under intimidation. When properly equipped, the villagers were more than prepared to defend their own hamlet and could demonstrate real resistance against insurgent attack. Phillips recounted a visit to Phu Yen province and detailed how, with limited means, the hamlet residents repelled one such assault:

> For several nights a small party of Viet Cong had tried to break through the bamboo fence around the hamlet. The militia had scared them off by beating gongs, shouting and throwing rocks and home-made spears. Realising the Viet Cong would return in greater strength the hamlet sent a delegation to the District Chief for help. He gave them what he had – four shotguns and one hand grenade. That night the Viet Cong came again, this time in three parties each with several men on different sides of the hamlet. They tried to break in simultaneously. As soon as the militia heard them the weapons were divided and three groups were dispatched to where the Viet Cong were trying to enter. Two groups fired their shotguns and scared off the Viet Cong. The group confronting the largest party of Viet Cong waited until they had partially broken down the fence before they fired and threw the single grenade. One Viet Cong was killed outright and bloodstains on the ground indicated that two more had been wounded.[131]

Many South Vietnamese were reluctant to leave their ancestral lands – even in the face of Viet Cong assault. Here a young family are being airlifted to safety aboard US Army H-21 helicopters. (Albert Grandolini collection)

This clearly shows that the Viet Cong attacks could be resisted and there was a will to fight against the insurgents even when supplies were limited. It also demonstrates that if the population felt secure then they would resist assaults on their hamlets.

Viet Cong Tactics – Night Battles, Home-made Weapons and Ambushes

Unfortunately, any limited successes gained in security were undermined by the effectiveness of Viet Cong tactics. The insurgents skilfully used natural conditions to intimidate and frighten people. One way this was done was through attacks at night. Cochran, in his analysis of the tactics used against the strategic hamlets, claimed that a 'strong correlation' existed between 'VC incidents and natural light conditions.'[132] Cochran estimated that more than '80 percent of all incidents were initiated at night and 46 percent in the dark of both sun and moon.'[133] He discovered that the insurgents correlated the size of their assault with the extent of the cover that darkness provided and 'the more serious the incident, the later at night the VC began it.'[134] He also said that there tended to be a deliberate timetable that determined the nature of the attack on the hamlet: he claimed that 'the mean time of initiation for half the propaganda incidents was 2030 hours, for terror incidents 2230 hours, and for attacks on the hamlets, 0100 hours.'[135] These night time attacks were used not only because the darkness provided cover but they also created a restlessness and fear in the hamlets. The timing of these

Viet Cong guerrillas plant these nails in thousands around their positions; they attempt to drive the enemy onto these nails by the direction of their firing. A nail is cheaper than a bullet.

Viet Cong villages in the area have "fields" of nails around them, with safe-paths through them, in much the same manner as defensive mine-fields. Safe-paths are marked with twigs, tied grass, or in other inconspicuous ways. When a ground attack is launched on a Viet Cong village, the guards on the outer perimeter retreat along these paths, pulling up the markings.

It was noticed that soldiers going through the mud on patrol moved forward with a sliding motion that looked as though they were ice-skating.

Naily Boards used to inflict damage on enemy soldiers. (Used with Permission)[140]

assaults also meant there would be a considerable delay in the time it took reinforcements to arrive in the darkness.[136] The confusion that a night time attack caused may also have triggered even greater fear in the defenders of the hamlet. For example, one villager noted that when his hamlet was attacked, 'all the members of the combat youth succeeded in escaping to the countryside' and abandoned their posts.[137] This was an intelligent use of the natural conditions by the Viet Cong that also helped to perpetuate a narrative that the government could not protect people under attack.

Night time attacks were not the only method that the insurgents used to instil fear into the local population. Home-made weapons were also used effectively. Lansdale noted, in a 1961 study of insurgent tactics used in Binh Hung village in the Ca Mau Peninsula, that 'in looking over captured Viet Cong weapons, one is struck by the ingenuity of some of their ordnance' and in some cases the firing pin of a weapon was 'activated by rubber bands.'[138] Lansdale claimed that the Viet Cong had 'jungle arsenals' which turned out home-made weapons that caused crippling injuries and perpetuated the narrative of terror and fear.[139] A particularly unpleasant home-made weapon and tactic was the use of 'naily boards' which were simply nails hammered into boards.

The boards were turned upright so that the nails became spikes and then the boards were hidden around the villages: the aim being to cause crippling foot injuries to the victim.[141] Sometimes these were used as defensive barriers around an insurgent village or stronghold and at other times they would be used as simple 'booby traps' to injure unsuspecting soldiers. Indeed, soldiers on patrol were encouraged to move forward with a sliding motion as if 'ice-skating' in order to avoid injury.[142]

These 'naily boards' were particularly useful because not only 'was a nail cheaper than a bullet,' they were also placed around insurgent-held villages and could be mass-produced cheaply and quickly.[143] The boards were particularly useful as a tactical defensive measure: if attacked, the Viet Cong would try and direct their fire to make the soldiers move onto the 'naily boards' and cause crippling injuries.[144] These boards would be marked by twigs and branches to make them apparent to the insurgents and they would pull up these markers as they retreated under attack. Also, the insurgents would often hide the 'naily boards' by making footprints 'in mud moulds, then dry them out.'[145] These moulded foot prints were then 'used to cover implantations of nails, to give the appearance of a safe-path' and provide further protection for inhabitants of a village.[146] In fact, these 'naily boards' were so effective and numerous that by 1962, the insurgents had a slogan of 'one naily board for each square of land.'[147] Indeed, one account of their usefulness noted how during a fight with an ARVN patrol, two soldiers were wounded, the attack slowed and this gave the insurgents a chance to escape.[148] The report stated that one of the soldiers 'stepped on two boards of spikes, and fell down at the spot' and he was evacuated by his colleagues afterwards whilst the other was 'lightly wounded.'[149] These boards not only created fear but also left an impression of ineffectiveness: if an attack had to be halted due to ARVN casualties, it gave the insurgents a chance to escape and made the attackers appear particularly inept.

Finally, the insurgents also staged frequent ambushes as a tactic that aimed to destabilise ARVN and create uncertainty and insecurity. The ambush tactic was particularly useful because even as the Saigon regime claimed it was protecting the people, ambushes would further 'discredit and undermine the position of the Saigon government' because they helped create confusion and fear.[150] The effectiveness of the ambushes resulted in 'ARVN casualties (perhaps 90 percent)' coming from these tactics.[151] This problem was made worse because the slow response time of ARVN units – who often arrived 24 to 36 hours after an attack – gave the Viet Cong time to prepare and plan their attack and their ambush method: the insurgents simply launched an attack and waited for the troops to arrive.[152] Another favourite Viet Cong technique was 'to set an ambush for a unit on its return from a patrol.'[153] Having passed through the area earlier and having seen no evidence of insurgents, 'the returning unit feels that the area is safe' and the patrol became vulnerable to ambush and attack.[154] As a result of these type of tactics the insurgents were able to pin down ARVN on defensive missions and this helped to create a 'pervasive sense of insecurity and frustration' amongst government forces.[155] Taylor noted how this failure to effectively protect people led 'to a drying up of the basic sources of intelligence' and limited 'the government's ability to raise recruits.'[156] This again undermined government claims to be protecting the population, made the people feel even more insecure and reduced the likelihood of them supporting the government even further.

Overall, this chapter has shown that the Diem regime was successfully implementing social, political and economic reform in order to win over the support of the people of Vietnam. However, the insurgents were – in addition to their tools of persuasion – simultaneously trying to win the backing of the people by using terror and force. The paradox is that whilst the counterinsurgents were stressing winning popular support, their methods failed to adequately protect the population from a legacy of terror that began before 1961. In fact, these measures may have accelerated their decline. This was because a highly visible but ineffective government presence confirmed the view that the government was incapable of protecting all the population. Consequently, the more the government built schools or other visible signs of progress, the easier it was for the insurgents to destroy them. This created the impression that the government could not protect its own people and reinforced the power and threat of the Viet Cong in the minds of the South Vietnamese. To make matters worse, the government were alienating their own supporters too …

2
BE STILL

Why the Strategic Hamlets made things worse

> God damn it, we had to lie down quietly or else they would blow our heads off. No one dared move. We had to close the doors and stay in the houses. Pardon me, we even had to urinate inside the house. There were many people [Viet Cong]: we don't know where they came from. We could not recognise their faces because it was dark. Let them do what they wanted, but we had to be still.
>
> A strategic hamlet resident describes how being grouped together made them easier targets for Viet Cong attack.[1]

Why Helping People Can Make Things Worse …

One of the intractable problems encountered when assessing the Strategic Hamlet Programme was this: it was possible that the very measures designed by the Diem regime to protect people made the situation worse. As previous chapters of this book (and series) have shown, there were many indicators of progress which gave the counterinsurgents cause for optimism and a belief that their programme was working. For example, a Department of State Research Report summarised the situation on 1 July 1963 and claimed that 'on balance, however, the strategic hamlet has been a success.'[2] Unfortunately, this analysis did not tell the full story: there were many faults in the programme too. One problem was illustrated by the comment in the opening of this chapter as the villager recalled how he had been forcibly relocated into a strategic hamlet. As a result, he and his fellow Vietnamese were concentrated together in greater density and this meant more casualties were inflicted because it was easier for the Viet Cong to attack, intimidate and rob them.

To help illustrate these ideas, the chapter uses – in addition to the usual range of sources – a report entitled *The Vietnamese 'Strategic Hamlets': A Preliminary Report* which was written in 1962 by John Donnell and Gerald Hickey for the RAND Corporation.[3] Donnell and Hickey were anthropologists, academics and field researchers who were commissioned to investigate the effectiveness of the hamlet programme and convey their findings – via RAND – to the United States Air Force. Their report gives a detailed account of some of the problems the Strategic Hamlet Programme faced and helps explain some of its failures.

Even though many advisors had a good working relationship with their ARVN counterparts, ultimately the US influence allowed the Viet Cong to promote an anti-colonial narrative in their operations. (Albert Grandolini collection)

American aid took many forms; not only did it manifest in the form of troops providing close air support, it was also apparent in materiel too. These three photographs show a helicopter gunner involved in a troop training drop (.30-cal machine gun in the door of a H-21) and … (Albert Grandolini collection)

Poor Standards of Construction

Planning After the Event …

Donnell and Hickey found that the Strategic Hamlet Programme contained many paradoxes. One of these was the way in which the construction of the hamlets often caused resentment and anger amongst the very people the hamlets were designed to protect. Poor standards of construction undermined the protection offered by the hamlets because fortifications were often of variable quality. The poor design of several of the hamlets also meant that the population were more, rather than less, exposed to insurgent attacks and indoctrination. The result of this was that the people lost confidence in the government's ability to protect them and this undermined the Diem regime's claims to be a strong, viable administration. It also reinforced the belief in rural areas about the insurgents' military strength.

In theory, the hamlets were constructed to a criteria drawn up by the Interministerial Committee for Strategic Hamlets. In terms of hamlet facilities, this criteria included 'completed fences, spikes, communication trenches, hidden trenches in all houses, etc.'[4] It also stated that work would be 'divided' amongst the local population and that the hamlet militia were to be 'organised, trained, and armed.'[5]

Unfortunately, the committee was established *after* the programme had started and this reflected some of the short-sighted thinking involved in the programme which often created as many problems as it solved.

Ignoring Local Economic Needs

Another problem was that planners were often ignorant of the local economic and cultural conditions and were unaware of how these were affected by hamlet creation. This meant that there was much resentment in rural communities caused by the overuse and misuse of important cash crops for hamlet construction. An example of this was the use of bamboo in constructing fences and buildings in and around the hamlets. Farmers felt that valuable bamboo had been sacrificed in order to create ineffective village defences that managed to obstruct 'the defender's field of fire' rather than protect those inside the hamlet.[7] Also, in the rush to construct these defences, immature bamboo was used which was unlikely to provide much protection as it was 'likely to become brittle' and thus reduced any deterrent value of the fence to be 'within one year.'[8] This was opposed to waiting

… Aircraft in protective wrapping being sent to South Vietnam on a 'jeep' carrier, and … (Albert Grandolini collection)

ICSH SO #0192/LB/ACL/TV/3 dated 19 July 1962

Interministerial Committee for Strategic hamlets Criteria for Completed Hamlets

1. Cleared communists from area, and have coordinated with the Surete Commune Committee hamlet chief to control personnel, equipment, and strength at the strategic hamlet.
2. Have coordinated with a Civil Affairs information service to mobilise the population, and successfully organised all the people.
3. Have instructed, and divided the work of all people as to their common obligations when there are disasters.
4. Have completed fences, spikes, communication trenches, hidden trenches in all houses, etc.
5. Have secretly organised 2 special forces cells for each strategic hamlet.
6. Have organised the election of the executive committee and established a constitution.

Further criteria and refinements of the six points:

1. Hamlet militia is organised, trained, and armed. The hamlet no longer requires outside emergency assistance.
2. Homes of relocated persons are complete.
3. Construction work on schools, community houses, dispensary, and information hall is complete.
4. An outside communication system or alarm system has been installed.
5. Hamlet defense plans have been prepared and rehearsed.
6. Some type of dedication service or ceremony has been conducted by the district chief or higher official.[6]

… A US-supplied A-1, fully bombed up and ready for next mission, inside a protective revetment, on a surface made of pierced-steel. (Albert Grandolini collection)

for the bamboo crop to mature which would have resulted in fences that would have lasted 'at least ten years.'[9] This meant that the hamlet fences rotted away quickly and became almost useless as a barricade. It also contributed to making the farmer poorer as the bamboo used in construction of hamlet perimeter fencing formed much of a cushion or secondary income: its use led to 'adverse economic developments' in many areas.[10] This not only resulted in a feeling of economic insecurity but, as Nighswonger noted in his study of rural pacification, built up resentment at an apparent waste of a crop of real worth: bamboo was 'always someone's property' and it had market value.[11] In addition, farmland was cleared around the hamlet for defensive fortifications and to provide areas for firing on attackers. This was intended to 'permit fields of fire and to avoid giving guerrillas and terrorists hiding places close to the hamlet.'[12] However, this also reduced land available for farming and helped lower income even further. A photo clearly shows areas of land cleared in order to provide lines of sight for defending militia should the hamlet be attacked. Unfortunately, it was also using up fields that could be used to grow bamboo or tobacco and increase village wealth.

ARVN troops listen attentively to a briefing about the Strategic Hamlet Programme. (Albert Grandolini collection)

In addition to the issues caused by using immature bamboo and taking up precious farmland, the hamlet construction standards were not always of the highest quality. Many of the hamlets were constructed using 'inefficient and unstandardised construction methods.'[13] Philips reported that many hamlets were of 'dubious quality, and there are probably not a few hamlets which are a liability rather than an asset to the counterinsurgency programme.'[14] Indeed, at a conference in Hawaii, 23 July 1962 it was put simply that some of the hamlets were 'not particularly good' and there was a lot of 'short-sighted planning' involved in hamlet construction.[15] One elderly villager even noted how the hamlet fence posts – aimed at securing

The strategic hamlets formed only part of the South Vietnamese Government strategy. Conventional warfare also played a major role. This photo shows a major troop deployment with H-21 and H-34 helicopters – probably in preparation for a large-scale battle such as Ap Bac. (Albert Grandolini collection)

A US pilot escapes from a crashed H-21 helicopter: the apparent failure to protect the people whilst being attacked by the VC undermined government claims to be able to defend the population. (Albert Grandolini collection)

the walls in place – were easily removed by pouring water into the foundations.[16] He remarked how 'as old as I am now, I can still pull up four or five posts at a time.'[17] He also said the fences offered very little protection from attack and claimed that the Viet Cong were 'even able to destroy the protected parts of the government hamlets, such as hamlet fences. They are able to destroy the whole thing. They knock down all the iron fence posts. They cut, chop, tear down, destroy everything.'[18] This inadequate construction also had a psychological effect because the insurgents appeared 'able to attack individual hamlets almost at will' and as a result the hamlet lost most of its intended protective value.[19] This failure to protect the population meant that the Viet Cong could 'come in and capture the people' as before: there was no incentive to resist attacks or infiltration.[20]

The issue of poor construction was further compounded by the variable speed and ineffective way in which the hamlets were being built around the country. For example, a USOM report in 1963 noted that whilst there was headway being made in many provinces, this was not true in the Delta where 'the programme has suffered serious reverses in many provinces, is in effect at a standstill in others and moving ahead slowly in only a few.'[21] Even in areas where the programme was making steady progress, USOM reported that 'no more than 50 percent of the hamlets can be considered satisfactory from the point of view of possessing a true will to resist the Vietcong.'[22]

Lack of Equipment Inside the Hamlets

Complementing this variable standard of implementation was a lack of equipment in several hamlets. William Shelton commented that the execution of the hamlets in many areas was 'not worth a damn' and that often the only protection available was a radio which could be used to request help.[23] Describing the ineffectiveness of these measures, he went on to say:

> They'd put up this little hamlet and they'd put a fence around it for protection from the Viet Cong but they would not really give them a hell of a lot in the way of defending themselves in case of an infiltration or an assault by a Viet Cong unit. They were pretty much stuck out there and told, "Look, we are going to put this barbed wire or this bamboo fence around you and it is going to protect you," and they'd leave them with a radio. As long as it worked that was fine. They could notify a higher headquarters that there was an attack underway and by the time the relief forces got there the attack was over and the Viet Cong had already gotten out of the village or the hamlet.[24]

The lack of equipment also extended to weapons. Hilsman reported that many hamlets were 'inadequately equipped and defended' and that there was a 'chronic shortage of weapons for strategic hamlet defenders.'[25]

One villager reported to Rufus Phillips that all they had to defend their hamlet was 'four shotguns and one hand grenade.'[26] What is

The construction of strategic hamlets was supported by regular patrols. Here an ARVN group is accompanied and advised by a US soldier armed with a Thompson submachine gun and a knife. (Albert Grandolini collection)

ARVN and hamlet militia undergo weapons instruction. Again, despite a lack of weapons in many villages, the South Vietnamese government were well resourced – as Roger Hilsman pointed out. (Albert Grandolini collection)

ARVN, militia and self-defence forces involved in jungle fitness training. (Albert Grandolini collection)

interesting to note though, is that Hilsman also claimed there were more than enough weapons in the country as a whole but they seemed to be lost amongst government supplies.[27]

One reason given for the varying standards of construction and lack of equipment in the hamlet programme was attributed to the over eagerness of Nhu and his desire to quickly instigate the hamlet programme. The speedy implementation of the hamlet initiative may have caught the insurgents off-guard but it also meant that rapid construction often started a race between the province chiefs to 'frantically build these installations with attendant imposition on the villagers.'[28] This also reduced security because according to Cottrell the 'security infrastructure had not been set up concurrently' with the hamlet construction.[29] Another result of this quick implementation was that the organisation of defence militias was often ignored and there was a 'lack of a co-ordinated defence effort to accompany' hamlet assembly.[30] As a result 'only a few hamlet militia' had been trained and armed and this meant that attacks would encounter little resistance.[31]

Corruption in the Provinces?

It was also apparent that rather than fulfilling the hamlet building criteria, some province chiefs simply dumped the resources they were given and claimed the hamlets had been constructed. One example, given by Colonel Jonathan F. Ladd, noted how this fraud was observed in operation in the Delta. This meant that although some province chiefs claimed that the hamlets were being built, their duplicity gave the insurgents further ammunition to use in their propaganda campaign. Ladd explained:

Despite a lack of equipment in some villages and hamlets, ARVN were well supplied. The photo here shows .30-cal machine gun firing practice and instruction. (Albert Grandolini collection)

An instructor demonstrates to watching militia how to throw a hand grenade. (Albert Grandolini collection)

paradox was being created. Whilst aid was pouring into many provinces, it was not being used correctly and instead was helping supply the insurgency. This resulted in more wasted resources, unfilled promises and a further erosion of trust in the government and its ability to manage the country.

Overextended? How Do You Defend a Canal?

In addition to the rapid pace of construction and poor building standards, the hamlets were often poorly designed or did not use the local environment to the advantage of the hamlet residents. A USOM report noted that the ideal hamlet needed certain characteristics in order to be effective. Firstly, 'walls or fences should be as close as possible to the dwellings' so that they could be quickly manned in the event of an attack and these fences should be far enough away from the village to offer 'clear fields of fire for at least 300 meters in every direction.'[33] The report also suggested that the perimeters should be circular to allow good vision around the hamlet.[34] However, the same report then went on to claim that many hamlets were indefensible, were cited in poor defensive positions and often made the people inside more vulnerable to attack.[35] The report said far too few hamlets met the defensive criteria and described some hamlets that were 'several kilometres long, but only one or at most two hundred meters deep' or were built surrounded by higher ground that gave attackers an advantageous viewpoint.[36] The report also suggested that many hamlets had 'forests, or cane brakes, or swampy areas coming right up to the fence' and some were so poorly designed that a clear field of fire was apparent inside the hamlet but 'not outside the defensive works.'[37] This may have been a reflection of the fact that the people in the hamlet misunderstood the nature of the building programme, it could also have shown that they did not feel threatened by the insurgents or it may have been a simple failure to adapt to local conditions. For example, Ladd, who was stationed in the Delta from 1962 onwards, explained how the hamlets were simply inappropriate for the conditions of a river delta area. What is interesting is that Ladd does acknowledge – in common with Phillips – that the hamlets could work in the north of the country.[38] However, Ladd explained that, in the Delta, 'it was not like Washington, D.C. where there's a house every ten feet. But maybe a hundred yards, two hundred yards apart, there would be a home and they would farm the lands out on either side of the canals.'[39] As a result of this failure to acknowledge the locality, Ladd went on to explain that whilst it would be relatively easy to corral people into large hamlets in the north – because they already lived in villages and 'you could put a fence around it' – this was next to impossible to do successfully in the Delta.[40] Ladd explained how as a result of this inappropriate adaption to the terrain, the hamlets were overextended, poorly designed and created even greater resentment. Describing how one hamlet fence went on for over 40 miles alongside a canal, he explained:

The aid and advisory mission saw numerous American personnel advise and support ARVN in the field. Here we see a joint planning/briefing trying to establish the location of Viet Cong bases. (Albert Grandolini collection)

> They had the Vietnamese river forces who in one case had taken up maybe fifty tons of barbed wire on these rolls and dumped it off at a canal junction, and it was sitting there rusting except for what the VC used. I mean, they'd take it themselves, a little bit. But they called it a strategic hamlet and there wasn't a goddamn soul, living soul, there; it was just a big pile of barbed wire rusting away on this canal bank.[32]

Ladd's comment here is particularly interesting because it indicates that hamlets were not being built and that the wasted resources were supplying the Viet Cong war effort too. Thus, another

Troops in the process of embarking an early UH-1A or B for a flight in the middle of a farmer's field. Such lack of care caused resentment as crops were destroyed in the process. (Albert Grandolini collection)

> Along the canal may live three hundred people in those houses, well, how do you put a damn fence around them? Well, the only way to do it is to congregate them all in one place…they'd have two or three hundred people corralled. But the guy's farm was thirty kilometres down the canal. He couldn't work his farm. So what you had was a bunch of disgruntled farmers…they couldn't do anything; they couldn't even make any money; they couldn't raise their rice, couldn't get to it and back and walk down and back.[41]

Ladd concluded his assessment by claiming that 'it was just utterly hopeless…it was just ridiculous to think of a strategic hamlet' in the Delta.[42] However, in fairness to the counterinsurgents, it should be recognised that not every hamlet needed elaborate defences. Whilst some fences were 'flimsy, half-hearted bamboo barriers' and were 'often the subject of scornful criticism by our people,' this was often in response to local security conditions.[43] Also, some hamlets did adapt to the locality. For example, one hamlet was described as being 'bordered on three sides by a stream and canals, a wall and a ditch were being constructed outside the remaining side.'[44] In addition, a '"strategic road" was being cut through the coconut palms at the water's edge to permit easier patrolling around the hamlet.'[45] Heavner made a valid point about the variation in hamlet quality when he stressed that there was 'no point in demanding elaborate perimeters everywhere before we really know how important the perimeter is.'[46] Whilst Heavner had a justifiable argument about resource allocation and context-relevant defences, poorly constructed fortifications undermined the claim of protection for all.

The result of this was that confidence in the hamlets and the ability they had to protect the population was severely undermined: the hamlets themselves actually symbolised the government's inability to defend the people. This point was emphasised in a USOM report from June 1963 which noted that 'the reactions and attitudes of the population are closely bound to the progress of the programme' and a perceived lack of protection undermined government support.[47] Interestingly, the same report went on to note that where the people felt secure they tended to fully back the programme and even began to 'establish their own strategic hamlets' when protection could be guaranteed.[48] This would clearly indicate a link between secure provision and the enthusiasm for the strategic hamlets. Similarly, the report noted that where the welfare of the population was being ignored or security was not adequate, the population 'reacted negatively' to the lack of security infrastructure.[49] Pearce also noted

ARVN storming and destroying a suspected Viet Cong-supporting village: the thatched roofs of the buildings were easily set fire. These attacks were often mirrored by Viet Cong on isolated or poorly defended strategic hamlets. (Albert Grandolini collection)

An ARVN soldier waits and watches in defence of a strategic hamlet armed with a .45-cal Thompson submachine gun. (Albert Grandolini collection)

President Diem tours a strategic hamlet accompanied by American officers. (Albert Grandolini collection)

in a report for RAND, that rather than providing additional security, many villagers now felt that by being clustered together 'they were even better targets for the Viet Cong mortars and bullets' than when they were spread out across an area or province.[50] One villager also noted that relocation meant people were often grouped with strangers and this unfamiliarity led to a lack of solidarity and made it easier for the insurgents to take advantage of the villagers and sow dissent and suspicion.[51]

A Big Success?

Population Resettlement

Another problem that the hamlets created was anger caused by forceful resettlement and forced labour. Although the tactic of forced relocation had been used successfully by the British in the Malayan Emergency, South Vietnam had a different culture and relationship with the rural landscape. For example, the movement of over eight million people into strategic hamlets was described as 'the big success story in South Vietnam' and a 'story that has not yet been fully told.'[52] Unfortunately, many of the South Vietnamese who were moved into these hamlets did not share this view.

Initially, much of the relocation into the hamlets was accompanied by terror and violence. For example, during Operation Sunrise it was acknowledged that in order to make the hamlets work, there would be times when the South Vietnamese authorities were 'obliged to use some of the same arbitrary techniques as the Communists themselves.'[53] Unfortunately, this meant that the distinction between insurgent and counterinsurgent blurred and made gaining the support of the local population even harder to achieve. Michael Forrestal recalled that many peasants were taken from their homes and without any warning saw 'their individual farms burned' behind them 'so as to deny their houses to the Viet Cong.'[54] They were then 'forcibly incarcerated' into 'half-built villages.'[55] This forced relocation also had an unintended effect of providing a morale boost to the insurgents who used it in their propaganda. The compulsory removal allowed the insurgents to present the hamlets as yet another example of government oppression and they claimed that the 'enemy has done a highly unpopular thing that is the concentration of the civilian population.'[56] One civilian prisoner noted that the result of this population movement was that the strategic hamlets were 'all considered to be the Ngo Dinh Diem invented prison': when the Viet Cong eventually destroyed the strategic hamlet people 'were only too happy to co-operate' in its destruction.[57] The government's image was harmed further because threats were used against recalcitrant villagers and once inside the hamlets the 'movement of the villagers was checked closely' and regularly monitored.[58] In a series of letters written in 1962 to relatives in the North, one writer, identified only as Tran Xuan described the scenes inside a hamlet. The hamlet is identified only as B.V. strategic hamlet but Tran Xuan described how people were 'herded together' in overcrowded conditions:

> People, fowl, cattle, pigs…lived under the same roof, relieving themselves without regard to hygiene. The place, infected with diseases, stunk…from time to time hooligans rushed in to rape women. The shopkeepers went bankrupt for the Diem's soldiers did not pay for the goods they took.[59]

Considering the probable influence of propaganda in the letter, it still illustrated how some of the Vietnamese perceived the Strategic Hamlet Programme. It also fed into the propaganda distributed by the Viet Cong which stressed the poor living conditions in the hamlets.[60] Xuan's account cannot be corroborated but it would have been read by those fighting against the Diem regime and may have provided additional incentive to oppose the hamlet strategy.

In addition to the violence that often accompanied forced relocation, families also resented the movement away from their own homes and ancestral holdings. The breaking of the link between villagers and their ancestral land was a cause of much unhappiness amongst the rural population. One villager noted how

ARVN troops return to base across a railroad bridge after a successful patrol. (Albert Grandolini collection)

Initially, ARVN soldiers and the self-defence corps might be stationed at a strategic hamlet. Their presence allowed the Viet Cong to weave stories about the mistreatment of villagers by these forces – not the sentry duty undertaken by the soldier here. (Albert Grandolini collection)

the response to being moved was mixed as 'some like to move in to avoid bombs and bullets dropping on their houses, but others say they don't want to go away from their forefathers' graves and lands.'[61] The villager explained that people would rather fight and die on the land of their ancestors and relocation made this difficult.[62] Interestingly, as the conflict developed, some of these issues began to surface in American reports too. General Krulak reported that many inhabitants of an unnamed hamlet constructed under Operation Sunrise were 'there under duress' and that the intended protection and organisation of the hamlet 'did not really extend far beyond a system of strong physical defences' which helped undermine the goals of the programme.[63] Reports also noted that the Viet Cong would often build upon the unhappiness at this forced relocation and stressed to the villagers that they would be able to 'return to live in their old hamlets' once the war was won.[64]

Whilst it may have been necessary to construct new hamlets because individual homes were 'too widely scattered' to allow organisation of a common defence system, forced movement created other issues too.[65] One problem was that although compulsory relocation and regrouping into hamlets affected only a 'minor percentage' of the population, many of those forcibly resettled were promised subsidies and compensation for their work and losses.[66] They had not received this compensation and as a result, were in debt.[67] This again created anger towards the programme. To compound matters, some villagers were forced to live inside the hamlet but work on land over a kilometre away whilst others were denied the protection of the hamlet and left in outlying areas. The aim was to have them serve as 'intelligence outposts' to report Viet Cong movements within a particular province.[68] Thus, a situation was created whereby some villagers were protected whilst others were left undefended within the same province. This perhaps helps explain why some villagers, when interviewed, were happy with the hamlets whilst others were clearly disaffected. For example, one villager openly expressed his happiness at being in his hamlet and commented that he was given supplies of rice, beans and fabrics.[69] There was also a recognition that as the conflict developed, many of the rural population came 'willingly – in some cases having actually sent deputations to request the development of a hamlet' – and that USOM aid programmes such as 'pig raising, seed and fertiliser distribution, fruit tree planting, well digging and education' were well underway and yielding significant support.[70]

Forced Labour?

Another problem was the use of obligatory communal labour. This labour would, in some cases, last between 45 to 90 days during mid-December and mid-March, with 'only a five-day break for the New Year in February.'[71] This had a negative effect on the overall rural economy and the ability of peasant farmers to manage their crops and subsequent incomes.[72] In addition, many workers were sent up to 100 kilometres away from their own homes to work on hamlet construction, whilst others worked for periods of up to

Despite the propaganda surrounding the Strategic Hamlet Programme – being celebrated here as a success – the VC often undermined the strategy through posters, talks and literature. (Albert Grandolini collection)

49 consecutive days on the projects.[73] Whilst many rural workers built their own homes and constructed the hamlets themselves, construction projects so far from home stoked additional resentment.[74] Donnell and Hickey again noted that the effects on the rural communities were not understood by those in charge because there was both an economic and psychological cost to the work. For example, they recorded that 'the farmers themselves talk about the drastic reduction of the tobacco crop this year (it will be about one-tenth the normal yield) as a "defeat," which they attribute mainly to their heavy communal labour schedules.'[75] They went on to explain that 'one bad crop year can put a Vietnamese farmer in debt for several years afterward because he tends to live on a very narrow subsistence margin' and this helped undermine support for the programme.[76] Whilst there were times, particularly before the rice planting season began, when peasants may have been happy to work away from their fields, this was not the case throughout the hamlets construction.[77]

In addition, although corvee labour had been used before in Vietnam and was a traditional feature of many public works, it had not been used so frequently or for such extensive periods on projects so far away from people's homes.[78] The use of this labour – although necessary in hamlet construction – had several negative consequences. Firstly, much of this labour was associated with French colonial practice and as a result many peasants resented their own government demanding they take part in the Strategic Hamlet Programme.[79] It also helped feed into Viet Cong propaganda about American colonialism and expansionism.[80] Donnell and Hickey claimed that the result of this was that the building of the hamlets often came close to 'arousing peasant dissatisfaction over the programme' and undermined the goal of establishing popular support for the regime.[81] Secondly, advisors in the field found that in several areas, people were 'openly resentful' of the material and labour demands made on them during construction of the strategic hamlets.[82] This situation was exacerbated because whilst there were areas where the government supplied barbed wire and wooden stakes for hamlet defences, the people often had to supply wood and other building materials themselves.[83] Thirdly, many did not receive any pay for their efforts: one refugee farmer noted that the villagers had to give up their own time and 'go to the mountain to cut the bamboo to build Strategic Hamlets by themselves. They didn't receive any money' whilst constructing the village defences.[84] Although local chiefs claimed that workers were paid for their efforts, private interviews often revealed that they received neither food nor the nominal pay rate of 10 piasters per day.[85] It is also telling to note that the Donnell and Hickey report of 1962 recommended that promises of payment for work done and raw materials used should be kept (which indicated they were being broken).[86] Finally, in addition to the monetary outlay, the drain on manpower and the limited resources within the rural communities was also commented upon by RAND interviewees. One noted that the construction costs 'represented the greatest handicap to their occupation and their normal way of living, not speaking of the drain it had on the people's manpower and economic resources.'[87] The result of all of this was a growing burden on rural communities which was reported back to officials in Saigon. For example, Heavner stated that 'the burden on the local population is heavy' and that local families were being required to buy their own nails for traps that they had to make instead of receiving support from the government.[88] The CIA also recognised problems with hamlet financing and noted that 'the district chiefs depend on the local population to finance the programme' and that after paying the costs of construction 'there is usually very little left over for the other aspects' of the hamlet strategy.[89] The CIA also observed that villagers were becoming 'irritated at being forced to contribute to something that produces no tangible results' and that this was reducing morale within these communities.[90]

Neighbourly Aid?

Another reason for unhappiness was that often the people were constructing hamlets for other villages and did not necessarily have the opportunity to live in the hamlets they had built. This led to bitterness and anger as the 'the people who had to live in the strategic hamlet were exempted from building it.'[91] This was because there was often no reciprocal principle involved in the construction process. It was entirely possible for one village to be built with unpaid labour from a neighbouring community which did not receive similar help in return.[92] As a result, the building of a hamlet – which was seen as a positive display of community cohesion – was actually an opportunity for the insurgents to sow division and resentment. One district chief commented that this unhappiness was acceptable because it gave the people of the province a common interest in protecting each other and that a well-constructed hamlet would serve as model for others to copy.[93] Despite these complaints, there was evidence even in the provinces discussed here that 'the people generally seemed to like the idea of strategic hamlets, particularly because the better security made it possible for relatives to visit during Tet' and in some areas 'people seemed almost enthusiastic' about the strategic hamlets themselves.[94] Indeed, in Hoa Hao areas, the rural communities even acknowledged that the hamlets were useful as they helped to stop Viet Cong infiltration and provided security for the local population.[95] Comments such as these highlight one of the problems in analysing the hamlet programme. It was entirely possible to find rural communities who were happily living in constructed hamlets alongside communities who were resentful at having to either build structures for other villages or who were denied access to the hamlets themselves. It is perhaps telling that the signals of disaffection came from in-field reports whilst the signs of enthusiasm were relayed to Washington from officials higher up the command chain. This disconnect between those on the ground in South Vietnam and the administrators in government helps explain why the hamlets were not always reported accurately. Indeed, Pike went so far as to say that one reason for this apparent disconnect was that the hamlet programme was set up 'essentially for the benefit of Saigon and was administered in terms of pay-off for Saigon.'[96] He went on to claim that 'it did not have any particular pay-off for the villager himself.'[97] This meant that problems such as the resentment of the work burden within rural communities were not really tackled in a satisfactory manner. Additionally, the very act of hamlet construction – which was designed to reassure people about government attempts to safeguard them – could divide the general population not only from the insurgents but from their friends too. For example, barricades such as fences offered an 'immediate psychological value' because they made the 'hamlet a visible geographical entity' and created division amongst the population.[98]

Finally, this bitterness also reflected the quality and reliability of province leadership. Reports commented that the manner in which the programme was being carried out and its overall success seemed to be determined 'primarily on the quality of local leadership and their understanding of the programme.'[99] Where the leadership was good the programme was working, but where leadership was poor the programme was failing.[100] There was also a suggestion that some province officials and visiting advisors were covering up the extent of these problems in order to retain their own political position. A CIA memo described how several advisors who visited the hamlets were unwilling to travel great distances and so were content to be 'guided to only those areas which the local officials wish them to see.'[101] This meant that a distorted picture about hamlet construction and effectiveness was being presented to many travelling advisors. It also meant that, in many cases, problems with the abuse of the rural workforce and oppressive actions undertaken by province chiefs were ignored or simply went unnoticed.[102] What is interesting is that before these reports were written, an earlier memo had commented upon the fact that the presidency was 'concerned over the continued misuse of the peasants by the province chiefs in building strategic hamlets.'[103] There was also an awareness of 'the harsh, dictatorial approach' used by the province chiefs which was turning the peasants against the central government.[104] However, there seemed to be little appetite for change. It is perhaps a telling comment on the ineffectiveness of much of the South Vietnamese government that these warnings were not acted upon. Instead, in many provinces, the Strategic Hamlet Programme appeared to be a 'pet project' of the elite that had very little benefit for the villagers themselves. There were other problems too …

A focus on pleasing Saigon and impressing the Americans meant that many hamlet residents felt detached from central government. Here Robert McNamara embarks on a whistle-stop tour of South Vietnam aboard a C-123B airplane – much to the chagrin of many involved in the field. (Albert Grandolini collection)

Again, as an indication of the detachment of Saigon from the rest of the nation, ARVN troops display ample equipment and ammunition whilst many villages lacked even a single gun. (Albert Grandolini collection)

Air Strikes and ARVN

In addition to the issues raised by forced labour, resettlement and poor use of resources, the military strategies and tactics adopted by the counterinsurgents were also unimpressive. One military problem was the ineffective use of air power. When it came to air strikes, many advisors were aware that in a guerrilla war they were often counterproductive. Thompson advised against the bombing and shelling of occupied villages as it would 'leave an indissoluble legacy of bitterness' and would boost support for the insurgents.[105]

Hilsman also recognised that air strikes needed to be used carefully and noted that 'contact must be made with the enemy before the air strike, not after' and that better intelligence was needed to make the tactic effective.[106] It was also acknowledged that air strikes often gave the insurgents a warning of an imminent attack: the three to five minute period taken for air units such as paratroopers to engage with the enemy was often 'time enough for a guerrilla unit to escape to the jungle.'[107] Finally, air strikes had the potential to kill 'innocent or at least persuadable villagers' and thus recruit 'more Communists than were killed' in the initial attack.[108]

Despite an ability to rapidly respond to Viet Cong attack, the insurgents learned to recognise the sounds of oncoming helicopter rotor blades and had often disappeared before troops arrived. (Albert Grandolini collection)

Unfortunately, whilst these problems were recognised, they were not always acted upon and as the war progressed, air power continued to be used, often in a counterproductive way. One reason for this may simply have been indifference. Cottrell, in a 1962 memo, noted that whilst air strikes had 'crippled Viet Cong freedom to attack in large formations and has had a telling effect on Viet Cong morale,' the effect of the accidental killing of villagers in these strikes 'probably depended upon how other villagers reacted.'[109] Cottrell also observed that the impact could be lessened because the villages were 'fairly self-contained units psychologically' and were 'relatively indifferent to the fate of the other villages' within South Vietnam.[110] Cottrell's comments unwittingly indicated the extent of the task facing the Diem regime: village loyalty could be more important than regional harmony and could undermine attempts to build national unity.

Air Strikes and 'Collateral' Damage?

The worry that air strikes would diminish popular support was continued into 1963 when Hilsman noted the paradox the counterinsurgents faced. He claimed that whilst 'there is no doubt that the Viet Cong fear air attacks and that some interdiction is necessary and useful' on the other hand, it was 'impossible to assess how much resentment among persuadable villagers is engendered by the inevitable accidents.'[111] The almost casual use of the phrase 'inevitable' is telling here in that it was unlikely that a similar attitude would be taken to American civilian casualties. This outlook was even more apparent in an airgram of March 1963 which went on to say that although reports had been received that revealed civilian casualties, the difficulty in separating the Viet Cong from the general population meant that this was 'to be expected.'[112] The solution was – rather than change tactics – to balance the casualties inflicted on civilians against insurgent losses.[113]

To be fair, many advisors such as the Director of the Vietnam Working Group (Wood), noted how counterproductive bombing could be. Wood remarked that bombing 'will probably cost us more in good will than it is likely to achieve in destroying VC installations.'[114] He also went on to note – almost as an afterthought – that 'we recently bombed a strategic hamlet by mistake' and this reduced popular support.[115]

Here an airstrike takes place on hidden Viet Cong jungle targets – an A-1E dropping napalm canisters. (Albert Grandolini collection)

Unfortunately, the use of tactical air strikes did not appear to diminish as the campaign progressed. In his report on his 1962 trip, Hilsman commented with evident frustration that there was 'still the same emphasis on air power as there was before'

Troop transports (H-21Cs seen with M-60 sling-mount door guns) deploy into the field in an attempt to target Viet Cong bases. (Albert Grandolini collection)

A US Air Force A-1 attack airplane being loaded in preparation for a bombing raid on a VC-supporting village. (Albert Grandolini collection)

and that 'almost every operation so far as I can tell still begins with an air strike which inevitably kills innocent people and warns the Viet Cong that they should get moving for the troops will be coming soon.'[116]

Another example of a plane being prepped and maintained in readiness for a bombing raid – an A-26. (Albert Grandolini collection)

Bombing raids also meant that aircraft were a target for VC attacks. Here a US Air Force B-57 sits on the ramp having been disabled in a VC attack. (Albert Grandolini collection)

The response of military planners was to argue that they were getting better at targeting the enemy and civilian losses would diminish as tactics and information improved.[117] For example, another airgram of April 1963 stated that:

> Continued refinement of target selection, marking and operational control techniques has reduced insofar as possible the likelihood that interdiction missions will cause casualties among innocent civilians.[118]

Unfortunately, it then went on to suggest that 'there is no way to ensure that interdiction missions will avoid such casualties altogether' and that air strikes would continue.[119] There was also a belief that even though innocent people were being killed, the civilian population would eventually 'seek GVN protection' and therefore deny 'their resources and their energies' to the Viet Cong.[120] The most telling phrase in the airgram though, was that the government of South Vietnam had not yet won the 'loyalty' of the population but it had denied the insurgents a chance to win their support: seemingly missing the point that air strikes were making that support even harder to obtain.[121]

Also linked into the air campaigns was the use of napalm and defoliants. The destruction of crops actually increased the credibility of Viet Cong claims about American involvement in the conflict.[122] Mansfield claimed that by using chemical weapons, the Diem regime was fitting the insurgent narrative of colonial oppression because 'during the Indochina War Napalm was considered here as white colonialists' weapon against yellow "natives".'[123] The use of chemical weapons may have helped reveal insurgent hideouts but it further undermined the claim to legitimate government and reinforced in some minds the link between a colonial America and Diem himself.

Were ARVN Too Defensive?

In addition to the use of chemicals, the strategies adopted on the ground often undermined the notion that the hamlets provided security for the general population. This manifested itself not only in a failure to adequately defend each hamlet but also in the wider conduct of the war. In an airgram to the Department of State, 23 March 1962, it was noted that the first essential purpose of the

More A-1 Skyraiders fully loaded and ready to go! (Albert Grandolini collection)

Defoliants formed a major part of the counterinsurgency strategy. Here the defoliant is sprayed from a C-123 adapted to the task. Unfortunately, they caused more problems than they solved; not only did the chemicals enter the Vietnamese ecosystem, they also poisoned American pilots and created inadvertent fields of fire for the Viet Cong ambushes. (Albert Grandolini collection)

government was to 'provide the villagers with a minimum of effective protection against VC terror and pressures. Only with this can the Government hope to obtain the co-operation and intelligence of the villagers.'[124] The belief here was that the Strategic Hamlet Programme was the way to 'restore a sense of security among the villagers.'[125] Unfortunately, the military units assigned to protecting the hamlets were not suited to the task and gave little indication that the government could protect the people.[126]

One reason for this was the defensive nature of ARVN and the hamlet militia. Maxwell Taylor commented that within the Vietnamese military there was 'a defensive disposition of forces to guard against Viet-Cong attack.'[127] This meant that it forced '80 to 85 percent of ARVN, including the bulk of the specially trained Ranger Force, into essentially static tasks' rather than being involved in search and destroy and patrol operations.[128] This was an important point because the Viet Cong were establishing their own presence in many villages and by acting so defensively, the South Vietnamese military were giving the impression of being unwilling to engage with the insurgents. As a result, this made them appear weak and ineffective. Phillips noted that even a brave province chief such as the leader of Quang Ngai, had lost the respect of the people 'because of his inability to protect them.'[129]

There were many reasons given for the defensive nature of the military. One was that it was unclear how ARVN intended to deal with elements inside the hamlets who were not actively supporting the Viet Cong, but who were 'basically sympathetic to the Communists': it was not apparent if these people should be arrested or left alone.[130] This may have paralysed decision making within the hamlets and reduced the effectiveness of attempts to gain government support. There was also confusion about the strategy itself. Heavner claimed that having spoken to Thompson, the actual concept of the strategic hamlet was not completely understood in the various provinces and as a result the tactics adopted put 'less stress on patrols outside the perimeter' of the hamlet and more on static holding operations.[131] This led to more defensive tactics which resulted in 'an extension of the static defence approach' which had 'dotted the countryside with Beau Geste towers.'[132] The CIA also observed in 1962 that too much of the military were forced into static defensive positions as opposed to be being out on patrol trying

An ARVN briefing for the 21st Tactical Division. Notice that the Strategic Hamlet Programme (the apparent centrepiece of government strategy) appears sixth on the list of topics discussed. (Albert Grandolini collection)

An image reinforcing the perception of ARVN: resting and relaxing between missions. This idea about ARVN was not a fair reflection of the reality. Shown are paratroopers preparing for a jump from waiting C-47s. (Albert Grandolini collection)

An ARVN soldier out in the field: armed, prepped and ready for action. (Albert Grandolini collection)

to disrupt insurgent activity.[133] This was because the province chiefs often believed it was 'their responsibility to protect the population and installations of their areas' and therefore many of the armed forces remained in their bases.[134] These tactics, which were too defensive, created an impression of a force that was unwilling to attack the insurgents.

This approach to maintaining a static defensive posture got worse as time progressed and by 1963 – as Phillips later claimed – the Buddhist Crisis meant that the troops were kept 'in the barracks' because people were afraid of a coup.[135] As a result, ARVN soldiers were stationed in their bases in Saigon as opposed to patrolling the Delta. The effect was that no single organisation was providing any security, hamlets were vulnerable to attack and consequently, the hamlet programme was 'being destroyed.'[136] The Viet Cong were also using the vacuum created by the Buddhist Crisis to move into 'a lot of the hamlets at night, getting the people to take down all of the barbed wire security fences, take the roofs off their houses' and dismantle the Strategic Hamlets.[137] Phillips went on to claim that the Vietnamese Army at this time was not 'providing any security at all' and this further undermined ARVN's claim to be protecting the people of South Vietnam.[138] Indeed, Phillips suggested that the Buddhist Crisis was a significant factor in damaging the hamlets 'in at least two provinces.'[139]

According to USOM, the Buddhist Crisis caused problems as it 'undoubtedly turned the population against' the Diem regime and further undermined claims to government legitimacy.[140] Although outside the scope of this book, both Philips in 2012 and Colby, in an interview in 1983, went so far as to claim that the war was going well until the Buddhists began setting themselves on fire: it was the defensive attitude caused by these events and not the war being fought out in South Vietnam that led to the collapse of the regime.[141] In fact, Phillips later claimed that 'we got off to a good start. Counterinsurgency was working but then the Diem government got itself into big difficulties over the Buddhist affair. This became a huge problem.'[142]

Another example of ARVN aggression; this time as part of a tank assault on Viet Cong emplacements. The M24 Chaffee light tank was common in the ARVN. (Albert Grandolini collection)

Despite their reputation for defensive operations, ARVN were constantly hunting down and attacking the VC. Here soldiers prep a light mortar before an assault. (Albert Grandolini collection)

ARVN Terror and Harassment?

However, even if there had not been a Buddhist Uprising and the troops were out of their barracks, they may have made the situation worse. The conduct of the SDC and ARVN within the villages and hamlets often alienated them from the local people. Although a military presence was needed to show that the government could protect the local population, use of force and an apparent show of strength did not always have the desired effect. It was claimed by one Party Committee Member that the violence towards villagers had been common since 1954.[143] The villager said that he joined the National Liberation Front as a result of the intimidation and the fact that 'the Ngo Dinh Diem family regime arrested, beat-up, and threw a lot of villagers into jail.'[144] It appears from other RAND interviewees that this violence and intimidation continued through to the period under study and its legacy left an underlying feeling of distrust and anger towards the government.

For example, one ex-Viet Minh reported that he was constantly hassled by ARVN and the only 'chance to avoid arrest was to accept the risks of the anti-government struggle' and re-join the insurgency in 1961.[145] Another villager commented that on occasions when the villagers who were building hamlets did not work hard enough, some supervisors 'handled the peasants roughly' to try and increase their productivity.[146] The villagers were also being 'cursed and threatened' if they failed to contribute financially to village programmes.[147] In addition, they faced being 'locked up in the communal house for one or two days' as punishment.[148] This continued throughout 1961 to 1963 and neither the young nor old were spared from violence.[149] One Viet Cong prisoner recalled that the government officials called for free labour and 'had no regard for anyone, not even the elderly. They caught and beat youngsters who strolled around in the evening.'[150] This attitude towards villagers was described as 'violent and arrogant' and it was even noted that if a villager was considered to be looking at a SDC official in a disrespectful way in 'public places such as restaurants or theatres, he would be called out and beaten.'[151] This overuse of intimidation was important because several interviewees commented that the official's bad behaviour was the reason why the GVN was 'losing the people's support.'[152] Some villagers also stated that theft was commonplace during ARVN hamlet searches.[153] Cochran, in his study of motivation and morale, commented that even in 1961, government repression was causing problems as it played 'into the hands of the Viet Cong' and forced many villagers to join the insurgency because they were afraid of punishment from the government if they voluntarily surrendered.[154]

The result of all of this repression was that the behaviour of ARVN and village officials just reinforced Viet Cong propaganda and people began to believe stories about government violence and oppression.[155] This conduct also helped the insurgents because the Viet Cong profited from dissatisfaction with GVN local officials and their 'heavy-handed management' of the strategic hamlets and related community programmes.[156] The stories of violence allowed the insurgents to develop a counter narrative and stir up resentment by claiming that the rural inhabitants were not protected by the counterinsurgency strategy and were being exploited by the government. For example, one villager noted that when the Viet

The self-immolation of Buddhist monks sparked further unrest and made it seem that Diem was losing control of the nation: here Thich Quang Duc self-immolates. The monks would drink a herbal infusion aimed at minimising the pain and then be set alight in full view of the invited media. (Albert Grandolini collection)

Cong entered a village and provoked an attack, rather than blame the insurgents for this, the villagers 'blamed the GVN.'[157] The villager explained that people felt forced into the hamlets, they were not protected by them, they thought they had wasted their labour, effort and money and in the end 'they lost everything.'[158] Propaganda issued by the insurgents also played on this theme of abuse of power. For example, one report on the programme stated that the villagers 'became very angry, because the enemy imposed on them oppression, labour work, torture, terrorism and rape, they could do nothing' and this helped to further develop a narrative of a repressive regime.[159]

ARVN patrol the waterways in armoured boats to withstand and return fire from the shore. There were complaints of heavy-handed behaviour, threats and brutality within the organisation. (Albert Grandolini collection)

ARVN – A Complicated Evaluation: Brave and Tough but Disorganised and Cautious?

However, the situation was not beyond rescue because ARVN were a capable fighting force. In contrast to the image presented in some historical accounts of an incompetent, almost amateur-like organisation, ARVN were experienced soldiers who – if used properly – could have been more decisive in the conflict. Their strengths were admired by, in particular, the CIA. A Special National Intelligence Estimate of August 1961 observed that the major strength of the South Vietnamese Army was its 'extensive combat experience in counter-guerrilla warfare. It has largely been trained

Most US advisors worked well with their South Vietnamese counterparts. (Albert Grandolini collection)

ARVN pictured around a defensive fortification and gun emplacement overlooking open fields and mountains. (Albert Grandolini collection)

under fire.'[160] It went on to detail how ARVN troops had 'a good knowledge of the terrain' in which they fought and had developed, through training and experience, 'the ability to move and fight under difficult conditions.'[161] The Vietnam Task Force supported these positive claims and noted that ARVN were considered to 'have the capability of continuing the suppression of the insurgency and even making considerable headway against it' as they possessed 'an outstanding record of success in jungle war.'[162]

Despite these obvious abilities, the military counterinsurgency effort of ARVN was hindered by several factors. Firstly, there was an ineffective use of manpower and a poor co-ordination of resources. For example, there were many different military groups within South Vietnam and these formed a 'confusing multiplicity of separate armies.'[163] These were listed by Hilsman in a memo to President Kennedy in 1963:

ARVN forces await collection and deployment aboard H-34 assault helicopters. (Albert Grandolini collection)

> In addition to the regular forces (the ARVN), there are under arms the Civil Guard, the Self-Defence Corps, the Civilian Irregular Defence Groups (CIDG), the Hamlet Militia, the Montagnard Commandoes, the Force Populaire, the Republican Youth, the Catholic Youth, several independent groups under parish priests, such as Father Hoa's Sea Swallows, and even one small army trained, armed, and commanded by a private businessman to protect his properties in Cap St. Jacques.[164]

The total number of men in these forces added up to over half a million soldiers which, if organised properly

Father Hoa on patrol with the Sea Swallows. (Albert Grandolini collection)

Sea Swallow forces patrol a river delta. Unfortunately, they were often working in isolation from other South Vietnamese forces. (Albert Grandolini collection)

'would come to the astounding total of 51 divisions.'[165] The problem therefore was not a lack of soldiers but a lack of planning and co-ordination and the fact that these armies were 'not apparently meshed in any way with the strategic hamlet programme.'[166]

This resulted in an inefficient use of manpower and so-called 'friendly fire' incidents. In one case, the Force Populaire 'got itself into a lively fire fight with the Civil Guard through this lack of co-ordination.'[167] This also led to a poor allocation of units around South Vietnam and unrealistic expectations regarding the ability of forces to protect and defend a region. For example, Heavner reported in 1962 that 180 soldiers were guarding an area of over '250 square miles' whilst also trying to keep open 'a 20 mile stretch of highway.'[168] He also described how, at another post, unreasonable requirements meant that 'a 12-man American Special Forces team had trained a 200-man strike force of Montagnard and a patrol group of 150.'[169] Their patrol area 'was 1,800 square miles.'[170]

Poor co-ordination and resource management were compounded by another issue: the slow response times to insurgent attack. The insurgents would attack at night in order to make it difficult for the counterinsurgents to react. However, Taylor noted poor response times to these assaults, claiming that when 'enemy attacks take place, forces are brought up from reserve too slowly to be effective, due to a lack of effective command and control, communications, and mobility.'[171] These problems were compounded by other, more practical issues. Farmer, for example noted that the typical American soldier carried 36 percent of their bodyweight in equipment when out on patrol, in contrast, the average ARVN soldier – usually being considerably smaller – carried around 75 percent of their bodyweight when on patrol.[172] The result of this was slow speeds and short patrol ranges.[173] Another simple problem was the inadequate communications system that the counterinsurgents possessed. Farmer again noted that radios often took a long time to put together and this allowed the insurgents to escape capture.[174] He claimed 30 minutes was the quickest he had seen a radio put together in the field.[175] A final factor here was the way in which ARVN felt it was perceived by outsiders. Many in ARVN had fought valiantly against French colonialists and felt that this experience was ignored. This may also have affected ARVN's approach. For example, Farmer claimed they had 'humbled the elite of the French army' and it was entirely possible that the apparent inability of ARVN to respond in ways demanded by American advisors was a cultural response. They were a force who felt – justifiably – that they had more experience of battle in South Vietnam than their American counterparts.[176]

Perhaps the final reason for the apparently ineffective response of ARVN was the perception that the military culture of South Vietnam often discouraged engagement in battle. Whilst ARVN contained many soldiers and officers who were 'personally brave' they had also suffered, from 1 January to 30 July 1962, nearly 7,500 casualties.[177] These were 'rather heavy losses in fighting a guerrilla war' which did not involve 'large-scale major engagements.'[178] However, there was still a belief in some American circles that ARVN did not really want to fight.[179] For example, Hilsman was informed of the 'reluctance on the part of the ARVN really to engage in a battle.'[180] He was told that ARVN 'do not really want to tangle with the enemy, they want to be completely safe and not have any really serious fight.'[181] This was in part due to the attitude of Diem who wanted to maintain a positive propaganda line and avoid setbacks. This meant that 'there must never be a defeat even a small one, but only one long series

Despite extensive training, the patrol area of many groups could not be adequately monitored – even with helicopter support (UH-1 photographed). (Albert Grandolini collection)

Again, American forces supporting ARVN in the field. Despite some tension, most American and South Vietnamese soldiers worked well together. (Albert Grandolini collection)

of victories' to maintain the perception of success.[182] An example of how this played out in reality was given by Hilsman. He recalled how a successful commander was reprimanded for a victory that was considered an apparent defeat:

> One of the much better commanders, more aggressive commanders, took a group out, killing three Viet Cong officers and 60 regular Viet Cong troops capturing their weapons in a stiff battle in which the ARVN lost one officer and several men. Diem was furious at this "defeat"; to lose an officer is a defeat in his eyes.[183]

These culturally enforced views about the nature of 'defeat' resulted in 'pressure for only victories and only total victories at that' and this led to 'excessive caution' on the part of ARVN.[184] This caution was often manifested in elaborate operations that were 'preceded by bombing, warning the VC and proceeding so slowly as to give the VC ample time to escape' and this reduced the effectiveness of the military operation.[185] This reluctance to engage with the enemy would also help explain the overuse of air strikes: they warned the insurgents of impending attack and meant a confrontation could be avoided and save both sides from combat.

This chapter has discussed another major paradox in the counterinsurgency campaign: the more the Diem regime promoted the hamlets initiative, the more vulnerable they became to attack. Thus, the counterinsurgents faced a conundrum because they were clearly building hamlets at a great rate across South Vietnam, they were establishing new communities and (they thought) improving the life and security of the rural Vietnamese. Unfortunately, they were also increasing rural resentment and making themselves even less popular amongst the South Vietnamese people. This was because many of the construction methods and techniques used undermined the rural economy, moved people off their ancestral land and were inadequate in providing protection for the local population. In addition, labour was used in such a way as to reinforce perceptions of unfairness and many communities lacked a convincing stake in the hamlets they were being forced to build: often they were constructed for other villages. There were also differences in the quality of strategic hamlets from area to area and province to province. For example, those built in the Delta region were not protecting the rural population and were creating resentment towards the Diem regime whilst those in the north of the country were more effective. Finally, these problems were made worse by the conduct of ARVN and SDC and their failure to protect people from attack. These Government forces were often oppressive in the way they treated the rural poor and then were deemed to be 'hiding' in their bases when the insurgents attacked. This further undermined government claims to be protecting and supporting the local people. It seemed that the more the government did, the less effective it became. Often the insurgents simply had to wait for a hamlet to be built. Then they used the very building process and the conduct of the military against the people to further their campaign.

Having looked at how the insurgents were gaining the perceived upper hand in the conflict, the next chapter will explain why the counterinsurgents could not adjust their strategies to build upon their successes. It will examine why they continued to lose a war they were more than capable of winning …

3
THE BEGINNING OF THE BEGINNING?

What was really going on? Why was the picture in South Vietnam so complicated and contradictory? Who was winning? Who was losing?

> Indeed, it was distressing on this visit to hear the situation described in much the same terms as on my last visit although it is seven years and billions of dollars later... in short, it would be well to face the fact that we are once again at the beginning of the beginning.
>
> Senator Mike Mansfield reports back to President Kennedy after his trip to South Vietnam in 1962.[1]

Mansfield's comments, although referring to the situation in South Vietnam in 1962, encapsulate much of what this chapter will discuss: the problems faced by South Vietnam did not, despite military support and social reform, appear to change. This chapter will examine why the counterinsurgents could not alter the direction of the war and why they were unable to capitalise on the limited successes of their strategy. It will show that many of the issues and problems faced by the counterinsurgents were deeply entrenched within South Vietnamese culture and would be familiar to, mirror and pre-empt many of the problems faced by the Johnson Administration later in the conflict. Indeed, Mansfield noted that despite 'new concepts and a new American approach in Vietnam' little appeared to have altered in terms of national security.[2] He went on to explain that South Vietnam, 'outside the cities, is still an insecure place which is run at least at night largely by the Vietcong' and the government in Saigon was still seeking political acceptance in the countryside.[3] Although this book has shown that Mansfield was not entirely accurate in his assessment of the situation on the ground, he was correct in highlighting the problems that the Diem regime faced.

Circles of Interlocking Problems: Taylor's Assessment

Although the following sections will detail aspects of failure in the counterinsurgency operation, the issues raised did not exist in isolation from each other: rather they were interlocking and interconnected. This caused one of the major problems in the analysis of the Strategic Hamlet Programme: it was possible to succeed in so many areas but failure of the whole programme could be caused by difficulties in just one part of the plan. The multi-faceted nature of the issues that South Vietnam faced were described by the Taylor Mission in 1961. Reporting to President Kennedy after his visit to South Vietnam, Taylor described these interlinked problems as forming several 'vicious circles' which undermined support for the Diem regime.[4] Unfortunately for Diem, these continued to cause difficulties throughout the final years of his rule. These circles were described as being both military and political and they had knock-on effects for policy, planning and strategic implementation.[5] The first circle Taylor described was a defensive military strategy made worse by limited intelligence.[6] This meant that over 80 percent of the Vietnamese military were essentially tied down in defensive operations awaiting an attack.[7] This, Taylor conceded, gave the 'initiative' to the enemy.[8] This also resulted in diminished ARVN activity and a counterinsurgent force that was essentially too defensive in nature. The second circle

Protestors confront the army and the police to demonstrate against the Diem regime. Many of these groups were infiltrated by Viet Cong agents. (Albert Grandolini collection)

The Army stand guard outside the Presidential Palace in response to yet another protest. (Albert Grandolini collection)

was characterised as being political. Taylor explained that Diem wanted to keep control of all aspects of government and this limited the initiative of commanders in the field, impeded the distribution of the flow of intelligence and led to poor relationships between the various province chiefs and military commanders.[9] This chapter will explain why these problems were not solved.

'Did you two guys go to the same country?'[10]

Even President Kennedy Was Confused!

The Australian counterinsurgency expert, Dr David Kilcullen, commented that information and intelligence were 'the basis for all other activities' when combating guerrilla forces.[11] This meant that within a counterinsurgency environment the gathering, interpretation and distribution of information was crucial for success.[12] In South Vietnam accurate intelligence gathering was hard. This was a combat arena where accurate analysis of events was difficult and, as the French analyst Robert Trinquier noted, there was 'an interlocking system of actions – political, economic, psychological, military' that all fed into the anti-guerrilla campaign on the ground.[13] Therefore, good intelligence was needed because, as General Wheeler observed, 'the more good intelligence that is forthcoming, the greater the number of successful operations that can be undertaken.'[14] A self-regenerative trend would be created which would ultimately see a 'greater willingness on the part of the people to support the government cause with information.'[15]

Female members of the Civil Guard on parade. Diem and his brother, Nhu hoped to establish self-sustaining military forces to fight off Viet Cong attacks. (Albert Grandolini collection)

Unfortunately for the Diem regime, as the counterinsurgency campaign intensified, the information gathering and application of intelligence was hindered by a number of aspects; it was slow, examined many irrelevant and diametrically opposed factors and was culturally ignorant of the environment in which the conflict took place. Analysts managed to provide information that was so contradictory it provoked President Kennedy to question how these differences could be explained. In fact, Kennedy famously asked, 'did you two guys go to the same country?' when confronted by contradictory reports from his advisors (Krulak and Mendenhall).[16]

The first point to note is that deficiencies in intelligence were acknowledged by the counterinsurgency forces and it was felt that the problem was being addressed as the conflict progressed. However, conflicting analysis meant that many obstacles were never identified and often over-optimistic evaluations of progress resulted in difficulties being ignored. There were several reasons for this. For example, Lansdale discussed problems with the information gathering operation as early as 1961 and Hilsman noted that whilst there was an intelligence deficit in South Vietnam it was one of 'combat' rather than strategic intelligence.[17] However, General Wheeler claimed that by the beginning of 1963, progress had been made to such an extent that the 'development of an effective intelligence system stands near the top in terms of progress achieved during 1962.'[18] Wheeler went on to say that the United States intelligence advisory programme had 'grown into a reasonably effective mechanism' for analysing the progress in the campaign.[19]

Although ARVN performed admirably in the campaign, the intelligence supplied to commanders and senior civil servants was often manipulated or simply incorrect. (Albert Grandolini collection)

Unfortunately, this optimistic appraisal hid several key failings. Firstly, analysis of information was often too slow for a 'timely tactical reaction' and this often ceded the initiative to the Viet Cong.[20] Secondly, the very nature of intelligence in an insurgency meant it was often gathered through informant networks, prisoner interviews and captured documentation: this meant there was a time lapse between activity and action. It was far easier to monitor the movement of a large battalion on the battlefield than it was to follow and assess the intentions and actions of a small insurgent cell that moved between several locations. Thirdly, as Hilsman noted after his visit to South Vietnam in December 1962, co-ordination was 'not really being accomplished' amongst the various agencies

The Civil Guard at graduation with equipment and vehicles designed to help them hunt and capture the Viet Cong. (Albert Grandolini collection)

Police attempt to break up a protest with tear gas. Using violence to disrupt peaceful rallies was a source of much criticism of Diem. (Albert Grandolini collection)

in South Vietnam and the responsibility for this belonged 'with the Americans' in that nation.[21] Notably, Hilsman's comments were in contrast to those of General Wheeler and further underscored the contradictory nature of the assessments taking place at this time.

Lies, Damn Lies and Statistics: Why Target Setting Never Works …

There were many reasons why the intelligence gathered could be reliable, unreliable and contradictory all at the same time. One explanation was that the reports often tended to focus on areas that were irrelevant or not really significant to the overall campaign. This was because of a demand for quantitative data over qualitative data. Phillips claimed that the reason for this was that McNamara wanted to hear about the number of 'regular army operations, how many bodies did they count and how many weapons did they recover, and all that was not relevant to anything.'[22] The result was an abundance of information that actually hindered effective analysis. Pike coined the phrase 'information pollution' to describe this mass of data and although he was discussing a later time period, the basic principle that information overload hindered effectiveness has relevance here. Thompson also discussed the problems of gathering information and claimed that 'there was a plethora of statistics designed to show whether the war was being won or not. Most of them were quite meaningless in this context.'[23] Thompson argued that the intelligence operation should have focussed upon areas such as the ability to grow rice securely or the happiness of the people.[24] Rather scathingly, Thompson went on to claim that 'these indicators were not something McNamara could readily grasp. He wanted figures' to help his analysis.[25] Thompson went on to assert, in agreement with Pike, that the explosion in information collection was a hindrance to effective action because 'if everyone starts collecting intelligence and running agents (and all love to), they end up spying on each other and there is no intelligence.'[26]

This made an accurate assessment of the circumstances on the ground difficult and also created a situation whereby counterinsurgents may have responded to the wrong problem or failed to react at all. The lack of reliable information meant that this problem was exacerbated. For example, even before the Diem coup, there had been a debate in the US administration around the effectiveness of the 'Counterinsurgency Plan' and the hamlet strategy. This was caused, in part, by reports such as the memo from the Department of State, 22 October 1963, that questioned the reported successes and claimed that the war was going badly in South Vietnam.[27] The report alleged that the Diem government was at a 'point it occupied six months to a year ago' in its progress against the insurgency and the counterinsurgency programme had gone backwards.[28] However, the report was countered quickly and it was suggested that it was taking a very narrow, military view of a complex situation on the ground.[29] This meant that two key reports were providing a completely different perspective on events in South Vietnam in the same time period. This was just one example of the

In June 1963, the Farm Gate Detachment was officially separated from the Viet Nam Air Force and redesignated the 1st Air Commando Squadron, USAF (callsign 'Hobo'). By this time, and Douglas B-26 Invaders had been largely replaced by Douglas A-1E Skyraiders (formerly AD Skyraiders) drawn from surplus stocks of the US Navy. Modified for a counterinsurgency role, and capable of carrying up to 14,491lbs (6,573kg) of ordnance, this type proved best suited for operations against the Viet Cong. In addition to attack roles, the type was used for the training of South Vietnamese pilots and for combat search and rescue for downed crews. (Artwork by Tom Cooper)

This A-1E (serial 52-132649) was delivered to the 1st Air Commando Squadron in early 1964. It went on to serve with the unit for years and on 10 March 1966 was flown by Major Bernard Fisher who rescued a downed USAF pilot by landing in enemy territory to fly him to safety: the only known fixed-wing operation of this kind during that war. Serial 132649 was one of relatively few A-1Es to survive the mission: badly damaged in combat and then repaired, in 1968 it was eventually donated to the National Museum of the United States Air Force. (Artwork by Tom Cooper)

As well as A-1s, the 1st Air Commando Squadron also received a new batch of North American T-28 Trojans. This T-28B – assigned to the 'Soc Trang Angels' detachment of the unit – was painted in USAF gray colour (FS36473) with a shallow anti-glare panel in front of the cockpit, VNAF roundels in four positions, and received the quasi-South Vietnamese serial TL-371 on the rear fuselage (a South Vietnamese observer still accompanied USAF pilots on every mission in 1963–1964). The armament illustrated here included a 500-round pod for a 7.62mm machine gun, and CBU-26 cluster bomb units. (Artwork by Tom Cooper)

The 8th Transport Company, US Army, arrived in South Vietnam equipped with Piasecky CH-21B Shawnee helicopters in mid-December 1961. It continued operating this type (and some Bell OH-13E Sioux light helicopters) throughout its deployment at Qui Nhon, which ended in late June 1963. While originally painted in a glossy olive drab (FS14087), by 1963 most of its CH-21Bs had disruptive camouflage patterns. This example – FY-serial 56-2036 – received 'stripes' in light green (FS34102), dark green (FS34092) and coal black (FS37038), and was operated from Qui Nhon as of 1963. (Artwork by Luca Canossa)

Later in 1963, apparently following an overhaul or repairs due to combat damage, and although still based at Soc Trang, the same CH-21C (FY-serial 56-2038I) was repainted in olive drab (FS14087), tan (FS30219), and light green (FS34102), and reassigned to the 121st Aviation Company. This unit arrived in South Vietnam in June 1963, and – after replacing its surviving CH-21Cs with new UH-1Bs, later on – remained in the country until 1970. (Artwork by Luca Canossa)

Starting from early May 1962, the 57th Transportation Company was deployed to Son Dong Air Base, while equipped with CH-21C Shawnees. Its 57th Medical Detachment – deployed at Nha Trang and, later on, Qui Nhon – became one of the first units to be equipped with Bell UH-1A Huey helicopters, which were primarily tasked with casualty- and medical evacuation. Early Hueys were pained in glossy olive drab (FS14087), with a wide yellow stripe around the rear boom, in front of which the service title was applied in white, accompanied by the national insignia. The full service title and the FY-serial (58-2081) were applied in yellow on the fin. (Artwork by Luca Canossa)

One of many minor helicopter units of the US Army to serve in South Vietnam during the early 1960s, before the fleet was consolidated, was the 12th Aviation Company. This was also one of the first units to receive the Bell UH-1B variant of the Huey, including the example illustrated here. As usual, all were painted in glossy olive drab overall, and had a wide yellow stripe around the rear boom. Because the type was new, and due to the local climatic conditions and intensive use, availability of UH-1s was relatively low. On average, an aviation company was assigned 25 Hueys, but only about 50 percent were fully mission capable at any one time. Therefore, units usually sought to have enough helicopters ready for action to simultaneously lift around 60 troops. (Artwork by Luca Canossa)

The Sikorsky CH-37 Mojave was a heavy-lift helicopter, capable of lifting up to 26 troops or 24 stretchers, or up to 3,000kg of freight. It entered service in 1954 and by 1960 all the US Army-operated examples were upgraded to the CH-37B standard through the installation of a Lear auto-stabilisation equipment and the ability to load and unload while hovering. Three units operating this type were deployed in South Vietnam: the 56th Transport Company at Tan Son Nhut starting in May 1963, A Flight of the 19th Aviation Company starting in 1964, and the 611th Transport Company. All their mounts were painted in olive drab overall, and wore only the usual set of national markings, service titles, and warning insignia. (Artwork by Tom Cooper)

Thanks to extensive aid from the USA, through 1963 and 1964 the VNAF continued expanding its helicopter component, which was of crucial importance for the capability of the ARVN to rapidly deploy its troops in reaction to the appearance of any bigger concentration of the Viet Cong. Deliveries of Sikorsky UH-34D Seahorse helicopters enabled an increase in number of VNAF squadrons operating this type to five (211th, 213th, 215th, 217th and 219th). This example – FY-serial 54-2903 – served with the 213th Helicopter Squadron in 1964–1967. It retained its flat/medium green (FS34102) overall livery, but received no national insignia. As usual, the serial consisted of the 'last five' of the former US-serial: in this case (5)4-2903 of the US Army. (Artwork by Tom Cooper)

The CMP CT15A was an armoured truck developed by General Motors Canada following a similar idea to the M3 Scout Car, but based on the chassis of the Chevrolet C15 Canadian Military Pattern truck. Over 3,900 were manufactured between 1943 and 1945. Several dozen were deployed by British forces in Vietnam during 1945–1946 and then taken over by the French, which used them intensively before transferring surviving vehicles to the Army of Vietnam in the mid-1950s. In Vietnamese service, they retained their overall olive drab colours, and wore a bare minimum of other markings. (Artwork by David Bocquelet)

Most strategic hamlets were surrounded by deep trenches and a bamboo fence, made of sharpened bamboo beams. Due to the lack of material caused by a diminishing harvest, this was anything but thick. Nevertheless, it frequently proved adequate to prevent the Viet Cong from entering the villages unobserved, and prevented or stopped small-scale attacks on a number of occasions – especially when reinforced with barbed wire. (Artwork by Anderson Subtil)

Developed and produced by the FMC Corporation, the M113 is a fully tracked armoured personnel carrier, designed to have aluminium armour thick enough to protect the crew and passengers from small arms fire, but light enough to remain amphibious and air portable. The basic M113 was armed with a single .50-calibre M2 machine gun. It was introduced to service with mechanised rifle squadrons of the ARVN in 1962 and proved highly successful. Nevertheless, combat experience soon led to a number of modifications, the most important of which was the addition of the Armoured Cavalry Assault Vehicle kit (ACAV), consisting of additional machine guns and armour plates protecting their operators. (Artwork by David Bocquelet)

Generally, the Viet Cong were merciless against any form of resistance, and would regularly assassinate or severely torture anybody daring to oppose them: the resulting body was usually dumped near the gates of the strategic hamlet in question. Whenever this was impossible, insurgents would mine the gate with hand grenades, aiming to maim or kill anyone careless enough to open these without proper inspection. (Artwork by Anderson Subtil)

The Cadillac/General Motors Corporation M114 was a lightweight, low-silhouette armoured fighting vehicle, designed to complement the M113 in command and reconnaissance roles. Constructed of aluminium, it weighed only 13,100lbs (5,900kg) empty and was equipped with a commander's cupola that had a .50-calibre M2 machine gun: the improved M114A1 allowed the firing of the machine gun from the inside, utilising manual traverse and elevating mechanisms. The ARVN received a total of 80 M114s which it deployed in four reconnaissance squadrons, starting in 1962. However, the type proved mechanically unreliable and vulnerable to mines, and was completely replaced by M113s by November 1964. (Artwork by David Bocquelet)

Another favourite method of the Viet Cong to terrorise the population into submission – or disrupt the patrolling activity of the ARVN – was to mine the jungle paths with the help of simple traps including hand grenades. (Artwork by Anderson Subtil)

Patch of the AATTV.

This member of the Australian Army Training Team Vietnam is shown wearing his distinctive slouch hat, the Australian version of the British OG uniform, and modified jungle combat boots. On his sleeve is the unmistakable patch of the US Military Assistance Command, Vietnam (MACV), and his combat gear is a mix of US-made and the Australian Army regulation backpack. His firearm was the Paratrooper version of the standard M1A1 carbine with folding buttstock and adjustable sight. (Artwork by Anderson Subtil)

This Montagnard from the early 1960s is shown wearing only his traditional clothing, an M1956 North American canvas belt with a bag for magazines for his weapon, and an old but reliable .45ACP M3 submachine gun, known as the 'Grease Gun' or simply 'the Greaser' to the Americans. Camouflage uniforms like the 'Duck Hunter' or 'Tiger Stripe' became common only after 1964. (Artwork by Anderson Subtil)

This Colonel of the ARVN is shown commanding his troops from an Asian elephant, while wearing the standard uniform of the early 1960s, including a fatigue cap with gold rank insignia, camouflage scarf wrapped around his neck, and GI boots. His gear includes an M7 shoulder holster for his Cold M1912 pistol: although revolvers were more common this was considered a status symbol. His 'driver' is a member of the Regional Forces and shown as armed with an old French MAS rifle. (Artwork by Anderson Subtil)

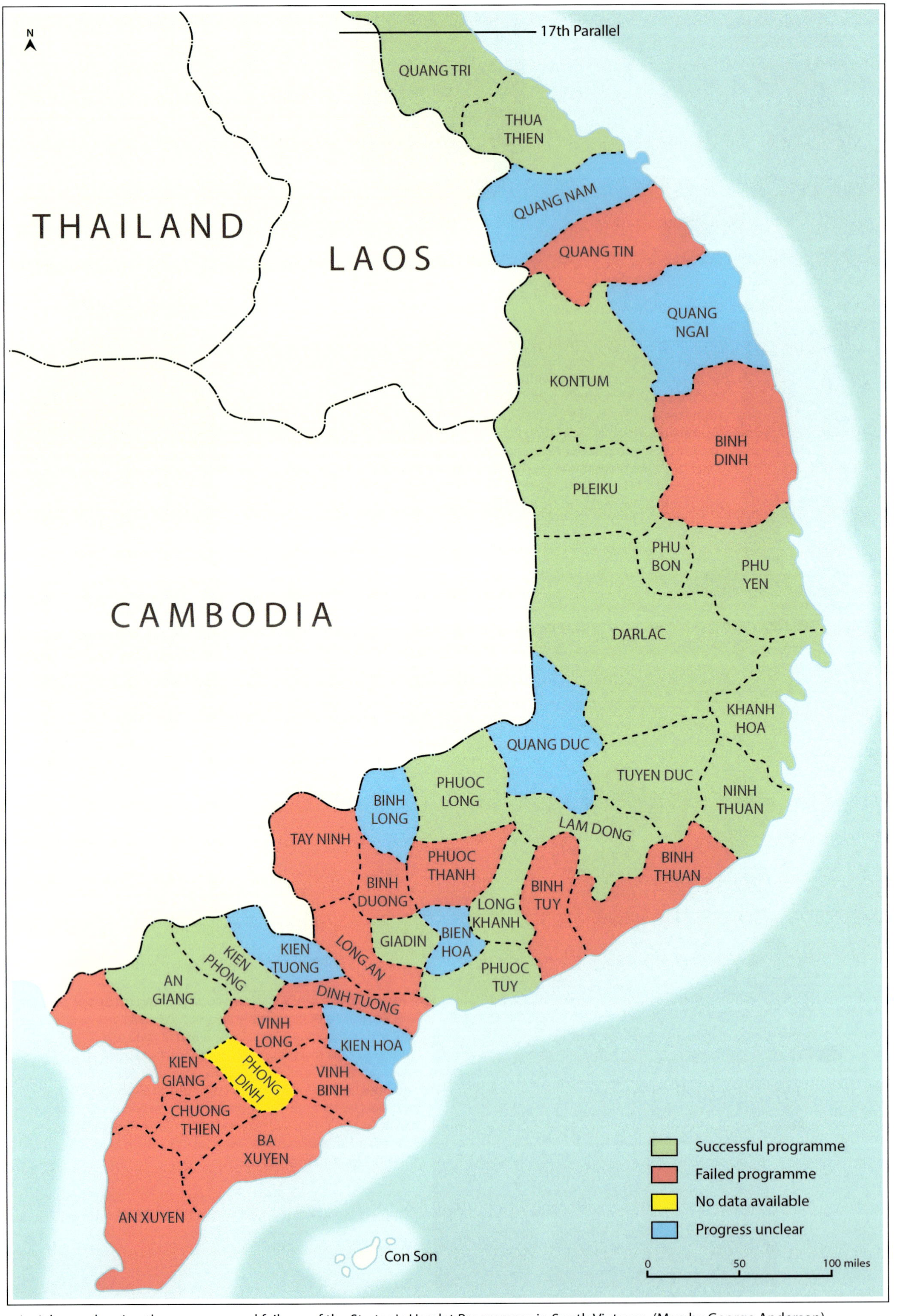

A provincial map showing the successes and failures of the Strategic Hamlet Programme in South Vietnam. (Map by George Anderson)

Protestors being manhandled and arrested. Accusations of prisoner torture and beatings were rife. (Albert Grandolini collection)

conflicting nature of much of the reporting and helps to explain why determining progress was so difficult. It is also worth noting that there was some deliberate inflation of success indicators on the part of the Vietnamese too.

Another problem with statistical data analysis was that it would often distort understanding of the conflict. Again, in his memoirs, Thompson commented that the cost of war was 'not symmetrical on both sides' and so to compare the losses of the insurgency vis-a-vis the losses of ARVN was not comparing like with like.[30] This would lead to incorrect assumptions being made and poor policy being devised.[31] Statistical data collection also resulted in target setting imposed from either Saigon or Washington that distorted reporting and analysis. Again, Phillips explained how people would simply adjust their data collection to meet the targets set:

> Of course, the Vietnamese, like anybody else, if that is how you are going to measure my performance, I am going to exaggerate. Anybody who gets in the line of fire is a VC, so that's a body. And of course that just proliferated to the nth degree when we got big forces in there; it is the same thing.[32]

Phillips went on to allege that many province chiefs 'tended to exaggerate their progress to Saigon, to look good' and this further hindered the effectiveness of intelligence gathering as inaccurate reports flooded Saigon.[33] This became apparent after Diem's death when illusions were 'shattered' and many advisors realised that the exaggerated claims of hamlets being built did not match reality.[34]

However, despite this focus on statistical data, other reports were available for analysis. The USOM reports and informal appreciations of the Strategic Hamlet Programme were sent to the Secretary of Defence for analysis. McNamara claimed never to have seen these reports and Phillips says this was because he (McNamara) had created such a conventional reporting system that the reports did not 'get into the reporting system as it existed.'[35] This was because the nature of the reports – being almost an unconventional analysis of the situation on the ground – were qualitative assessments of progress rather than quantitative data. Indeed, another advisor in South Vietnam at this time, Bert Fraleigh, went so far as to claim the blame for following 'conventionality to certain defeat' lay with 'the highest level military and political leaders' (particularly McNamara) because of the arrogant attitude that they displayed in their analysis of the situation on the ground in South Vietnam.[36] In fairness to McNamara, it should be noted that USOM also sent their reports to President Diem, General Harkins, the United States Ambassador and 'to everybody' so the blame for ignoring their contents does not rest solely with the Secretary of Defence.[37]

Whilst statistical data collection may have distorted the overall analysis, another problem faced by the counterinsurgents was that reports on the success of the campaign in South Vietnam could vary depending on the focus or background of the person involved. It was, as Thompson's quote used at the start of Volume 1 of this series suggested,[38] possible for anything to be proven in the war. The issue was not that the people involved were poorly informed, rather that they were talking to a narrow group of individuals who confirmed

President Diem examines an early counterinsurgency initiative at the start of the 1960s. (Albert Grandolini collection)

McNamara attends another briefing about the situation in South Vietnam. Many of these were almost informal in nature and the Americans were criticised for failing to understand Vietnamese culture: taking the wrong lessons from each meeting. (Albert Grandolini collection)

their own world view or supported their political or military agenda: it was almost as if a self-selecting information gathering process was taking place. For example, in the Kennedy briefing discussed earlier, Mendenhall had visited Central Vietnam and talked to anti-Diem dissidents whereas General Krulak had visited the Delta and spoken to military personnel.[39]

The resultant reports they produced reflected this difference in tone and outlook. Interestingly, in an interview in 1970, Krulak claimed that after the Kennedy briefing, the president invited him into his office and said to him, 'I just want to tell you I believe you.'[40] Krulak also recounted further details of the meeting with President Kennedy and his explanation given for the contradictory nature of the reports was due to Krulak claiming he was reporting on 'national' attitudes whilst Mendenhall was commenting upon urban attitudes.[41] This would again support the idea of different provinces yielding different perspectives. The record also showed that Ambassador Nolting questioned the validity of Mendenhall's assumptions whilst Phillips explained that the Vietnamese would be reluctant to express their true feelings to foreigners, such as Krulak, whom they hardly knew.[42] Kennedy's exasperation at the situation was entirely understandable!

McNamara arrives at the Presidential Palace in Saigon for another meeting with South Vietnamese officials. (Albert Grandolini collection)

There was also a suggestion that deliberate manipulation of data was taking place. In an interview in 1984, General John Michael Dunn claimed that these contradictory reports should not have surprised anybody:

> Because, in the first place, they frequented different haunts and they talked to people with entirely different orientations. And they did it deliberately and with malice, aforethought in my judgement in both instances. They knew exactly what they wanted to hear and they knew where to go to get it. And that was not just an isolated instance.[43]

Urban unrest was reflected in Mendenhall's report and here police arrest student protestors at a Saigon rally. (Albert Grandolini collection)

Dunn's claim of almost deliberate distortion in the reporting was supported by Phillips. He recalled a briefing given to Krulak that later formed part of the General's report to President Kennedy. Phillips described how, when challenged on the accuracy of his reporting, the colonel in charge simply said that he was told to present information in a particular way (original spellings included):

> Krulack went down to the Delta and got a bunch of military briefings. I had gone to one of those damn briefings up in Bien Hoa just north of Saigon where they carried out an operation in the Iron Triangle in which the Vietnamese Army had run a bunch of tanks over the place and hadn't encountered anything. Nothing came out of this operation. I happened to go to this meeting at which the division advisor, Colonel Miller, gave this incredible briefing to Krulack about how it was a great victory. Afterwards

Unrest in 1963 culminated in an attack on the Presidential Palace and the overthrow of the Diem regime. (Albert Grandolini collection)

One success story in the counterinsurgency campaign was the training of the Montagnards in the Highlands. They were enthusiastic campaigners against the Viet Cong and were the victims of insurgent massacres too. Here a Montagnard volunteer is being trained in the use of firearms by one of the numerous American advisors in South Vietnam. (Albert Grandolini collection)

> I went up to Miller, because I knew him, and said, "How the hell can you tell a guy like Krulack what you just told him? You know that is not true." He said, "Well, that is the way they wanted it presented."[44]

This would seem to indicate some form of deliberate distortion of the facts which would add further difficulty to the analysis being attempted in Washington.

Ignoring Local Knowledge and Experience

Whilst an obsession with statistics and dubious reporting methods all helped to cloud the intelligence gathering operation, a lack of cultural or contextual awareness also hindered effective information operations. One reason for this was that American attitudes and ideas did not always co-exist happily with Vietnamese cultural values. This was, unfortunately, often expressed through ignorance and a lack of local knowledge. For example, Thompson recalled his shock upon arriving in South Vietnam and finding that 'at this stage no one had looked at the French record and no American we met had read Mao' and this limited their understanding of the nature of the war.[45] Whilst Thompson's assertion was too sweeping a statement to make, it did illustrate how counterinsurgents had to really understand the theatre in which they operated and indicated that some United States personnel felt they could rectify any problems encountered without reference to past historical experiences. For example, the Taylor Report noted how even though the war had to be won by the Vietnamese, their performance 'in every domain can be substantially improved if Americans are prepared to work side by side with the Vietnamese on the key problems' and the Vietnamese listened to their American counterparts.[46] Unfortunately, this 'side by side working' often meant imposing ideas from the top down – usually with little understanding of how South Vietnam worked – or with any regard for the needs of the local population. It also ignored the vast experience accrued by ARVN during the Indochina War against the French. Lansdale remarked upon this tendency for top-down imposition in 1981 when he commented on the major problems of policy, planning and implementation in the war. He

Local recruits were vital. Again, the Montagnards formed units in the Highlands that rooted out and killed Viet Cong insurgents. They developed a ferocious reputation. (Albert Grandolini collection)

claimed that relatively few initiatives came from the Vietnamese on the ground:

> The essential trouble with every last one of them was that they were made in Saigon or made abroad, outside of the area and dictated from above. I learned very early on, you do things locally and have it go from bottom to the top and accepted at the top to have them work. A lot of them were American ideas.[47]

This tendency to impose ideas and plans was noted by Phillips who said one of the problems in South Vietnam was a tendency for controlled management that was completely unsuited to the country and the rural population. He wrote about how plans, theories and a lack of 'real-world' experience led to unrealistic agendas:

> The notion that you could impose a hierarchical structure covering everything in South Vietnam was some notion that you might get if you were in the State Department or the Pentagon but it had nothing to do with reality.[48]

The result of this imposition of policy and attitude was that a lack of understanding developed in the field. This hindered interpretation of intelligence gathering and created one-dimensional thinking that may have been 'good for the spleen but it is not contributory to thinking aimed at defeat of the Viet Cong.'[49] Indeed, in his report of 1962, Mansfield commented that the 'temptation to extrapolate our own reactions on to the Vietnamese' was dangerous and would damage the overall war effort.[50]

Western notions of democracy and fairness did not always manifest themselves in the South Vietnamese government. Here, advisors and government officials await the President's arrival. Many were appointed through secret elections and confrontational, adversarial politics was an anathema to many South Vietnamese. (Albert Grandolini collection)

This was illustrated most clearly by an account of an election taking place in a hamlet, where Western concepts of democracy actually undermined the local traditions. The adversarial nature of Western politics was alien to many South Vietnamese and one province chief openly admitted to rigging the local elections in order to maintain control of the village.[51] A missionary also pointed out that the Vietnamese found confrontational, Western-style elections 'repugnant' as the Vietnamese would rather make informal decisions behind closed doors and 'save face.'[52] Indeed, the same missionary went on to say that 'of course the elections are decided in advance. The people would be very uncomfortable if they were not.'[53] Phillips noted that this misunderstanding was 'kind of typical, that is that we come into a country and we don't know what they are doing, so we dream up a lot of ideas of our own.'[54] This lack of cultural knowledge hindered the counterinsurgency campaign and revealed one of

The popularity of President Diem is often understated. Many rural Vietnamese still respected him as a man, even if they felt he was a flawed leader. This photo from 1956 shows the President being greeted by admirers as he undertakes a tour of the country. (Albert Grandolini collection)

Another way in which outsiders misunderstood South Vietnamese culture was in the portrayal of Madame Nhu. Often depicted as a 'Dragon Lady', many of the accusations about corruption and nepotism were not borne out by the sources used in this book. (Albert Grandolini collection)

Montagnards enrol in counterinsurgency training. Lansdale pointed out to McNamara that much of this needed to be standardised and the Americans had to have a way of evaluating the success of their approach in the nation. (Albert Grandolini collection)

the problems of imposing values from one culture onto another: it developed inappropriate and counterproductive policy.

Lansdale Writes to McNamara – a Missed Opportunity?

There were, though, efforts made to correct this lack of knowledge and experience. In July 1962, Lansdale sent a memo to McNamara, which he titled 'The "X-Factor," Vietnam' and listed questions that people in the field should be asking in order to determine the success of the war effort.[55] Lansdale wrote the memo because he wanted to encourage ways 'of getting a sharper picture of how we are doing in Vietnam.'[56] He listed ways in which the questions should be framed, to whom they should be addressed and when and where they should be asked.[57]

The questions included such seemingly basic information as the location of the village being attacked and progressed to more in-depth analysis that attempted to understand what happened in the hamlets themselves. For example, questions such as 'how did the military forces behave and how did people become stakeholders in their communities?' were common.[58] The list of questions was extensive, ran to over thirteen hundred words and was an attempt to use Lansdale's experience in the Philippines to try and bring some qualitative analysis to the situation on the ground. Some additional examples of the type of questions asked included:

> What happens to civilians who come to a Vietnamese military unit with complaints, problems, or questions? Does the commander talk to them? A special officer on the staff? Are they turned away by the guards? If there are wrongs complained about, what redress is given? How? Do the local people hear about this? How?[59]

McNamara's response was to write 'an excellent set of questions Ed – it is this kind of info I need and am not receiving.'[60] This would support McNamara's assertion earlier in this section that he did not receive reports such as those compiled by USOM but it also raises several points of interest. Firstly, Lansdale clearly felt that there was a problem with the gathering of information in South Vietnam and by drawing up a list of questions was suggesting a remedy to the problem. Secondly, the very straightforward nature of some of the questions, for example, 'which weapons do the troops like best?' would suggest rudimentary information gathering in extremis and a limited knowledge of the combat theatre by some counterinsurgents. Finally, Lansdale's memo raises the issues as to why, if he felt he was not getting such basic information, McNamara did nothing to address this in subsequent months? Many of the USOM reports discussed were published after the 7 July date of the memo so it appears that systems were not in place that enabled the content of these reports to get to the Secretary of Defence.

Internal Conflict

Whilst issues in information gathering such as the cultural ignorance, dubious reporting and an obsession with statistics all hindered the counterinsurgents' response to the situation in South Vietnam, there were also failings in the internal workings of the military and political establishments that exaggerated the problems encountered. Hilsman, in 1962, noted that a major difficulty with the United States Missions and their allies in South Vietnam was that 'they do not always work as a team. Each agency has its own views and concepts which have led to inter-agency jealousies and bickering' and this limited the effectiveness of policy on the ground.[61]

Establishing a 'Special Group for Counterinsurgency'

Attempts were made in 1962 (with National Security Action Memorandum, NSAM, 124) to counter this problem. It established a special group for counterinsurgency and attempted to co-ordinate actions around anti-guerrilla campaigns.[62] The aims of the group were to 'to establish broad lines of counterinsurgency policy,' to

The multitude of different organisations tackling the Viet Cong within South Vietnam is illustrated in these three photographs. The first one shows the Civil Guard who would respond to and defend strategic hamlets … (Albert Grandolini collection)

… the second shows the Montagnards cleaning weapons and preparing for a patrol … (Albert Grandolini collection)

… and the third photo shows Father Hoa's Sea Swallows on parade. Unfortunately, the assortment of militias, groups and organisations lacked a cohesive, organising force. (Albert Grandolini collection)

ensure 'a co-ordinated and unified approach to regional or country programmes' and verify 'progress in implementation thereof.'[63] It also had to 'make decisions on interdepartmental issues arising out of such programmes.'[64] It did not bode well for the future of the group that Komer wrote – in response to finding out about the initiative – 'as for me, I didn't even find out about NSAM 124 (which I initially drafted) until well after it was out' and he went on to say that 'someone has fallen down on the job.'[65] This would appear to indicate that communication was a problem embedded in the White House office even in this early stage of the conflict (January to February 1962).[66]

A lack of co-ordination of activities and weak analysis was commented upon by Krulak in a memo to Gilpatric on 26 March 1962.[67] In the memo Krulak discussed how one of the main problems facing the counterinsurgents was that each particular faction in the campaign had their own agenda and as such, this distorted their view of the conflict and resulted in each department wanting to tackle the problem in their own way.[68] Krulak then showed foresight in that he recommended the solution to this problem and noted that the counterinsurgents had to synthesise their approaches and 'blot out the organisational lines and function as a single matrix of power.'[69] He claimed that confusion was damaging the campaign and 'the time is past when we can hope to meet the Communists with a system in which diplomacy, guns, propaganda, and dollars all seek to function alone.'[70] Krulak went on to suggest that the way forward was for each group to assign deputies to the Counterinsurgency Group established by NSAM 124 in order to speed up decisions made.[71] Interestingly, he finished his memo by claiming that 'this whole CI Group idea is wrong, in as much as it transgresses organisational lines.'[72] This would perhaps indicate his real view on how the various bodies involved in counterinsurgency should stick to their special areas of interest.

Too Many Cooks Spoil the Broth?

Krulak's analysis was supported by many of the papers found in the Kennedy Library and in the Foreign Relations of the United States papers. Firstly, in terms of sharing equipment, Hilsman was scathing in his assessment of the Air Force versus Army-Air Corps and the support for helicopter missions. He highlighted how he had been told by Major General Edward L. Rowny, that the Air Force was 'very reluctant' to provide escorts for helicopters in the field of battle and was placing a very high priority on 'retaining command of the air,' which he noted, rather dryly, was a priority even though 'there is, of course, no air opposition.'[73] Secondly, General Wheeler noted that within ARVN there was a tendency to 'hold planning very closely within the armed forces' and this inhibited complementary air support planning.[74] As a result the pre-operational advantages that air support could bring, such as 'photo, weather and visual reconnaissance and observation' were not forthcoming.[75] Thirdly, this poor co-ordination got in the way of effective action. Again,

The Sea Swallows in operation aboard an aircraft. In this case operating a Medevac procedure in support of ARVN. (Albert Grandolini collection)

Hilsman noted that Rowny's information had revealed how the counterinsurgency programmes required 'precise and efficient co-ordination of the different activities of many different American agencies' and unfortunately, Hilsman had the impression that this co-ordination was not really being achieved.[76] This lack of co-ordination was not helped by the workings of the Kennedy administration in Washington. Thompson noted in his memoirs that on arriving in Washington to discuss the Strategic Hamlet Programme 'the impression left with me was of a vast machine completely uncoordinated, rather like a large four-engined aircraft with its engines unsynchronised' which resulted in chaos and poor planning.[77] Thompson's assessment was supported by Arleigh A. Burke, Admiral on the Joint Chiefs of Staff, who was scathing of the organisation in the White House.[78] In a 1967 interview, Burke claimed that as soon as Kennedy took office, 'immediately there was chaos.'[79] He went on to say that the politicians did not seem to have 'an overall objective' regarding the conduct of operations in South Vietnam and there was a lack of leadership as 'nobody knew who was in charge of a particular item' and this contributed to internal conflict and division.[80]

These issues and problems began to be recognised and addressed as the conflict progressed. By 1963, Hilsman had acknowledged difficulties within the overall counterinsurgency effort, claiming that whilst 'individual agencies are doing a superb job (e.g., Rufus Phillips, Richardson of CIA and the Special Forces)' it could not be claimed that there was a 'wide understanding' or a 'clear conception' of the nature of the counterinsurgency effort.[81] As Hilsman was one of the conceptual planners this was rather a scathing self-critique.

Hilsman and Forrestal went on to suggest that the size of the American effort in South Vietnam caused a lack of direction.[82] This was because there was 'no one man' in charge and this resulted in a lack of cohesion. Additionally, the size and competing nature of much of the American input created unnecessary problems in the war:

> The US effort, although massive, is fragmented and duplicative. An example is the chronic shortage of weapons for strategic hamlet defenders. There are more than enough weapons in the country, but they get lost in Vietnamese government depots. The full effort of the American community is rarely concentrated on breaking such bottlenecks.[83]

The solution was, according to Hilsman, to promote an overall commander for counterinsurgency operations: 'ideally, what we need is what the British had in Malaya – a Gerald Templar who has absolute authority to hire and fire anyone in any agency or department and through whom all reporting and all orders are transmitted.'[84] This would, Hilsman felt, result in effective teamwork and an increased efficiency in the counterinsurgency campaign.[85] Phillips felt that Lansdale would have been an ideal candidate but that he was considered to be difficult and Lansdale was not appointed because bureaucrats in Washington did not want someone in South Vietnam that they could not control.[86] Even though the organisation and co-ordination arguably improved as the war progressed, the result of these internal conflicts and organisational issues meant that there was 'no overall planning effort that effectively' tied together the civilian and military activity.[87] As a result there was little or no long-range thinking about the 'kind of country that should come out of victory' and little concept of the ultimate goal.[88] Thus, separate organisations were hindering effective progress and were also allowing the South Vietnamese to, in Colby's words 'play one off against the other a bit' and this added confusion in the war effort.[89] Successful implementation required firm and accurate monitoring of progress and this was often missing during the campaign. This was further hindered by inaccurate reporting from the South Vietnamese. This over-exaggerated success, distorted the nature of the programme and misrepresented what was occurring in large parts of the country. Indeed, as the next section will demonstrate, it was not just events in Washington that caused problems: proceedings inside the government of South Vietnam were also undermining the effectiveness of the counterinsurgency strategy.

Sabotage in the South

Micro-management within the Diem regime

Although issues of organisation and the chain of command were hindering counterinsurgency success, the problems were made worse by the situation on the ground in South Vietnam. The American support for Diem was part of a political process aimed at defending his regime, increasing democracy and suppressing Viet Cong activity. Unfortunately, the Diem regime was not always able to implement the reforms needed and had to deal with many problems. The difficulties that Diem's government faced were summed up by a Special National Intelligence Estimate of March 1961 which stated that the Vietnamese Army was starting to question Diem's ability to lead, corruption was increasing and many in the countryside were disillusioned by the lack of protection they were receiving against Viet Cong attack.[90]

Although Diem has received a lot of criticism from historians, he was respected by many of the Americans who worked with him.[91] Taylor described him as a man with 'extraordinary ability, stubbornness, and guts' and McGarr styled him as 'pro-US, definitely

Madame Nhu poses inside the Presidential Palace. She was often the target of press attacks and – it could be argued – served as a proxy target for the government. (Albert Grandolini collection)

Madame Nhu played a prominent role in the Diem regime's propaganda material. Here she inspects strategic hamlet militia. Notice that the militia are only armed with spears; in many hamlets this was the only weapon of defence against Viet Cong guns and grenades. Despite this the hamlet militias often fought incredibly bravely in defence of their homes and family. (Albert Grandolini collection)

anti-Communist' and said he had 'done a remarkably fine job during his five years in office against terrific odds.'[92] McGarr went on to say that Diem was 'the most tough-minded, dedicated practicing anti-Communist leader among our friends today.'[93] However, even though there was praise for Diem, in his letter to President Kennedy in 1961, Taylor noted that Diem was also a problem because he was trying too hard to keep centralised control of the whole government.[94] This was in keeping with the style of a traditional Asian ruler: power was centred on him and his family.[95] Unfortunately, this resulted in Diem micro-managing many of the policies he was trying to implement, it weakened the chain of command and undermined the decision making processes of those out in the field. The result of this was that his government displayed an 'inability to mobilise intelligence effectively' which hindered operational development and undermined devolution in the provinces.[96] The centralisation of power was not the only reason for Diem's unpopularity within parts of South Vietnam.

Another reason for disapproval was the heavy-handed nature of the regime: torture, imprisonment, press suppression and intimidation were all used against political opponents. The regime was also, arguably, too heavy-handed in its approach to relatively minor incidents of protest and disruption. For example, Pike recalled how one officer in the army had told him of the arrest of his sister. The story illustrates the character of the regime and the indiscriminate nature of arrests:

> In August of 1963, which was three or four months before Diem was overthrown, a South Vietnamese army lieutenant colonel that I knew very well, a very respected combat soldier, came to me and said, "Diem's police have just arrested my sister. She's eleven years old." She'd been out at a Buddhist demonstration. He said, "What should I do?"[97]

Arresting children was not the only problem with the administration. There were also allegations of violent assaults on American journalists. One such account described an attack on correspondents in Saigon and noted how the police intimidated the press and destroyed equipment. This caused further anger and resentment towards the regime:

> This Sunday morning at the entrance to Chantareansay Pagoda in Saigon nine representatives of American news organisations were subjected to a swift unprovoked and violent attack by government plain clothes police while covering an otherwise peaceful Buddhist religious ceremony. One correspondent was knocked down and kicked. Other newsmen were shoved, jostled and struck by rocks thrown by the plain clothes men – all in full sight of forty to sixty uniformed metropolitan policemen and a squad of riot police. In the course of the attack one camera was smashed and several damaged.[98]

Attacks on the foreign media reinforced Viet Cong propaganda portraying an out of touch despot who was not only attacking his own people but intimidating foreign nationals too.

The Philosophy of Diem: 'Personalism' in Action?

Unfortunately, the Ngo's own adopted philosophy – Personalism – also helped cement the image of a Third World leader obsessed with his own personal theories and out of touch with events in his country. Personalism was developed by the French philosopher, Emmanuel Mounier and was intended as a path between communism and liberal capitalism: Diem and Nhu saw it as a way of empowering the South Vietnamese to take charge of their own destiny.[99] In 1963, *The Times* described Personalism as being a complex idea that drew upon Confucian principles to try and develop loyalty to the state through civic duty. The article claimed that Diem wanted to develop an ideology that confronted the inability of developing countries to make progress. Diem, it was argued, felt that democracy was not vital for economic or social progress in the early stages of development. Instead, Diem was seeking to develop an attitude that recognised the

Diem tried to promote his own philosophy. 'Personalism' mixed South Vietnamese and Asian tradition with individual, modernising collective responsibility. (Albert Grandolini collection)

individual within the context of their responsibilities to the wider, collective whole.

This would incorporate traditional Vietnamese values of Thanh and Tin whilst helping the country progress towards becoming a modern nation. When discussing these principles, *The Times* journalist reported how Diem had spoken of incorporating traditional Asian tenets into a modern philosophy:

> Of the traditional Vietnamese civic virtues of Thanh and Tin. The first expresses the concept of duty towards the Creator and the state; while the second defines the courageous practice of that duty. These Confucian ideas are incorporated in the theory of "personalism," which is, in effect, the official ideology of South Vietnam. Personalism is a complex doctrine which affirms the absolute value of the human person, but at the same time emphasises that this value is realised only in the context of civic duty.[100]

This merging of individual and community allowed Diem to justify using forced labour to build the strategic hamlets. It also enabled him to claim he was developing an Asian philosophy that could, had he lived, helped promote the values of his regime and dilute insurgent claims of American colonialism. Unfortunately, many rural Vietnamese did not share his enthusiasm for the Personalism agenda or the compulsory labour it entailed. One noted how Diem's image and popularity begin to decline after 1961 as a direct result of this agenda, whilst another, perhaps getting to the financial crux of the matter, claimed he no longer supported Diem because of the cost of pictures bought to support the cause:

> He [Diem] required every house to buy one photo of him and to hang it up in his house as if to worship him. He did it as if he was the father of the people, and each picture cost from 50 to 80 piasters. How much money did they get from all the houses of this village?[101]

In addition to issues raised by Personalism, Diem's family also contributed to the unpopular nature of his regime. Phillips claimed that the real problems in South Vietnam were not with Diem but with his brother, Nhu.[102] This was supported by villagers who claimed that they felt the difficulty was 'his brother, Nhu and his sister-in-law Madame Nhu.'[103] One villager claimed that 'all the corruption and trouble was caused by Madame Nhu. He [Diem] listened to her and collected very heavy taxes from the people. I feel sorry for Mr. Diem, if only he did not listen to his sister-in-law.'[104]

Again, Diem's family caused him problems. Here Madame Nhu inspects Civil Guard training – giving some the opportunity to suggest she was overstepping her boundaries. (Albert Grandolini collection)

This would support claims by Phillips made earlier in this book that Diem was not as unpopular as the perception in the media suggested. However, Diem was unwilling to remove his brother because he trusted him and as Rostow noted, to remove Nhu 'would be a traumatic experience for Diem' and weaken his grip on power.[105] As an adjunct to this, it should also be recorded

One reason for Diem's fear and isolation was that violence in South Vietnam was not a new phenomenon. This photo from 1955 shows troops preparing for possible disorder in the face of an oncoming protest march and the Binh Xuyen criminal gang attacks during the Battle of Saigon. Diem had to use an 'iron fist' to control large parts of the nation but his attacks on criminal organisations also brought him credit with the average South Vietnamese citizen. (Albert Grandolini collection)

Troops rest during a lull in the fighting in the 1955 Battle of Saigon. Diem's crackdown on criminal gangs helped shore up American support for his regime. (Albert Grandolini collection)

that the alleged corruption of the Ngo's was dismissed by Elbridge Durbrow. After the murders of Diem and Nhu, Durbrow claimed Madame Nhu lived a life that did not reflect her supposed riches. He recounted the lifestyle the supposedly wealthy and corrupt Madame Nhu was leading after the coup:

> In Paris, when I was later on in Paris, she lived with Brother Nguyen – that was the youngest brother of the Ngo family – in one of these great big French apartments where you have got lots of room. The Nguyens had eleven children. She had two, and herself. Then one of our military guys on the NATO staff lived literally right below her. He saw her go up in the elevator and knew the concierge. They were living like peasants in this room, just stacked in like sardines in a tin in this fairly big apartment in a nice part of Paris. Finally, they had to move. She moved down to Rome where the oldest brother of the family, the Archbishop, was able to get a little place for her to live out in Frascati, just outside of Rome. I checked that with my CIA friends, and they checked on it. She was living very frugally. She lost the key to all these riches or they didn't know where it was or they didn't tell her. But this idea of corruption was greatly exaggerated, but our press just fell for it hook, line and sinker.[106]

Durbrow's account illustrated how the perception of what was happening in Vietnam was not always borne out by the reality.

Sympathy for Diem?

Perhaps the final point to note in relation to Diem was that his centralisation of power was borne out of necessity. Diem had been the subject of a military coup in 1960 and as such could not 'be expected to delegate concentrated authority to the military' who he felt were plotting his removal.[107] Secondly, the very act of a coup occurring had, in the words of a Special National Intelligence Estimate, 28 March 1961, made Diem 'now more suspicious of the army as a potentially serious source of anti-government activity' whilst also opening 'the eyes of many army officers to their political potential' and encouraging them to consider future plots.[108]

Diem was convinced that the 1960 plot had been sponsored by the CIA and that there were ongoing discussions within the Kennedy administration regarding removing him from office. Indeed, Nolting claimed that many in the State Office wanted to give Diem 'enough rope to hang himself.'[109] In addition, Diem had survived several assassination attempts and seen many of his followers killed. For example, *The Times* reported that 'President Diem of South Vietnam faces an abnormally complex and difficult situation, as so many local officials in the South Vietnamese administration have been killed by communist guerrillas' and this helps explain his authoritarian actions: he was using force to remain in power.[110]

It is also easy to forget that Diem faced a ruthless insurgency: the Viet Cong were capable of beheadings, disfigurement and murder.

Troops open fire from an M8 armoured car during the 1960 coup attempt. Diem believed the CIA had instigated the coup against him. (Albert Grandolini collection)

In fact, Moyar has argued that force was the only option to 'restore order' to the nation and Nagl has suggested that Diem needed to assure 'himself a check on army power' to avoid a military coup.[111] The limited nature of social and political reform was also about protecting Diem's power base. Higgins claimed that Diem and his brother were very aware of their narrow support and whilst putting loyalists in key command posts may have created inefficiency, it also acted as a 'buffer against future plots' aimed at the regime.[112]

In addition, there was also potentially inappropriate pressure put on Diem to reform his government: his resistance to change could be seen to be part of a misplaced application of Western values and a misunderstanding of the South Vietnamese context. For example, as noted previously, the introduction of local village elections offended village elders, disrupted centuries of tradition and created resentment towards the regime. This not only helps explain the failure by American officials to understand the situation in South Vietnam but also why the Ngo's French-derived Personalism philosophy was unsuited to South Vietnam. Therefore, a vicious circle was being created. The counterinsurgency strategy relied on democratic reforms being introduced but Diem's fear of creating a strong alternative to his rule prevented some of these changes from happening. Whilst this was taking place, the American administration was trying to pressure him into change but they were also fearful of undermining him. This led to an increasing democratic deficit and even more unrest. This in turn made Diem more fearful of his position and more resistant to change. Taylor commented that this resulted in even less delegation and actions which would 'further complicate' Diem's problems.[113] Unfortunately, the threat or fear of another coup, the gossip in Saigon and the talk of a removal of American support for Diem led to a situation that Hilsman described as 'clearly very dangerous.'[114] Hilsman went on to explain why the talk of Diem's overthrow caused so many problems:

> It tends to be in the nature of a self-fulfilling prophecy – talk about neutralisation disheartens those who must fully and vigorously implement the strategic concept and encourages those who are plotting for a neutralist coup.[115]

This proved to be a prescient prediction considering what happened to Diem and illustrated how the situation in South

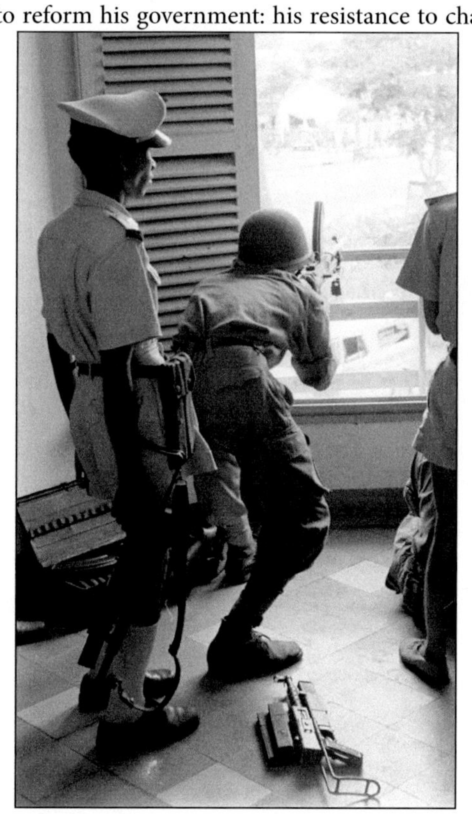

The army open fire on Binh Xuyen followers in 1955 – again illustrating the fragility of Diem's position and the legacy of uncertainty it left in the early 1960s. Many of the Binh Xuyen escaped to the Delta and later joined the Viet Cong. (Albert Grandolini collection)

Here the police and army try to quell the 1955 uprising from the rooftops. (Albert Grandolini collection)

Vietnam was so unstable: talk of a coup could lead to a coup and the denial of a plan for a coup could result in suspicion that a plan was in place. The perception of events was crucial.

Problems of Perception

People See What They Want to See …

The penultimate part of this chapter examines how important these perceptions were to the progress of the war in the rest of South Vietnam. Misunderstanding and misinterpreting a complicated situation on the ground further undermined the counterinsurgency effort and hindered the effectiveness of the Strategic Hamlet Programme. Several narratives were developing in South Vietnam that may not have matched the reality. Consequently, the counterinsurgency programme often appeared to be less successful than it actually was. This was because of flawed perceptions.

One reason for all the differing perceptions of events on the ground was that different groups wanted diverse things from the programme and these goals were not always compatible. For example, Thompson claimed that the Vietnamese were unable to understand that the hamlets could not be implemented in isolation of other measures such as democracy, protection or uniting the population and this meant that the Vietnamese 'tended to confuse the means with the end.'[116] The result of this was that clear strategic goals became lost and the strategic hamlets 'became the purpose in itself' rather than a tool to support counterinsurgent action.[117]

In their analysis of the Strategic Hamlets, The Department of Defence claimed that three distinct groups in Vietnam were inadvertently working against each other; the military wanted a mobile army and objected to clear and hold type operations required by counterinsurgency, American politicians saw political progress as the pre-eminent objective and worked towards this goal whilst Diem himself simply wanted to reinforce his own regime, suppress rebellion and avoid being seen as a colonial puppet.[118] Apart from the fact that this analysis ignored the input of the Viet Cong, it was correct in pointing out that competing goals often hindered the progress and evaluation of the programme. This confusion made it difficult to ascertain any improvement in the situation on the ground and created several problems of perception.

ARVN soldiers take a break in mid-patrol. (Albert Grandolini collection)

An Important Landmark – Phillips' Reports on the Strategic Hamlets

The first problem of perception was the claim that, by 1963, the hamlets were failing to protect the population in South Vietnam. However, reports by Rufus Phillips called this analysis into question. He produced several informal summaries of the Strategic Hamlet Programme and the contents of each report cast doubt on the idea of complete failure in the programme.[119] In his reports, Phillips used his position at USOM to undertake a province by province analysis of the Strategic Hamlet Programme. Whilst never claiming that the hamlets were an outstanding success, Phillips did present a far more nuanced analysis of progress being made in South Vietnam at that time: he discussed both the accomplishments and the failures of the strategy. Phillips' views and opinions are interesting because he was clearly considered by many people involved in the conflict to have a good grasp of the situation in South Vietnam. Hilsman said he was doing 'a superb job,' General Wheeler 'spoke well of him' and Major General Rowny described Phillips as 'excellent.'[120]

Phillips discussed leadership, resources used and general security. He was also unafraid of being critical of provincial officials or of highlighting failures in the programme. In fact, on 4 September 1963, Phillips even tried to prevent the expansion of further hamlets in the Delta and said consolidation was needed for the strategy to be successful in that region.[121]

There were two informal appreciations of the Strategic Hamlet Programme. The first was for the period up to June 1963, the second for the period June to August 1963 and was used to construct the map of South Vietnam shown in the colour section of this book.[122] The information contained in the second report was used here because it discussed a more developed hamlet strategy. The map shows that the hamlets were not a universal failure and reveals several key geographical results. Firstly, the effectiveness of the hamlets varied

The Sea Swallows and Father Hoa had their own counterinsurgency policy. They successfully chased and attacked Viet Cong insurgents as part of their own anti-communist ideology. (Albert Grandolini collection)

Hoa Hao forces patrol the Delta region. They were so successful in their anti-VC activities that serious consideration was given to hiring them as an effective mercenary task force to be employed in rooting out insurgents in heavily-populated Viet Cong areas. (Albert Grandolini collection)

from Corps area to Corps area and from province to province. Of the data that Phillips provided, 17 of the provinces could be considered to be running successful hamlet programmes; that is to say they were building the hamlets successfully, were implementing necessary political and social reform or were generally successful in protecting the population from attack. In contrast, 15 of the provinces were judged to be running failing hamlet programmes. The data on the remaining seven provinces was deemed to be inconclusive because in some provinces the hamlets had not been built or there were conflicting reports of successes and failures.

Phillips' analysis made several claims. His first assertion was that the majority of the population, by July 1962, were 'still neutral' in the conflict.[123] He suggested that many rural Vietnamese could not decide who to support and that where the government had been able to 'effectively assist the population in defending itself against the Viet Cong,' the population had started to change their allegiance.[124] His research revealed several other key points. Firstly, progress in Corps One and Two (in the north of the country) was generally good, progress in Corps Three mixed and the programme was clearly failing in Corps Four.[125] In Corps One, progress was being made in all the provinces with the exception of Quang Tin where there was poor local leadership which was hindering the programme.[126] Also in Corps One, USOM found discontent in Quang Ngai but were encouraged by the local population who were beginning to become informers and hand over the Viet Cong to the relevant authorities.[127] In the northern parts of Corps One, the provinces of Quang Tri and Thua Thien were not necessarily supportive of government action but these were Buddhist strongholds and the people were not considered to be sympathetic towards the insurgency either.[128] Secondly, in Corps Two the Montagnards tribes were providing momentum for the Strategic Hamlet Programme and most of the planned defences had been completed.[129] The only real exception in this Corps was the province of Binh Dinh which was a Viet Cong stronghold and Phillips commented that the 'astonishing light' reaction against the hamlets by the insurgents could have been an indication of high levels of hamlet infiltration.[130] Corps Two also provided other areas of encouragement. For example, in Phu Bon, refugees had been successfully resettled, not one strategic hamlet had been lost or overrun and there had been nearly 150 defections from July to August.[131]

Other provinces in Corps Two claimed similar successes. In Phu Yen all the recorded Viet Cong attacks had been repelled whilst in Pleiku the population were in secure hamlets of 'high quality.'[132] Thirdly, although problems began to emerge once Phillips' moved on to analyse Corps Three and Corps Four there was still cause for optimism. Although Corps Three was an insurgent stronghold there had still been over 2,000 defectors and in places (such as Tay Ninh) improvements were being made despite insurgent resistance.[133] Indeed, provinces such as Gia Dinh were making excellent progress: all of the strategic hamlets had been completed and the province was entering a booming economic development stage.[134] Finally, Phillips indicated that Corps Four and the areas around the Delta were where the real problems lay. Whilst provinces such as Chuong Thiem were under almost complete Viet Cong control, other provinces such as Kien Phong were able to successfully repel insurgent attacks and make good progress in hamlet construction.[135]

What was particularly striking about the reports that Phillips produced was that they did not claim that the hamlets were a panacea for all of South Vietnam's problems. However, they did indicate, as Donnell later claimed (after province reorganisation), that there were '45 provinces in South Vietnam and it has often been said that there are 45 different wars going on.'[136] This would suggest that success and failure varied from location to location and province to province. Fraleigh suggested that one reason for this not being acknowledged in the wider reports at the time was that far too many American advisors spent all their time in and around Saigon and the Delta.[137] He went on to explain that when he arrived in South Vietnam he found out that one American aid agency had 110 Americans in its employ but 'only three were stationed outside' Saigon.[138] This limited their experience and understanding of the wider war and influenced the reports they sent back to Washington.[139] Therefore, it could be argued that the positive achievements of the Strategic Hamlet Programme were not always recognised and this fed into a wider perception of failure. This also exacerbated the fear of the rural Vietnamese terrorised by the Viet Cong because their own experiences were not seen in the wider context of national successes in the programme. As such, they were unable to gain a picture of

Catholic refugees resettled in 1954. Many of these people were stridently anti Viet Cong and joined militia forces to wipe the insurgents out. (Albert Grandolini collection)

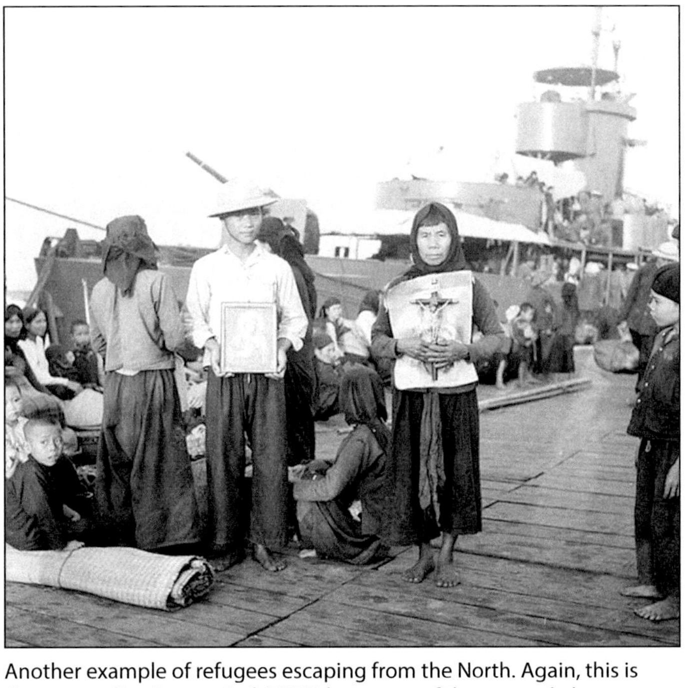

Another example of refugees escaping from the North. Again, this is from an earlier time period (1954) but many of these people became staunch anti-communists and helped drive forward government success. (Albert Grandolini collection)

accomplishments in the rest of South Vietnam and they could not be reassured of their own safety or security.

Was the Hamlet Concept Misunderstood?

Whilst the successes of the strategic hamlets may not have always been effectively transmitted to the population, the next point to make regarding perceptions and attitudes was that the very concept of 'Strategic Hamlets' may have been misunderstood: they may have been based on a mistaken assumption of successful practice in the Malayan Emergency. The Strategic Hamlets had worked well in Malaya and it was perhaps reasonable to assume they could have a positive impact in South Vietnam. However, this simplistic assumption of strategic transference was an indication of Western cultural ignorance: to assume that a single approach could be successfully transplanted from one South East Asian nation to another indicated a failure to understand the differing cultures, geography and problems of each nation. Malaya was vastly different in terms of geography (it was a peninsular), ethnic mix (insurgents were mostly Chinese) and political context (independence discussions were already underway): it was simply an unsuitable analogy for South Vietnam. The Department of State was warned about this in 1962 when staff at the American Embassy in India, cautioned in a telegram that 'the strategic villages plan, however plausible from a military point of view, is politically disastrous and based on false analogy by Thompson and others to (the) Malayan situation.'[140] The warning went unheeded.

Another problem of perception in regard to the Strategic Hamlet Programme was that it was not reported accurately in the media and this again shaped impressions of its failure. Diem himself considered many in the foreign media to be too inexperienced to be reporting on events in the country: this left them vulnerable to exploitation by disgruntled government officials and the insurgents' spy network. One problem with the inexperienced correspondents was not so much that they were against the pacification programme but that they did not understand it or wanted to write about other stories. Fraleigh noted that the press was more concerned with 'sensational war stories' rather than the slow but steady progress made in the counterinsurgency campaign and Hilsman claimed that 'the American press representatives are bitter and will seize on anything that goes wrong and blow it up as much as possible' which he believed helped distort the news agenda.[141] Fraleigh went on to explain that there was a real 'lack of understanding of unconventional warfare on the part of the many, many young American correspondents covering Vietnam at that time' which further distorted the news output.[142] Additionally, Phillips revealed the irritation he felt with what he called 'frequent and inaccurate' reports and Nhu went even further.[143] Nhu claimed that the Western press were not 'adapted to subversive war' and asked for media representatives to be of a higher intellectual standard noting that they needed 'minimum standards of intellect and of emotion' in order to grasp the problems faced by South Vietnam.[144] This was a not so subtle expression of his regard for their journalistic abilities.[145]

A Familiar Problem – the Misinformed 'Press'?

Another consequence of this relative inexperience, was that the press were often targets for United States personnel who had 'been in Vietnam too long and carry old grudges and frustrations, or are unduly influenced by the views of various South Vietnamese "dissidents."'[146] These people would feed 'defeatist talk' to the American press and also encouraged the 'dissidents' among the French-educated South Vietnamese intellectuals (concentrated in Saigon) to add to the perception of unrest and unhappiness.[147] To augment this negative perception was the deliberate Viet Cong tactic of exaggerating any unrest and using 'half-truths and insinuations' which were 'not supported by hard facts' to undermine the Diem regime.[148] Indeed, the insurgents appear to have actively targeted foreign news correspondents and special organisations and were sending material to the press with the aim of 'exploiting further' the insurgents' ability to control the news agenda.[149] To augment this negative perception was the deliberate Viet Cong tactic of exaggerating any unrest and using 'half-truths and insinuations' which were 'not supported by hard facts' to undermine the Diem regime.[150] The insurgents even went so far as to list the various foreign correspondents in Saigon who they felt might be sympathetic to their cause and provided addresses for their informants to contact them.[151]

Table 2: List of Possible Viet Cong Contacts Amongst Foreign Journalists[152]

Names and addresses of foreign journalists living in Saigon

1	Simon Michan	AFP (French)
2	Burfin	AFP (French)
3	Brown	AP (American)
4	Perry	UPI (American)
5	Smark	Reuter (British)
6	Nivolon	"Figaro" Newspaper (French)
7	Hudson	NBC Radio (American)
8	Jerry Rose	"Time", "Life", "New York Times" (American)
9	John Sterling"	"The Observer", 2London Times" Newsaper
10	Raks Hat Purl	"Hindustani Times", New Delhi (in India)
11	Guy Searls	CBS Radio (American)
12	Chin Hak Chong	Pan Asia News agency located in Singapore
13	Kalk	ABC (American)

All of this resulted in press coverage that was – at times – very negative about events taking place in South Vietnam. Crucially, it also impacted on perceptions of the success in the war and further undermined attempts to support the Diem regime. This news coverage was important because it affected 'the US and its ability to help South Vietnam' by damaging support for the war in America.[153] It also created an impression of chaos and dysfunction in the counterinsurgency campaign. This had the effect of weakening Diem's trust in the foreign press who he regarded as 'untrustworthy, prone to publish secret and false information derived from private sources and biased to the extent that the press writes up only the bad and not the good aspects of events in South Vietnam.'[154] This hindered attempts to reform his regime and furthered the impression that he was failing to rule the country effectively.

Final Thoughts on the Strategic Hamlets: Too Little, Too Late?

Finally, in addition to these problems, time was another factor influencing perceptions of the failure of the strategic hamlets: the belief that a quick victory was possible hindered policy implementation and distorted media interpretation. Two facets of chronology are important here; the hamlets may have been introduced too late in the conflict to save the regime and when implemented, the programme needed more time to be successful. In relation to the first point, although damaged, the insurgents were already entrenched within South Vietnam before the Strategic Hamlet Programme began. Ruane suggested that the North Vietnamese were actually compelled to step up their activities in 1959 and 1960 because Diem had been so successful in using what Ruane called 'dragnetting' techniques to kill communists in the period 1956 to 1959.[155] Ruane claimed that this oppression resulted in around 12,000 executions and 50,000 internments in prison.[156] He went on to say that the North Vietnamese were so worried about the effects of this repression that it spurred them on to formally pursue their armed struggle in 1960 and increase infiltration because they thought that no communists would be left in the south.[157] Also, Pike argued – in his review of the conflict – that two key dates before 1961 seriously altered the course of the war. He claimed that from around 1956 onwards Diem became more and more isolated from his people and that he gradually lost popularity as a result of a complete centralisation of power.[158] Pike went on to claim the second key date was the arrest of Doctor Phan Quang Dan in 1960 – who Pike regarded as the only legitimate threat to Diem in the National Assembly – was 'the Diem's government point of no return.'[159] Additionally, although some control measures – such as agrovilles – were introduced in the 1950s, it may have been that other reforms were needed that could have allowed a legitimate, rival democratic base to be established and for issues to be discussed in public. Instead, oppression meant that problems festered and resentment against the government grew.

Similarly, in relation to the second point about the duration of the war, there was often a lack of understanding regarding the length and nature of counterinsurgency conflicts. Anti-guerrilla campaigns were often 'measured in years not months' and even the most successful campaigns involved 'false starts, major operational mistakes' and, in the end, took 'years to achieve success.'[160] There appeared to be a failure to both acknowledge this prospect and inform the wider public that a long, drawn-out war was possible. The Americans hoped to win or be in the ascendency in the war by 1965 and this may have been a reflection of their hubris but it also represented a misunderstanding of the time it took to win a counterinsurgency struggle.[161] This rush to succeed also affected policy by putting pressure on Diem to reform faster than he was prepared to act and meant that the possibility of a lengthy, difficult campaign was not communicated to the American public. The Strategic Hamlet Programme did not offer instant victory and political and social reform would take several years

Many of the successes of the counterinsurgency campaign eluded media reporting. Here an advisor works with ARVN in the field. (Albert Grandolini collection)

to produce support for the government of Diem.

Phillips believed that all these various misunderstandings reflected what he called an 'Objective Reality' taking place in South Vietnam at this time.[162] 'Objective Reality' in this case referred to when different events were perceived in different ways by the many actors in the conflict. It was entirely possible to produce an honest, facts-based report or assessment of the state of affairs on the ground and still misinterpret or misunderstand what was actually taking place. As such, successes claimed by one side could be interpreted as a failure by another. This led to confusion, inaccurate reporting and a misunderstanding of the hamlet strategy and the positive effects it was having on parts of South Vietnam. All of these failures in perception meant that when Diem was assassinated, the violence that erupted in the countryside was seen by many as confirmation of the failure of the American-Diem strategy in South Vietnam. It also led to the end of the Strategic Hamlet Programme.

Violence erupts outside the Presidential Palace during the 1963 coup – an M24 tank set alight. (Albert Grandolini collection)

The End of the Hamlets

What Happened After the Murder of Diem?

The months after the Diem coup are outside of the remit of the book but they do illustrate that the hamlet programme did not suddenly collapse with the death of Diem. Instead, after his assassination, the Strategic Hamlet Programme gradually came to an end and was replaced by the New Rural Life Hamlets Programme.

Phillips claimed that the assassination of Diem was when 'things really began to fall apart' and the increased insurgent activity together with a lack of government support would seem to support this assertion.[163] Immediately after the coup, insurgent incidents rose by around 300 to 400 percent but then 'dropped down to normal' after November.[164] This would support the view that insurgents still saw the hamlets as a threat because they remained a focus for their attacks.

However, the insurgents also began to concentrate their strikes on strategic hamlets considered to be 'soft' or vulnerable which may have increased the perception of failure in the programme as these hamlets were relatively poorly defended and were quickly overrun.[165] Thompson noted that although many hamlets had a basic structure in place to prevent collapse and remained 'resilient' other 'vulnerable hamlets were immediately lost.'[166] In particular, this was because so many of the hamlets under assault were in Corps Three and Corps Four regions – areas which were already under attack from insurgents.[167]

This would again support the analysis made by Phillips in his comments about the Strategic Hamlet Programme.[168] Indeed, reports did acknowledge that although insurgent activity had increased in the Delta, 'this violent activity met with little success in the northern and central parts of the country' which would indicate some form of success in these provinces.[169]

The infamous photo showing Diem's dead body. President Kennedy was said to be appalled at the coup and blamed himself for not being in full control of his administration during the assassination – he left the running of the White House to his officials just before Diem was killed. (Albert Grandolini collection)

A major reason for the increased level of Viet Cong activity was because the insurgents wanted to destabilise the new regime. It was stated that the assaults were mainly intended for 'psychological impact and for testing the new regime' and to also encourage 'internal strains' in the post-coup government.[170] Whilst these attacks showed an impressive level of insurgent strength, they also indicated that they could not sustain a prolonged assault and supported the idea that the Viet Cong, at this stage, lacked the manpower for a prolonged, conventional military campaign.

The new Saigon government also appeared to be reluctant to support the Strategic Hamlet Programme. For example, General Don suggested that the Diem regime had 'gone about the Strategic Hamlet programme in the wrong way' – which was an implied critique of the Ngo family and its policies.[171]

This further manifested itself in a failure to support hamlets under attack from insurgent forces. It was claimed that in Long

Heavily armed troops patrol the streets in 1964 – a clear indication that tensions had not declined despite the fall of Diem. (Albert Grandolini collection)

Again, as indicated by this 1964 photograph – the removal of Diem did not decrease the level of threat or reduce the police and military presence on the streets of Saigon. (Albert Grandolini collection)

Troops patrol Saigon. Several historians have suggested that the post-Diem regimes deliberately let the Strategic Hamlet Programme fail in order to blame Diem for their own faults and allow them to claim they were a break from the past. (Albert Grandolini collection)

An for example, the failure of the Government to 'support and protect' the hamlets meant that military support simply 'never came' when needed: communities were left isolated and unprotected.[172] The US Embassy in Saigon described the results of this inaction saying, 'hamlet chiefs (were) murdered, the houses of all relocated families destroyed, the barbed wire fence is cut, and another hamlet is eliminated' and this led to a diminishing of the status of the Strategic Hamlet Programme.[173] Again, and particularly in the Delta, little was being done to support the counterinsurgency strategy and although the new government recognised they had problems, inertia had set in and limited efforts had been made to resolve the difficulties that the government faced.[174]

All of these factors combined to give the impression of a programme that was simply being destroyed. Both Thompson and Moyar have suggested that this neglect could have been part of a deliberate campaign to undermine Diem's reputation and justify the coup against him. Thompson discussed the wider need to 'smear' Diem in 'every possible way to justify his murder' whilst Moyar wrote that the new leaders of South Vietnam 'inaccurately claimed' that an 'abysmal situation' post-coup was no different to events before Diem's death in order to show they had not created new problems for the nation.[175]

However, new problems were created by the coup. In March 1964, McNamara presented a pessimistic appraisal to President Johnson in which he claimed that from September 1963, the situation had been 'growing worse' and much of the country was under Viet Cong control or 'predominant influence.'[176] McNamara went on to list 'high and increasing' ARVN desertion rates, failing and 'disarmed' strategic

Again, giving a lie to the claim of increased security, ARVN patrols Saigon in heavily manned M113 APCs. Notice the American observers in a jeep in the background. (Albert Grandolini collection)

Although this is an image portraying relative peace at the end of heavy guns (taken in 1964), is it instead, the calm before the storm? (Albert Grandolini collection)

hamlets and more active Viet Cong recruitment.[177] He also acknowledged that since the start of the year there had been a 'weakening' of the government's position.[178] McNamara noted how, since the Diem coup, 35 of 41 province chiefs had been replaced and this meant that the control structure from Saigon 'disappeared': a power vacuum in the Strategic Hamlet Programme was created.[179] In addition, McNamara indicated that post-coup, many hamlets had been damaged or abandoned, and around '40 percent of the countryside of South Vietnam' was under Viet Cong control.[180] This was particularly striking because in 1961, NSAM 52 claimed that 58 percent of the country was under insurgent control: McNamara was inadvertently indicating that progress had been made under Diem.[181]

The New Rural Life Hamlet Scheme

The end of the Strategic Hamlet Programme began when the New Rural Life Hamlet scheme was proposed to replace the original hamlets in January 1964.[182] The New Rural Life Hamlets appeared to recognise some of the problems inherent in the Strategic Hamlet Programme and the scheme curtailed rapid expansion and forced relocation and instead placed the emphasis on 'quality not quantity' when it came to construction.[183] This seemed to tacitly acknowledge some of the issues that led to the unpopularity of the Strategic Hamlet Programme but also recognised and retained some of the successes too.

For example, local elections were planned, community groups were to be re-established and better training for farmers, teachers and doctors would be introduced.[184] It was also stressed that 'the good features of the Strategic Hamlet Programme' were 'still valuable and should be retained' but adapted to more local conditions.[185] This meant that the New Rural Life Hamlets Programme would expand

1964: Peace and security return to Saigon enforced by tanks in the streets. (Albert Grandolini collection)

less rapidly and the hamlets would even be abandoned if they proved to be difficult to defend.[186] By March 1964, advisors and province chiefs in South Vietnam were being urged to 'push forward' with the new plans and the Strategic Hamlet Programme effectively ended.[187]

This chapter has shown why the counterinsurgents were unable to build upon the successes of the Strategic Hamlet Programme. Firstly, an information operations system was in place that generally analysed statistical rather than human data. This meant that there was often a focus on information that was irrelevant to the conflict or that misrepresented what was going on in South Vietnam. This was compounded by a culture of target setting, selective interviewing and a cultural ignorance that hindered wider analysis. Secondly, internal conflict within the military and a lack of overall co-ordination compounded these intelligence gathering failures. Thirdly, the Diem regime itself – as is often commented upon in the war literature – was repressive, inefficient and too centralised around Diem and his ruling family. Finally, there were problems in the way the hamlets were perceived. Even though there was clear evidence of progress in the programme, this was often not acknowledged in official reports, the media were ignorant of the general and specific counterinsurgency strategy and the Strategic Hamlet Programme itself may have been based around false assumptions of successful practice. The inability to understand events on the ground created a narrative of failure which further undermined the counterinsurgency effort. This in turn led to more pressure on Diem, a demand for more inappropriate tactics and greater failure in the programme.

Conclusion – Three Blind Men Describe an Elephant

> This is not the problem of the three blind men describing the elephant; it is the problem of men with different perspectives each moulding his own conception of a proper body to the same skeleton.
>
> A Department of Defence evaluation of the Strategic Hamlet Programme 1961–1963 (declassified, 2011).[188]

The opening chapters of Volume One in this series contained two key assertions: Douglas Pike's claim that the Viet Cong were being 'cut up' and Sir Robert Thompson's statement that anything could be proven in South Vietnam, nothing was as it appeared to be and if something could go wrong then it would do so. Both of the volumes presented here have attempted to unpick some of this confusion and explain why, to use Thompson's phrase, 'the roof fell in.'[189]

A Confusing Legacy?

In examining the Strategic Hamlet Programme and associated counterinsurgency strategy, this series has shown that it was entirely possible for the counterinsurgents to implement a successful, well-planned and theoretically sound counterinsurgency strategy and still be defeated. It has demonstrated how the insurgents could be seriously hurt by the campaign, lose troops, fear for their own insurgency and yet still emerge victorious. It has also established that so many of the factors that influenced success or failure were interdependent and often worked in counterintuitive ways. For example, building strategic hamlets was a sign of government power but their infiltration and destruction was an indication of their failure to protect the people and the potency of the insurgency.

Protestors celebrate the overthrow of the Diem regime. (Albert Grandolini collection)

These counterintuitive, counterproductive and paradoxical features all supported the need for a re-evaluation of the impact of the Strategic Hamlet Programme upon South Vietnam.

Why Is Evaluation so Difficult?

These books have deliberately avoided over-stating the case for the success or failure of the Strategic Hamlet Programme and the counterinsurgency strategy. They have shown that whilst there were many achievements in the programme, the claim that Diem was winning the war in 1963 cannot be supported by the historical record. The panic that led to the Diem coup and the rise in insurgent activity in the aftermath of his death were evidence that this was not what was happening in South Vietnam. However, it is also unrealistic to assert that the strategic hamlets were a complete failure. When implemented correctly, the Strategic Hamlet Programme provided impetus to the counterinsurgency effort and was capable of protecting the population from attack. This series has shown that the insurgents were being damaged and were made to re-assess and re-evaluate their approach to the struggle in South Vietnam.

The series has also illustrated how key failures in security provision and inadequate social, economic and political reform all merged together to undermine the Diem regime. These seemingly conflicting aspects of the analysis have demonstrated the paradox that underpins these books: it was entirely possible for both sides to be winning and losing at the same time. The actions of each side fed into and reinforced the actions of their opponents. The Diem regime was involved in a contest with the Viet Cong to destroy the insurgent infrastructure before losing all popular support. These books have shown that although Diem ultimately lost that race, the Strategic Hamlet Programme gave his government a chance in the fight.

Advisors work hard with their South Vietnamese counterparts to try and quell the insurgency. (Albert Grandolini collection)

Changing the Historical Narrative – What can we learn?

Challenging Academic Views About the Vietnam War

This series of books has demonstrated that several of the accepted beliefs surrounding the Strategic Hamlet Programme and the wider counterinsurgency policy need to be reassessed. Whilst not necessarily incorrect, the body of research surrounding the strategic hamlets is relatively slim and often lacks depth. As a result, it sometimes reaches conclusions based upon limited evidence, false strategic assumptions or misinterpretation of military trends. The books in the *Hunting the Viet Cong* series have attempted to address the limits of the historical record. The following sections will try and explain why things went wrong and show what we can learn from these events. They also present several new themes that add to and, in some cases, challenge the existing academic literature and our views of the war. Some of the concepts presented here are academic in nature but they are intended to try and explain why events unfolded in the way that they did …

Winning and Losing at the Same Time: 'Paradoxical Duality'

The first new theme to emerge and aid our understanding of events is an esoteric concept that I have called a *'Paradoxical Duality'*. What does this mean? Well, essentially, a strategy introduced to help the South Vietnamese win the war, could also help them lose that same conflict. When implemented correctly, the 'Counterinsurgency Plan' and the Strategic Hamlet Programme were working and, paradoxically, this also led to the downfall of the government. That is to say, the more the programme damaged the insurgency, the more likely it was to be attacked; the more the Americans offered aid, the more they appeared as imperialist conquerors and the more people were 'protected' by the strategic hamlets, the more they felt like prisoners in their own communities. In effect, the more successful the programme, the more it contributed to its own destruction (the paradox). The books have also demonstrated that

An American helicopter aircrewman poses for a picture in the door of a heavily armed UH-1 before embarking on a close air support mission. (Albert Grandolini collection)

as these paradoxes developed, both sides were simultaneously 'winning' and 'losing' the war: it was possible for the counterinsurgents to damage the VC operation whilst also losing the support of the rural Vietnamese. In contrast, the insurgents could lose many skirmishes and battles but at the same time wear out, over-extend and undermine the South Vietnamese military effort (the duality).

These 'paradoxical dualities' combined with poor information operations, a misunderstanding of strategy and many counterproductive initiatives to undermine and eventually neuter the programme across much of the country. A narrative took hold that suggested the hamlets were a failure, this spiralled into a perception of outright defeat and further undermined the Diem regime and its claim to be able to protect the people. The hamlets became more and more unpopular whilst at the same time, the insurgents suffered greater casualties. The Strategic Hamlet Programme was destroying Viet Cong infrastructure but it was also alienating much of rural Vietnam. It was, as Douglas Pike suggested, a race against time to defeat the Viet Cong without losing the support of the people. This concept of 'Paradoxical Duality' also helps to explain why traditional historical views of the strategic hamlets could consider them to be a failure whilst more recent viewpoints present the programme as a qualified success.[190] Both could be correct.

Several other new themes have also emerged from the research and help add to the historical debate…

Failure to Transfer Skills: Aka 'Dysfunctional Transference'

Another theme highlighted has been that of how skilled professionals failed to transfer learning and experience from one sphere (such as business) to another sphere (such as military planning). I've called this *'Dysfunctional Transference'*: in short, expertise in one field being unsuccessfully applied to another. This would again help to explain much of the contradictory nature of historians' analysis and show why many talented, experienced people (such as McNamara) were unable to influence events in South Vietnam. The people in charge of policy were not necessarily corrupt, ill-motivated, inept or inexperienced, rather they were applying the wrong skills to the problem.

McNamara has been criticised throughout these books but his approach was a classic example of a successful businessman transferring unsuccessfully to another area of operations – industrial to military – and using inappropriate methods and tools. McNamara's approach proved that what might work in American industry would fail in the jungles of South East Asia.[191] In a similar vein, Diem and Nhu's *Personalism* was a European-based philosophy that was unsuitable for South Vietnam. Again, the idea of personal independence merged with collective responsibility would, on first glance, appear to suit a South East Asian nation but it was abused by

McNamara undertakes an aerial appraisal on the counterinsurgency campaign. His refusal to listen, change his approach and inflexibility in the face of failure is often criticised in the literature. (Albert Grandolini collection)

province chiefs and was unpopular with the Vietnamese themselves. Another illustration of this concept was the transference of Thompson's Malayan experience to the South Vietnamese context. Again, a very successful approach was insufficiently adapted to another nation and it proved to be less successful than its predecessor. Perhaps the final example of *'Dysfunctional Transference'* was the way in which attempts to establish 'rice roots' democracy proved to be counterproductive. The rural Vietnamese disliked their village traditions being interrupted and secret ballots that appealed to Western advisors actually undermined the counterinsurgency campaign: unsuccessful candidates 'lost face' and social standing in the eyes of other villagers.

Not Adapting to Change: Aka 'Adaptable Campaigning'

In contrast to the 'Dysfunctional Transference' of the counterinsurgents, a third new theme illustrated by the research

William Westmoreland in consultation with his South Vietnamese counterparts. Westmoreland is another who is widely criticised for his failure to adjust strategy. (Albert Grandolini collection)

was how the insurgency was able to grow and adapt their approach as the campaign progressed. The literature about South Vietnam often overlooks the strengths of the insurgency and concentrates on US success and failure.[192] However, this repeatedly masks the very effective and adaptable enemy that the Americans and Diem faced. As a result, the third new theme to emerge is one of *'Adaptable Campaigning'* by the Viet Cong and their allies. In contrast to the counterinsurgents, they were able to transfer their previous experiences against the French to the new combat environment with far more success. They added to old fighting techniques and developed simple but effective methods of attack. They also maintained contact with the local population and used the intelligence they gathered to adjust their campaign throughout the war. The insurgency also underwent a period of self-evaluation and reorganisation. This was most apparent during a period of consolidation in the initial phases of the counterinsurgency campaign. From this, they recognised the need to challenge the Strategic Hamlet Programme, adjust their tactics and strategy and became more effective fighters.

They also introduced new anti-colonial narratives to try and win support for their insurgency and skilfully used hamlet initiatives for their own propaganda. Crucially, the insurgents recognised a need for change and were not wedded to inappropriate or ineffective techniques. This adaptation meant that as the war progressed they developed into the more formidable fighting force – even when the Strategic Hamlet Programme was causing them real harm. In contrast, the counterinsurgents tended to be committed to their relatively successful approach. Whilst this was understandable in the context of the war, there was a fluidity-rigidity paradigm in operation here: more adjustment to Viet Cong approaches was needed as the campaign progressed. This could have included changes in priority areas, increasing the tempo and speed of operations or even withdrawal of the hamlet strategy in some areas of the Delta. The ability to adjust was one of the major advantages that the insurgents possessed and this facet of their operation helped them win the war.

A major frustration when writing this book was realisation that success was not built upon. Here the Hoa Hao undertake another fruitful patrol. It is a *What if? of history* but their approach gave a template for hunting and killing the Viet Cong. (Albert Grandolini collection)

Ignoring Local People: Aka 'Network Dissonance'

This book series has also demonstrated that a fourth new theme was in operation at this time. I've called this *'Network Dissonance'*: there was often a failure by those in power to listen to people 'on the ground' and adjust strategy accordingly. The book has made extensive use of reports by Phillips, USOM and RAND because they often bypassed official Vietnamese and American military channels and talked to the people.[193] This meant that they had a far more accurate picture of events and were able to suggest problems and issues with the hamlet programme before Diem was killed. This was particularly apparent in Phillips' informal appreciations of the hamlet strategy: his analysis of successful areas and provinces under great threat was confirmed by the events following the Diem coup. Similarly, RAND reports highlighted the counterproductive nature of much of the hamlet programme and findings by anthropologists such as Donnell and Hickey were again confirmed after the 1963 coup.[194] The fact that several communities in the Delta dismantled their own hamlets or burnt them down was evidence of the unpopularity of the programme in that part of South Vietnam. This inability to use local knowledge also meant that areas of the Delta where the hamlets were a relative success – Phillips mentions Kien Hoa, An Giang and Kien Phoung – were not used to develop or enhance provision in other provinces.[195] Listening to the people 'on the ground' was not a feature of the counterinsurgency campaign.

Management in Chaos: aka 'Institutionalised Confusion'

The fifth new theme to emerge is one of *'Institutionalised Confusion'* within the American and Diem governments. In both cases, government structure facilitated rivalry, fragmentation of policy and ineffective analysis and planning. Whilst historical writers tend to stress faults in the Vietnamese regime, internal American divisions have also been highlighted by the research.[196] Much of the current analysis is rightly critical of Diem but the Kennedy Administration and the military structure in South Vietnam seemed to be equally dysfunctional.[197] For example, whilst not wishing to place all of the blame on McNamara, his arrogance and inability to accommodate alternative viewpoints was noticeable but not unique. Hilsman was often criticised for failing to listen to views that did match his own and Krulak has even been accused of deliberately misrepresenting data to further his own argument.[198] This situation was compounded by inter-agency rivalry, generals and politicians all reporting facts and figures that matched their own agendas and a failure to really work as a team.[199] The multitude of counterinsurgency plans adopted during this time period also illustrate this concept.[200] This lack of co-ordination was discussed frequently in reports at this time and was a recurring feature of the research.[201] In fact, Diem's centralisation of power meant he was arguably more informed about events in South Vietnam than many US officials. This failure to organise was made worse by the side-lining of people such as Edward Lansdale who had extensive experience in counterinsurgency warfare and the chaos which several observers claimed was a feature of the Kennedy White House.[202] A large amount of the literature about the Vietnam War has been written by American authors and because of this, it sometimes stresses Diem's failings too stridently whilst ignoring the conduct of the Americans in the war.[203]

Hoa Hao villages were well defended and hard to attack. This allowed their troops to harass and chase the insurgents. (Albert Grandolini collection)

Different Places, Different Results: 'Geographical Contradiction'?

The final new theme highlighted by the books was a concept I've labelled as *'Geographical Contradiction'*: essentially, the success of the Strategic Hamlet Programme varied from province to province and region to region. This demonstrated the conflicting and confusing nature of the Strategic Hamlet Programme. It was possible – as reports by Rufus Phillips have shown – to find areas where the hamlets were a success and where the insurgency was being blunted or diminished.[204] Equally, it was possible to find areas – particularly in the Delta – where the hamlets were a complete failure.[205] To make matters worse, different provinces had implemented the hamlet scheme with varying degrees of success and in various ways. For example, some province chiefs had built well defended, secure perimeter defences supported by improvements in social and economic aid.

Other local leaders had simply corralled people into inadequately constructed villages that offered little security or tangible improvement in peoples' lives. In the very worst cases, material for hamlet construction was either discarded or found its way into the insurgents' hands. This facet of the programme often went unrecognised and so was not acted upon. A major reason for this was the ineffective nature of the reporting system and the methods used to evaluate the hamlets and the counterinsurgency strategy: it was often unclear what was going on in South Vietnam. This further undermined Diem and created an impression in parts of Washington of chaos and confusion in the entire country. These geographical variations also help to explain why the press appeared to be reporting a different war to the military. Many correspondents tended to focus – understandably – on the Delta but this distorted much of the narrative because successes in other regions tended to be ignored. All of these geographical difficulties were compounded by failures within the Diem government and the selective gathering and assessment of data from the battlefield. As a result, the Strategic Hamlet Programme presented strategists with a complex, varied and often inconsistent set of variables to assess, interpret and act upon.

Correcting the Historical Record

In addition to these major new thematic additions to our historical understanding, the books have also shown that several aspects of the existing historical record need to be reconsidered. Academic historians often claim the Strategic Hamlets Programme was poorly planned, failed to deter the Viet Cong, people willingly supported the insurgency and insurgent violence is often dismissed or ignored. How should this record change?

First, the Strategic Hamlet Programme and the wider counterinsurgency campaign were well-planned – at least in theory – and were based around a solid understanding of the insurgency and the threat it posed to South Vietnam. The planning was developed, in part, from the British experience in the Malayan Emergency and the French in Algeria and the prototype hamlets were well-designed and capable of resisting assault.[206] The *crucial caveat* here is that the programme had to be implemented correctly for this planning to take effect. This also links to another correction to the history of the conflict: the claim that planners were simply re-fighting the Korean War and there were no experts to rely on at this point in time.[207] At this stage in the conflict the plans clearly demonstrate that a counterinsurgency strategy was being developed and there was an attempt to implement it. Also, in agreement with many recent historians' views, there was a substantial amount of counterinsurgency expertise to draw upon.[208] Not only did advisors such as Edward Lansdale have extensive experience fighting

ARVN equipment on display – an artilleryman sighting a field gun. The South Vietnamese army was well-resourced by its American allies. (Albert Grandolini collection)

guerrillas in the Philippines, Roger Hilsman had fought with the Office of Strategic Services in the Second World War and the British experience in Malaya was also utilised heavily.

Second, this series has demonstrated that the counterinsurgency programme was hindering insurgent activity; enemy losses were increasing, large areas of South Vietnam were being protected and the insurgents were often being cut off from their base of operations. Counterintuitively, the increased attacks on the strategic hamlets in late 1962 were a sign of the effectiveness of the programme. Indeed, there is a convergence of opinion in the insurgent and counterinsurgent documentation. Both agree that 1962 was a year when the Viet Cong suffered serious losses, defections were increasing throughout 1963 and even as late as June 1963, the insurgents admitted that they were having trouble with leadership and morale in their organisation.[209] The Viet Cong not only knew about the hamlet programme but it caused them great concern: the losses they were suffering actually spurred them on to increase their activities and become more violent.[210] Essentially, the more effective the programme became, the more aggressive the insurgent response. Some early historians are also rightly critical of the rapid expansion of the hamlet programme but these books have shown that initially, this caught the insurgents off-guard and hindered their attempts to gain popular support. This was because it quickly cut them off from local people and resources. This again illustrates the paradoxical nature of much of this analysis because government over-extension also damaged the Viet Cong.

The third point illustrated by the books is that historians' claims of willing village acquiescence to insurgent pressure and mass support for the insurgency are incorrect.[211] Many areas enthusiastically supported the insurgency but equally, many provinces and villages supported the insurgents out of fear for their lives: they were not eagerly championing the 'Revolution'. There were reports of villagers fiercely resisting Viet Cong attack, fighting bravely and stubbornly in the face of insurgent aggression and requesting aid and resources to build their own strategic hamlets.[212] Also, although many rural communities were alienated by the hamlet programme this was not the case across all of South Vietnam. Reports of enthusiasm for medical facilities, improved schooling and better roads and houses also feature in many sources and show that some popular, albeit limited, forms of nation building were underway.

The violence and terror undertaken by the Viet Cong has also been highlighted by this series. Much of the historical record almost casually mentions this facet of the conflict and tends to condemn Diem but ignore or underplay insurgent atrocities.[213] The brutality of much of the insurgents' methods has been highlighted here. The beheadings, mutilations and executions not only instilled terror into the rural population, they arguably gave the Americans a moral justification for interfering in the conflict. Indeed, some of the insurgent tactics would not be out of place in modern day campaigns conducted by ISIS or the Taliban. Although much criticised, American support and intervention was part of a wider 'moral' cause to neuter a violent insurgency and whatever the rights and wrongs of the Diem regime, this should not be ignored. In many areas of the country the hamlet programme was having a positive impact: schools, hospitals and roads were all being constructed. However, there were large parts of the nation – in particular in the Delta – where government control simply did not exist. Even though increased insurgent activity was an indication that they were being damaged by the campaign, it is unrealistic to claim that the war was being won. Instead, a more balanced appraisal would be that the balance of victory in the conflict was ebbing between both sides throughout 1961 to 1963. Diem enjoyed a slight advantage in 1962 – again supporting recent claims – but this was not maintained and could be attributed to the insurgents taking time to adjust to the new strategy and tactics.

This series has also helped illustrate why the historians disagree about events in South Vietnam: they are often approaching the programme from one particular perspective and their accounts reflect this focus. Many reports were looking at isolated aspects of the programme rather than seeing it as coherent, interconnected whole: failing to see how one aspect of the programme compared to or stimulated activity in another area of the conflict. For example, increased attacks in the Delta region were a sign of insurgent strength but also an indication that they were being cut off from their village supply bases: the attacks demonstrated both the prowess and the desperation of the insurgency. Depending on the viewpoint used, it was possible to present an account that recognised success or failure in a particular region or during a specific time frame.

This series has shown that Preston's earlier assertion (in Volume One) that the historical record was not so much 'incorrect as incomplete' applies to the Strategic Hamlet Programme too. It was a disorientating, diverse and often destructive initiative that was also well-planned, based on sound historical precedent and was hurting the Viet Cong. This book has added depth to the historical account and shown that the reputation of the Strategic Hamlet Programme – whilst not necessarily capable of rescue – does need to be reassessed.

CONCLUSION AND CLOSING THOUGHTS

Conclusion

In the final analysis, rather than being seen as a failure, it is perhaps fairer to claim that the Counterinsurgency Plan and the Strategic Hamlet Programme were squandered opportunities. When implemented correctly the hamlets were certainly effective and initially at least, caused the insurgents serious problems. The Viet Cong were losing troops, many parts of South Vietnam were being protected against insurgent attack and there was evidence of the people fighting back against the insurgency when they felt secure enough to do so. To dismiss the entire national strategy as a failure cannot be borne out by the historical record. Despite the many problems with the programme it was not a 'lost cause' or beyond redemption. However, neither can the programme be classed as a success. At the death of Diem, large parts of the country were still under Viet Cong control, many hamlets were incomplete and various reforms undertaken were often counterproductive. However, as this book series has shown, this illustrates further the many paradoxes within the Strategic Hamlet Programme: the constant interaction between insurgent and counterinsurgent resulted in a strategy that was difficult to assess in a meaningful or accurate way. Like so much of the subsequent conflict there were many complex actors and interacting environments in the country which were hard to define and harder to control. It seemed that the more the government did, the less effective it became and the Diem-American alliance was unable to adjust to changes on the ground and win the war. The tragedy of the Strategic Hamlet Programme was that it offered a chance for success that Diem and his American allies were unable to grasp.

Closing Thoughts from the Author

When writing the books in this series I was confronted with lots of material that did not match the historical consensus. Public opinion about the war in Vietnam is often distorted by events from 1965 onwards and this view often clouds academic judgement too. I hope my books have helped to correct some of the historical record. There have been many admirable attempts to try and amend the history of this time from people such as Philip Catton, Rufus Phillips and Edward Miller and I'd like this series to add to their sterling work.[214]

I would also hope the books have increased respect and admiration for those involved in South Vietnam at this time. It is very fashionable in some quarters to constantly critique the 'West' (and America in particular) for its involvement in foreign affairs. However, in this case, I believe these views are misplaced. This is because whatever their political stance or their view of the war, many of those serving in South Vietnam at this time believed they were doing the 'Right Thing'. American advisors, ARVN soldiers, South Vietnamese government officials and troops from nations such as Australia, all risked and gave their lives to try and halt a ruthless terrorist campaign; they tried to protect and help the South Vietnamese people and build a better nation. Whatever the results, their determination and sacrifice should be valued.

I also believe that a good deal of the critique of this time ignores one important factor that is essential for historical study: Context. What else could Diem, Kennedy and others have done? Should they have simply abandoned a country to its fate? Should they have let terrorists run riot? The Cold War, the threat of totalitarian communist expansion and the horrifying and brutal levels of insurgent violence were all reasons to act. We now know of the terror that the communist regimes inflicted on their own people and their legacy of pain and suffering. We can debate the implementation of policy (and should do so) but I feel some modern analysts – in their rush to impose our prevailing values on the time period – have forgotten the global context around the war. The men and women serving in South Vietnam were trying to make that nation safe, prosperous and free. That should not be forgotten or distorted by current fashions and trends.

In summary, researching this work left me with a huge amount of respect for those fighting the Viet Cong in South Vietnam at this time. However, one event in particular has remained in my memory. When I was a child, I watched a documentary on British television where a young woman was in Washington and was at the Vietnam Veterans Memorial Wall of Remembrance, paying her respects to her dead brother. She asked tearfully, 'what was it for? He died for nothing'. Words can never replace such a loss or repair the pain felt, but I hope these books offer some small comfort to that young lady (now probably in her 60s or 70s) in knowing that her brother died trying to do some good. Like so many involved in South Vietnam, he – and so many others – gave so much to try and make one small part of the World a better place. I hope these books have – in my own small way – been a fitting tribute to those who served.

BIBLIOGRAPHY

ARCHIVES AND MANUSCRIPT SOURCES

JOHN F. KENNEDY ARCHIVES, BOSTON, MASSACHUSETTS

PRESIDENTIAL PAPERS – PRESIDENT'S OFFICE FILES

Country Files

Vietnam: General, 1960–1961
Vietnam, General, 1961
Vietnam, General, 1962
Vietnam, General, 1963
Vietnam, Security, 1961
Vietnam, Security, 1962
Vietnam, Security, 1963
Vietnam Subjects, Jorden Report
Vietnam Subjects, MAAG, Counterinsurgency, Part I–VII

Counter-insurgency

31 March 1959–13 January 1962
Departments and Agencies
Justice: Counterinsurgency (U.S. Army report), May 1961
Air Force: Counterinsurgency, 1962

Countries

Vietnam: General, 1963: 22 September–5 October: Defense cables
Vietnam: General, September 1963: 18–21: State cables

MEETINGS AND MEMORANDA (GENERAL)

Key national security problems: General, 1961: March–September

National Security Council meetings, 1963: No. 519, 2 October 1963
Special Group (CI): Subjects: Meetings, 8 June 1961–2 November 1962

Meetings and Memoranda (Staff)

Rostow, Walt, 1961
Taylor, Maxwell, 1961: September–December

National Security Action Memoranda

NSAM 52: re: Report of the Vietnam Task Force
NSAM 65: Joint Program of Action with the Government of Vietnam
NSAM 111: First Phase of Vietnam Program
NSAM 124: Establishment of the Special Group (Counter-insurgency)
NSAM 163: Training Objectives for Counterinsurgency
NSAM 182: Counterinsurgency Doctrine

National Security Files (General)

Vietnam, General, 1961: January–March
Vietnam, General, 1961: August
Vietnam, General, 1963: September

PRESIDENT'S OFFICE FILES (GENERAL)

Departments and Agencies

Air Force: Counterinsurgency, 1962
President's Office Files
General Correspondence 1962: HA

Regional Security Files

Southeast Asia, 1961

Gilpatric, Roswell L., Personal Papers

Hilsman, Roger, Personal Papers

Countries Files, 1961–1964. Vietnam: "A Strategic Concept for South Vietnam, 2 February 1962"
Countries Files, 1961–1964. Vietnam: Hilsman trip, December 1962–January 1963: Basic report and "Eyes Only" annex
Countries Files, 1961–1964. Vietnam, 27 August 1963

Komer Series, Counterinsurgency

Oral History Collection

Ball, George W.
Bell, David
Bundy, William P.
Burke, Arleigh A.
Cooper, Chester
Forrestal, Michael V.
Gilpatric, Roswell L.
Krulak, Victor (Harold)
Lansdale, Edward G.
Rostow, Walt W.
Wheeler, Earle

Liddell Hart Centre for Military Archives, London

The John F. Kennedy National Security Files, 1961–1963
US Armed Forces in Vietnam. 1954–1975
Vietnam Documents and Research Notes Series: Translation and Analysis of Significant Viet Cong / North Vietnamese Documents

Miami University Library: Oxford, Ohio

OCLC Number: 1658815. Rand Vietnam Interview Series V, Microfilm Collection V: Viet Cong Organizational Activities at Hamlet / Village level

THE VIETNAM CENTER AND VIRTUAL VIETNAM ARCHIVE, TEXAS TECH UNIVERSITY, LUBBOCK, TEXAS

Colby, William Collection

Donnell, John Collection

Questionnaire (I) For POW's and Ralliers
Studies of the National Liberation Front of South Vietnam Interviews
The CRIMP Documents
The Strategic Hamlet Program in Kien Hoa Province, South Vietnam: A Case Study of Counter-insurgency

Drachnik, Joseph Collection

Lehovich, Vladimir Collection

Michigan State University Vietnam Advisory Group Collection

Nulsen, Charles (Bob) Collection

Oral History Project

Phillips, Rufus Collection

Pike, Douglas Collection

Assessment and Strategy
Democratic Republic of Vietnam
Insurgency Warfare
Intra Ministry Committee for Strategic Hamlets
Military Operations
Monographs
National Liberation Front
Other Manuscripts
Statistical Data
The Early History of Vietnam

Shelton, William Collection

US Marine Corps History Division Vietnam War Documents Collection

Vietnam Archive Collection

Captured Documents
Background Information and Areas of Knowledgeability

ONLINE ARCHIVES

CIA ARCHIVES, WASHINGTON D.C. [ONLINE]

CIA History Staff – Center for the Study of Intelligence Memoranda and Miscellaneous

FOREIGN RELATIONS OF THE UNITED STATES [ONLINE]

Volume I: Vietnam, 1961
Volume II: Vietnam, 1962
Volume III: Vietnam, January–August 1963
Volume IV: Vietnam, August–December 1961
Volume VII: Vietnam, 1961–1963 National Security Policy

LYNDON B. JOHNSON PRESIDENTIAL LIBRARY [ONLINE]

Oral History Interviews

Ball, George
Bundy, William
Colby, William E.
Cooper, Chester
Davidson, Phillip
Durbrow, Elbridge
Forrestal, Michael F.
Gilpatric, Roswell
Harkins, Paul D.
Hilsman, Roger
Lansdale, Edward G.
McNamara, Robert S.
Phillips, Rufus
Pike, Douglas
Wheeler, Earle G.

NATIONAL ARCHIVES, WASHINGTON D.C. [ONLINE]

US–Vietnam Relations 1945–1967, Volume IV.A.4: Evolution of the War. U.S. Training of Vietnamese National Army, 1954-59
US–Vietnam Relations 1945–1967, Volume IV.A.5: Evolution of the War. Origins of the Insurgency
US–Vietnam Relations 1945–1967, Volume IV.B.1: Evolution of the War.
Counterinsurgency: The Kennedy Commitments and Programs, 1961
US–Vietnam Relations 1945–1967, Volume IV.B.2: Evolution of the War.

Counterinsurgency: Strategic Hamlet Program, 1961–63
US–Vietnam Relations 1945–1967, Volume IV.B.3: Evolution of the War. Counterinsurgency: The Advisory Build–up, 1961–67
US–Vietnam Relations 1945–1967, Volume IV.B.4: Evolution of the War. Counterinsurgency: Phased Withdrawal of U.S. Forces in Vietnam, 1962–64
US–Vietnam Relations 1945–1967, Volume IV.B.5: Evolution of the War. Counterinsurgency: The Overthrow of Ngo Dinh Diem, May–Nov. 1963
US–Vietnam Relations 1945–1967, Volume IV.C.1: Evolution of the War. U.S. Programs in South Vietnam, November 1963–April 1965
US–Vietnam Relations 1945–1967, Volume V.A: Justification of the War. Public Statements. Volume I: C–The Kennedy Administration
US–Vietnam Relations 1945–1967, Volume V.B.4: Justification of the War. Internal Documents. The Kennedy Administration. Book I
US–Vietnam Relations 1945–1967, Volume V.B.4: Justification of the War. Internal Documents. The Kennedy Administration. Book II

RAND, SANTA MONICA, CALIFORNIA [ONLINE]

RAND Research Reports, Vietnam, 1962–1973
RAND Interview Series, Vietnam, 1965–1972

GOVERNMENT PUBLICATIONS

Military Reports and Handbooks

Armed Forces Information and Education Department of Defense, *Handbook for U.S. Forces in Vietnam* (Washington: US Government Printing Office, 1966)
MACV, *Counterinsurgency: Lessons Learned Number 61: Salient Lessons Learned* (San Francisco: United Stated Military Assistance Command, Vietnam, 1967)
MACV, *Counterinsurgency: Lessons Learned Number 63: Search and Rescue Operations* (San Francisco: United Stated Military Assistance Command, Vietnam, 1967)
MACV, *Counterinsurgency: Lessons Learned Number 68: Viet Cong Base Camps and Supply Caches* (San Francisco: United Stated Military Assistance Command, Vietnam, 1968)
Petraeus, General D.H., Amos, J.F., & Nagl, J.A., *US Army Marine Corps Counterinsurgency Manual* (Chicago: University of Chicago, 2007)
United States Army Special Warfare School, *Program of Instruction for Military Assistance Training Advisor* (MATA) (North Carolina: Fort Bragg, 1962)
United States Marine Corps, *FMFM–21: Operations against Guerrilla Units* (Washington DC: Department of the Navy, 1962)

RAND Research Reports

Anderson, M., Arnsten, M., & Averch, H., *RM–5239–1–ISA/ARPA – Insurgent Organization and Operations: A Case Study of the Viet Cong in the Delta, 1964–1966* (Santa Monica: RAND Corporation, 1967)
Carrier, J.M., & Thomson C.A.H., *RM–4830–2–ISA/ARPA– Viet Cong Motivation and Morale: The Special Case of Chieu Hoi* (Santa Monica: RAND Corporation, 1966)
Cochran, S.W., *16157–ISA/ARPA – Motivation and Morale: Some Questions – Some Answers* (Santa Monica: RAND Corporation, 1967)
Davison, W.P., *R–1024–ARPA – User's Guide to the Rand Interviews in Vietnam* (Santa Monica: RAND Corporation, 1972)
Davison, W.P., & Zasloff, J.J., *RM–4983–1–ISA/ARPA – A Profile of Viet Cong Cadres* (Santa Monica: RAND Corporation, 1966)
Donnell, J.C., & Hickey, G.C., *RM–3208–ARPA – The Vietnamese 'Strategic Hamlets': A Preliminary Report* (Santa Monica: RAND Corporation, 1962)
Donnell, J.C., *14436–IBA/ARPA – Viet Cong Recruitment: Why and How Men Join* (Santa Monica: RAND Corporation, 1966)
Goure, L., & Thomson, C.A.H., *RM–4699–1–ISA/ARPA – Some Impressions of Viet Cong Vulnerabilities: An Interim Report* (Santa Monica: RAND Corporation, 1965)
Goure, L., *RM–4517–1–ISA – Some Impressions of the Effects of Military Operations on Viet Cong Behavior* (Santa Monica: RAND Corporation, 1965)
Goure, L., *RM–5522–1–ISA/ARPA – Inducements and Deterrents to Defection: An Analysis of the Motives of 125 Defectors* (Santa Monica: RAND Corporation, 1968)
Kecskemeti, P., *'Insurgency as a Strategic Problem'* (Santa Monica: RAND Corporation, 1967)
Kellen, K., *RM–5013–1–ISA/ARPA – A Profile of the PAVN Soldier in South Vietnam* (Santa Monica: RAND Corporation, 1966)
Kellen, K., *RM–6131–1–ISA–ARPA– Conversations with Enemy Soldiers in Late 1968/Early 1969: A Study of Motivation and Morale* (Santa Monica: RAND Corporation, 1970)
Koch, J.A., *The Chieu Hoi Program in South Vietnam, 1963–1971* (Santa Monica: Rand Corporation, 1973)
Komer, R.W., *R–957–ARPA – The Malayan Emergency in Retrospect: Organization of a Successful Counterinsurgency Effort* (Santa Monica: Rand Corporation, 1972)
Pearce, R.M., *RM–552–1–ARPA – Evolution of a Vietnamese Village – Part I: The Present, After Eight Months of Pacification* (Santa Monica: Rand Corporation, 1965)
Pearce, R.M., *RM–4692–1–ARPA – Evolution of a Vietnamese Village – Part II: The Past, August 1945 to April 1965* (Santa Monica: Rand Corporation, 1966)
Sweetland, A., *17634–ARPA/AGTLE – The Analysis of the HES (Hamlet Evaluation System)* (Santa Monica: RAND Corporation, 1968)
Zasloff, J.J., *RM–4703/2–ISA/ARPA – Political Motivation of the Viet Cong: The Vietminh Regroupees* (Santa Monica: RAND Corporation, 1968)

Special National Intelligence Estimates 1960–1963

Special National Intelligence Estimate, *63.1–60, Short Term Trends in South Vietnam* (Washington DC: Director of Central Intelligence, No 344, 23 August 1960)
Special National Intelligence Estimate, *58–61 Probable Communist Reactions to Certain US Courses of Action with Respect to Laos* (Washington DC: Director of Central Intelligence, No 253, 21 February 1961)
Special National Intelligence Estimate, *50–61 Outlook in Mainland Southeast Asia* (Washington DC: Director of Central Intelligence, No 364, 28 March 1961)
Special National Intelligence Estimate, *50–61 Outlook in Mainland Southeast Asia* (Washington DC: Director of Central Intelligence, No 364, 03 April 1961)
Special National Intelligence Estimate, *10–2–61 Likelihood of Major Communist Military Intervention in Mainland Southeast Asia* (Washington DC: Director of Central Intelligence, No 320, 27 June 1961)
Special National Intelligence Estimate, *58–2–61 Probable Reactions to Certain Courses of Action Concerning Laos* (Washington DC: Director of Central Intelligence, No 69, 05 July 1961)
Special National Intelligence Estimate, *14.3 / 53–61 Prospects for North and South Vietnam* (Washington DC: Director of Central Intelligence, No 370, 15 August 1961)
Special National Intelligence Estimate, *TS 142405–c Probable Communist Reactions to Certain SEATO Undertakings in South Vietnam* (Washington DC: Director of Central Intelligence, 10 October 1961)
Special National Intelligence Estimate, *10–62 Communist Objectives, Capabilities, and Intentions in Southeast Asia* (Washington DC: Director of Central Intelligence, No 352, 21 February 1962)
Special National Intelligence Estimate, *10–62 Communist Objectives, Capabilities, and Intentions in Southeast Asia* (Washington DC: Director of Central Intelligence, No 86, 21 February 1962)
Special National Intelligence Estimate, *58–5–62 Probable Communist Reactions to Certain US Courses of Action with Respect to Laos* (Washington DC: Director of Central Intelligence, No 370, 31 May 1962)
Special National Intelligence Estimate, *68–5/1–62 Communist Reactions to Additional US Courses of Action in Laos and North Vietnam* (Washington DC: Director of Central Intelligence, No 371, 12 June 1962)
Special National Intelligence Estimate, *53–63 Prospects in South Vietnam* (Washington DC: Director of Central Intelligence, No 361, 17 April 1963)
Special National Intelligence Estimate, *14.3–63 The Impact of the Sino–Soviet Dispute on North Vietnam and its Policies* (Washington DC: Director of Central Intelligence, No 358, 26 June 1963)
Special National Intelligence Estimate, *53–2–63 The Situation in South Vietnam* (Washington DC: Director of Central Intelligence, No 354, 10 July 1963)

Memoranda and Miscellaneous

CIA Telegram, *Strategic Hamlets* (Washington DC: Director of Central Intelligence, 20 February 1962)
CIA Telegram, *Hamlet Programs* (Washington DC: Director of Central Intelligence, 03 July 1962)
CIA Telegram, *Strategic Hamlet Situation in Central Vietnam* (Washington DC: Director of Central Intelligence, 05 October 1962)
CIA Telegram, *Progress of Free Elections in Strategic Hamlets* (Washington DC: Director of Central Intelligence, 26 November 1962)
CIA Report, *Vietnam 1961–1968 Review of Judgements in INR Reports* (Washington DC: Director of Central Intelligence, Declassified 1985)
Memorandum for the Director, *South Vietnam's Leaders* (Washington DC: Director of Central Intelligence, 02 September 1963)
Memorandum for the Director, *Probable North Vietnamese Reaction to Certain Clandestine Operations* (Washington DC: Director of Central Intelligence, 20 December 1963)
CIA Documents, *Counter Insurgency Critical List* (Washington DC: Director of Central Intelligence, 25 July 1962)
CIA Documents, *Minutes of the Meeting of the Special Group (Counterinsurgency)* (Washington DC: Director of Central Intelligence, 21 August 1962)
CIA Documents, *Minutes of the Meeting of the Special Group (Counterinsurgency)* (Washington DC: Director of Central Intelligence 23 May 1963)
CIA Documents, *Minutes of the Meeting of the Special Group (Counterinsurgency)* (Washington DC: Director of Central Intelligence, 12 December 1963)

General

Commonwealth of Australia, *Parliamentary Debates: Melbourne and the Strategic Hamlets,* The Vietnam Center and Archive, Texas Tech University, 1963. [Online]. Available: http://www.virtualarchive.vietnam.ttu.edu/starweb/virtual/vva/servlet.starweb#

NEWSPAPERS, MEDIA AND PERIODICALS

The Times, London

Unknown Correspondent, 'American Guerrilla Experts for Vietnam', *The Times,* 15 May 1961

Unknown Diplomatic Correspondent, 'British Mission to South Vietnam', *The Times,* 18 September 1961.

Unknown Special Correspondent, Saigon, 'Vietnam Village Defence Pledge. 3M. Peasants Affected.' *The Times,* 21 April 1962

Unknown Correspondent, Saigon, 'Lessons of the War in South Vietnam', *The Times,* 21 January 1963

Unknown Correspondent, Saigon, 'Vietnam Dilutes its Democracy', *The Times,* 1 July 1963

Unknown Defence Correspondent, 'The American Strategic Revolution 3 – fierce Dedication of Fort Bragg.', *The Times,* 31 July 1963

Unknown Special Correspondent, Saigon, 'New Vigour in South Vietnam War on Communist. Popular Support for Regime leads to Aggressive Spirit', *The Times,* 12 November 1963

Unknown Special Correspondent, Saigon, 'Strategy in Vietnam', *The Times,* 31 March 1964

Unknown Correspondent, 'Vietnam as Seen from Peking', *The Times,* 29 March 1965

Unknown Defence Correspondent, 'Vietnam, The War No One Can Win', *The Times,* 16 July 1965

Unknown Correspondent, 'Strategy in Vietnam', *The Times,* 14 July 1967

MEMOIRS

Giap, Gen. V.N., & Dung, Gen. V.T., *How We Won the War* (Ypsilanti, Michigan: RECON Publications, 1976)

Herrington, S.A., *Silence was a Weapon. The Vietnam War in the Villages: A Personal Perspective* (Novato, CA: Presidio Press, 1982)

Luce, D. & Sommer, J., *Vietnam – The Unheard Voices* (Ithaca and London: Cornell University Press, 1969)

McNamara, R.S., *In Retrospect: The Tragedy and Lessons of Vietnam* (New York: Random House, 1995)

Neese, H. & O'Donnell, J. (eds), *Prelude to Tragedy: Vietnam 1960–1965* (Annapolis: Naval Institute Press, 2001)

Phillips, R., *Why Vietnam Matters: An Eyewitness Account of Lessons not Learned* (Annapolis: Naval Institute Press, 2008)

Sharp, Admiral U.S.G., *Strategy for Defeat: Vietnam in Retrospect* (Novato, California: Presidio Press, 1978)

Tang, T.N., *A Vietcong Memoir* (San Diego: Harcourt Brace Jovanovich, 1985)

Templer, R., *The Conduct of Anti-terrorist Operations in Malaya* (Third Edition), (Malaya: Director of Operations, 1958)

Thompson, R., *Defeating Communist Insurgency: Experiences from Malaya and Vietnam* (London: Chatto and Windus, 1966)

Thompson, R., *Make for the Hills: Memories of Far Eastern Wars* (London: Leo Cooper, 1989)

Thompson, R., *No Exit from Vietnam* (London: Chatto and Windus, 1969)

Truong, N.Q., *Territorial Forces* (US Army Center for Military History: Washington DC, 1981)

Zumwalt, J.G., *Bare Feet, Iron Will: Stories from the Other Side of Vietnam's Battlefields* (Jacksonville: Fortis Publishers, 2010)

PUBLISHED SECONDARY SOURCES

Books

Addington, L.H., *America's War in Vietnam – A Short Narrative History* (Bloomington: Indiana University Press, 2000)

Ahern, T.L., *CIA and Rural Pacification in South Vietnam* (Washington, DC: CIA History Staff – Center for the Study of Intelligence, Declassified, 2009)

Ahern, T.L., *CIA and the Generals. Covert Support to Military Government in South Vietnam* (Washington, DC: CIA History Staff – Center for the Study of Intelligence, Declassified, 2009)

Ahern, T.L., *CIA and the House of Ngo. Covert Action in South Vietnam, 1954–63* (Washington, DC: CIA History Staff – Center for the Study of Intelligence, Declassified, 2009)

Ahern, T.L., *Good Questions, Wrong Answers. CIA Estimates of Arms Traffic through Sihanoukville, Cambodia, During the Vietnam War* (Washington, DC: CIA History Staff – Center for the Study of Intelligence, Declassified, 2004)

Ahern, T.L., *The Way We Do Things: Black Entry Operations into North Vietnam, 1961–1964* (Washington, DC: CIA History Staff – Center for the Study of Intelligence, Declassified, 2005)

Ahern, T.L., *Undercover Armies. CIA and Surrogate Warfare in Laos 1961–1973* (Washington, DC: CIA History Staff – Center for the Study of Intelligence, Declassified, 2009)

Aldred, J., *British Imperial and Foreign Policy, 1846–1980* (Oxford: Heinemann, 2004)

Allen, C., *Plain Tales from the British Empire* (London: Abacus, 2008)

Anderson, D., *Shadow on the White House: Presidents and the Vietnam War, 1945–1975* (Lawrence: University Press of Kansas, 1993)

Anderson, D.L., & Ernst, J., *The War that Never Ends: New Perspectives on the Vietnam War* (Lexington: The University Press of Kentucky, 2007)

Arnold, J.R., *Jungle of Snakes – A Century of Counterinsurgency Warfare from the Philippines to Iraq* (New York: Bloomsbury Press, 2010)

Arreguin-Toft, I., *How the Weak Win Wars: A Theory of Asymmetric Conflict* (Cambridge: Cambridge University Press, 2005)

Asprey, R.B., *War in the Shadows: Classic History of Guerrilla Warfare from Ancient Persia to the Present* (St Ives: Little, Brown and Company, 1994)

Baker, M., *Nam: The Vietnam War in the Words of the Men and Women who Fought There* (London: Abacus, 1982)

Ballard, J.R., & Cordesman, A. H., *Iraqi Security Forces, A Strategy for Success, Terrorism and Political Violence* (Washington: The National War College, 2007)

Ball, S.J., *The Cold War: An International History, 1947–1991* (London: Hodder-Arnold, 1998)

Barber, N., *The War of the Running Dogs: How Malaya Defeated the Communist Guerrillas, 1948–1960* (London: Cassell, 1971)

Bayly, C., & Harper, T., *Forgotten Wars: The End of Britain's Asian Empire* (London: Penguin Books, 2007)

Beckett, I.F.W., & Pimlott, J., *Counter-insurgency: Lessons from History* (Barnsley: Pen and Sword Military, 2011)

Beckett, I.F., *Insurgency in Iraq: A Historical Perspective* (Carlisle, PA: Studies Institute, U.S. Army War College, 2005)

Beckett, I.F., *Modern Insurgencies and Counter – Insurgencies: Guerrillas and their Opponents since 1750* (London: Routledge, 2001)

Beckett, I.F. (ed.), *The Roots of Counterinsurgency: Armies and Guerilla Warfare, 1900–1945* (London: Blandford Press, 1988)

Berman, L., *Lyndon Johnson's War: The Road to Stalemate in Vietnam* (New York: W.W. Norton and Company, 1989)

Bew, J., Frampton, M., & Gurruchaga, I., *Talking to Terrorists: Making Peace in Northern Ireland and the Basque Country* (London: G Hurst & Co, 2009)

Birtle, A.J., *U.S Army Counterinsurgency and Contingency Operations Doctrine 1942–1976* (Washington, D.C.: Center of Military History, United States Army, 2006)

Boot, M., *Invisible Armies: An Epic History of Guerrilla Warfare from Ancient Times to the Present* (New York: Liveright, 2013)

Bourke, J., *An Intimate History of Killing: Face-to-Face Killing in the Twentieth Century* (London: Granta Books, 1999)

Bradley, M.P., & Young, M.B. (eds), *Making Sense of the Vietnam Wars: Local, National and Traditional Perspectives* (Oxford: Oxford University Press, 2008)

Bragg, C., *Vietnam, Korea and US Foreign Policy 1945–75* (Oxford: Heinemann, 2005)

Brigham, R.K., *Is Iraq another Vietnam?* (New York: Public Affairs, 2006)

Brown, A., Elder, S., Gilbert, A., & Williams, R. (eds), *War in Peace: Conventional and Guerilla Warfare since 1945* (London: Orbis Publishing, 1981)

Brown, T., *JFK: History of an Image* (London: I.B. Tauris & Co Ltd, 1988)

Browning, P., *The Changing Nature of Warfare* (Cambridge: Cambridge University Press, 2006)

Burleigh, M., *Blood and Rage: A Cultural History of Terrorism* (London: Harper Perennial, 2008)

Burleigh, M., *Small Wars, Far Away Places. The Genesis of the Modern World: 1945–65* (London: Pan Macmillan, 2013)

Callwell, C.E., *Small Wars: Their Principles and Practice,* 3rd edition (Lincoln: University of Nebraska Press, 1996)

Caputo, P., *A Rumour of War* (New York: Henry Holt and Company, 1996)

Carlton, E., *War and Ideology* (London: Routledge, 1990)

Carruthers, S.L., *Winning Hearts and Minds: British Governments, the Media and Colonial Counter-Insurgency 1944–1960* (London: Leicester University Press, 1995)

Carter, J.M., *Inventing Vietnam. The United States and State Building, 1954–1968* (Cambridge: Cambridge University Press, 2008)

Catton, P.E., *Diem's Final Failure: Prelude to America's War in Vietnam* (Lawrence: University of Kansas, 2002)

Cassidy, R.M., *Counterinsurgency and the Global War on Terror: Military Culture and Irregular War* (Stanford, California: Stanford University Press, 2008)

Cawthorne, N., *Vietnam: A War Lost and Won* (London: Arcturus Publishing, 2003)

Clodfelter, M., *The Limits of Airpower: The American Bombing of North Vietnam* (New York: The Free Press, 1989)

Clutterbuck, R., *The Long, Long War: Counterinsurgency in Malaya and Vietnam* (Westport: Praeger, 1966)

Conboy, K., & Andrade, D., *Spies and Commandos. How America Lost the Secret War in North Vietnam* (Lawrence: University Press of Kansas, 2000)

Cooley, J., *Unholy Wars. Afghanistan, America and International Terrorism* (London: Pluto Press, 1999)

Connable, B., *Embracing the Fog of War: Assessment and Metrics in Counterinsurgency* (Santa Monica: RAND, 2012)
Cordesman, A.H., *Rethinking the Challenge of Counterinsurgency Warfare: Working Notes* (Washington: The Center for Strategic and International Studies, 2005)
Cordesman, A.H., *The Long War: The United States as a Self-Inflicted Wound,* (Washington: The Center for Strategic and International Studies, 2007)
Corum, J.S., *Bad Strategies – How Major Powers Fail in Counterinsurgency* (Minneapolis: Zenith Press, 2008)
Cosmas, G.A., *MACV The Joint Command in Years of Escalation, 1962–1967* (Washington, D.C.: Center of Military History, 2006)
Cox D.G., & Bruscino, T., *Population-Centric Counterinsurgency: A False Idol?* (Fort Leavenworth, Kansas: Combat Studies Institute Press – US Army Combined Arms Center, 2011)
Crockatt, R., *The Fifty Years War: The United States and the Soviet Union, 1941–1991* (Abingdon: Routledge, 1995)
Croke, K., *Rethinking the War on Terrorism: The Lessons of Counterinsurgency Doctrine* (Washington: Progressive Policy Institute, 2006)
Dallek, R., *John F Kennedy: An Unfinished Life, 1917–1963* (London: Penguin, 2004)
Damms, D.V., *The Eisenhower Presidency, 1953–1961* (London: Pearson Education Limited, 2002)
Daugherty, L., *The Vietnam War – Day by Day* (Birkenhead: Snap Productions Ltd, 2002)
Davis, R.G. (ed.), *The U.S. Army and Irregular Warfare 1775–2007* (Washington, D.C.: Center of Military History, United States Army, 2008)
Deery, P., *Malaya, 1948: Britain's 'Asian Cold War'?* (New York: International Center for Advanced Studies New York University, 2002)
Dinh Tho, T., *Pacification* (Washington D.C.: US Army Center of Military History, 1980)
Dixon, N., *On the Psychology of Military Incompetence* (London: Pimlico, 1976)
Dorland, G., *Legacy of Discord. Voices of the Vietnam War Era* (Washington, DC: Brassey's, 2001)
Duiker, W.J., *The Communist Road to Power in Vietnam* (Colorado: Westview Press, 1996)
Dumbrell, J., *Rethinking the Vietnam War* (Basingstoke: Palgrave Macmillan, 2012)
Dumbrell, J., & Ryan, D. (eds), *Vietnam in Iraq: Tactics, Lessons, Legacies and Ghosts* (London: Routledge, 2007)
Edwards, O., *The USA and the Cold War, 1945–63* (Abingdon: Hodder Murrray, 2002)
Ellsberg, D., *Secrets: A Memoir of Vietnam and the Pentagon Papers* (New York: Penguin Books, 2002)
Elliott, D.W.P., *The Vietnamese War: Revolution and Social Change in the Mekong Delta, 1930–1975* (New York: East Gate Books, 2003)
Feaver, P.D., & Kohn, R.H. (eds), *Soldiers and Civilians: The Civil–Military Gap and American National Security* (Cambridge, MA: MIT Press, 2001)
Freedman, L., *Kennedy's Wars: Berlin, Cuba, Laos, and Vietnam* (New York: Oxford University Press, 2000)
French, D., *The British Way in Counter-insurgency, 1945–1967* (Oxford: Oxford University Press, 2011)
Fitzgerald, F., *Fire in the Lake* (London: MacMillan, 1972)
Fitzgerald, D., *Learning to Forget: US Army Counterinsurgency Doctrine and Practice from Vietnam to Iraq* (Stanford: Stanford University Press, 2013)
Gaddis, J.L., *Strategies of Containment: A Critical Appraisal of Post-war American National Security Policy* (Oxford: Oxford University Press, 1982)
Gaddis, J.L., *The Cold War* (London: Penguin Books, 2005)
Gaddis, J.L., *The Long Peace: Inquiries into the History of the Cold War* (Oxford: Oxford University Press, 1987)
Gaddis, J.L., *We Now Know: Rethinking Cold War History* (Oxford: Oxford University Press, 1997)
Galula, D., *Counterinsurgency Warfare: Theory and Practice,* 2nd edition (London: Praeger Security International, 2006)
Gardner, L.C., & Young, M.B. (eds), *Iraq and the Lessons of Vietnam* (New York: The New Press, 2007)
Gat, A., *A History of Military Thought from the Enlightenment to the Cold War* (Oxford: Oxford University Press, 2001)
Gelb, L., & Bett, R., *The Irony of Vietnam: The System Worked* (Washington DC: Brookings Institution Press, 1979)
Giglio, J.N., *The Presidency of John F. Kennedy* (Lawrence, Kansas: The University of Kansas, 1991)
Gilbert, M.J. (ed.), *Why the North Won the Vietnam War* (New York: Palgrave, 2002)
Gill, D.C., *How We are Changed by War: A Study of Letters and Diaries from Colonial Conflicts to Operation Iraqi Freedom* (New York: Routledge, 2010)
Goodwin, J., *No Other Way Out: States and Revolutionary Movements, 1945–1991* (Cambridge: Cambridge University Press, 2001)
Gompert, D.C., *Heads We Win: The Cognitive Side of Counterinsurgency (COIN)* (Santa Monica: Rand Corporation, 2006)
Gompert, D.C., & Gordan, J., *War by Other Means. Building Complete and Balanced Capabilities for Counterinsurgency* (Santa Monica: Rand Corporation, 2007)
Graebner, N.A., *The Cold War: Ideological Conflict or Power Struggle?* (Boston: D.C. Heath and Company, 1963)
Graessner, S., Gurris, N., & Pross, C., *At the Side of Torture Survivors: Treating a Terrible Assault on Human Dignity* (Baltimore: John Hopkins University, 2001)
Grob-Fitzgibbon, B., *Imperial Endgame: Britain's Dirty Wars and the End of Empire* (Basingstoke: Palgrave Macmillan, 2011)
Guan, A.C., *The Vietnam War, 1962–64: The Vietnamese Communist Perspective* (New York: McGraw Hill, 2000)
Gurman, H. (ed.), *Hearts and Minds: A People's History of Counterinsurgency* (New York: The New Press, 2013)
Gwynn, C., *Imperial Policing* (London: Macmillan, 1936)
Halberstam, D., *The Best and the Brightest* (New York: Ballantine Books, 1969).
Halberstam, D., *The Making of a Quagmire: America and Vietnam during the Kennedy Era, Revised Edition* (Lanham, Maryland: Rowman & Littlefield Publishers, 2008)
Hall, M., *The Vietnam War* (Harlow: Pearson Education Limited, 2000)
Hammes, T.X., *The Sling and the Stone: On War in the 21st Century* (St.Paul: Zenith Press, 2006)
Hammond, W., *Reporting Vietnam: Media and Military at War* (Lawrence: University Press of Kansas, 2000)
Hanson, V.D., *An Autumn of War: What America Learned from September 11 and the War on Terrorism* (New York: Anchor Books, 2002)
Hanson, V.D., *Why the West has Won* (London: Faber and Faber, 2001)
Head, W., & Grinter, L., *Looking Back on the Vietnam War: A 1990 Perspective on the Decisions, Combat and Legacies* (London: Praeger, 1993)
Hearden, P.J., *The Tragedy of Vietnam* (Abingdon: Pearson Education, 2016)
Hernon, I., *Britain's Forgotten Wars: Colonial Campaigns of the 19th Century* (Stroud: Sutton Publishing, 2002)
Herring, G.C., *America's Longest War: The United States and Vietnam* (New York: McGraw Hill, 2002)
Hess, G.R., *Vietnam and the United States* (Boston: Twayne Publishers, 1990)
Hess, M., *Then the Americans Came: Voices from Vietnam* (New York: Four Walls Eight Windows, 1993)
Heuser, B., & Shamir, E. (eds), *Insurgencies and Counterinsurgencies: National Styles and Strategic Cultures* (Cambridge: Cambridge University Press, 2016)
Hickey, G.C., *Village in Vietnam* (New Haven and London: Yale University Press, 1964)
Hilsman, R., *To Move a Nation. The Politics of Foreign Policy in the Administration of John F. Kennedy* (New York: Delta Publishing, 1967)
Hoffman, B., *Insurgency and Counterinsurgency in Iraq* (Arlington: RAND Corporation, 2004)
Holland, R.F., *European Decolonization, 1918–1981* (London: Macmillan Education, 1985)
Hosmer, S.T., & Crane, S.O., *Counterinsurgency: A Symposium, April 16–20, 1962* (Santa Monica: Rand Corporation, 2006)
Hunt, D., *Vietnam's Southern Revolution: From Peasant Insurrection to Total War* (Amherst: University of Massachusetts Press, 2008)
Hunt, M. (ed.), *A Vietnam War Reader: A Documentary History from American and Vietnamese Perspectives* (North Carolina: University of North Carolina Press, 2010)
Ives, C.K., *US Special Forces and Counterinsurgency in Vietnam: Military Innovation and Institutional Failure, 1961–1963* (London and New York: Routledge, 2007)
James Joes, A., *Resisting Rebellion: The History and Politics of Counterinsurgency* (Lexington: The University Press of Kentucky, 2006)
James, L., *The Rise and Fall of the British Empire* (London: Abacus, 1994)
Jennings, R.S., *The Road Ahead: Lessons in Nation Building from Japan, Germany, and Afghanistan for Postwar Iraq* (Washington: United States Institute of Peace, 2007)
Joes, A., *The War For South Vietnam* (Westport: Praeger, 2001)
Kahin, McT., *Intervention: How America became involved in Vietnam* (New York: Anchor Books, 1986)
Kaiser, D., *American Tragedy: Kennedy, Johnson and the Origins of the Vietnam War* (Cambridge: Belknap Press of Harvard University Press, 2000)
Karnow, S., *Vietnam: A History* (Harmondsworth: Penguin, 1987)
Kennedy, J. F., *Profiles in Courage – 50th Anniversary Edition* (New York: Harper Perennial, 2003)
Kilcullen, D., *The Accidental Guerrilla: Fighting Small Wars in the Midst of a Big One* (London: Hurst & Company, 2009)
Kitson, F., *Low Intensity Operations: Subversion, Insurgency, Peacekeeping* (London: Faber and Faber, 1971)
Kolko, G., *Anatomy of War: Vietnam, the United States and the Modern Historical Experience* (New York: The New Press, 1985)
Komer, W., *Impact of Pacification on Insurgency in South Vietnam* (Santa Monica: RAND Corporation, 1970)

Komer, R. W., *The Malayan Emergency in Retrospect: The Organization of a Successful Counterinsurgency Effort* (Santa Monica: RAND Corporation, 1972)
Lanning, M.L., & Cragg, D., *Inside the VC and the NVA. The Real Story of North Vietnam's Armed Forces* (New York: Fawcett Columbine, 1992)
Law, R.D., *Terrorism: A History* (Cambridge: Polity Press, 2009)
Lawrence, M., *Assuming the Burden: Europe and the American Commitment to War in Vietnam* (Berkeley: University of California Press, 2005)
Laqueur, W., *A History of Terrorism* (New York: Transaction Publishers, 2001)
Lembbcke, J., *The Spitting Image: Myth, Memory, and the Legacy of Vietnam* (New York: New York University Press, 1998)
Leffler, M.P., & Painter, D.S., *Origins of the Cold War* (London: Routledge, 1994)
Levy, D., *The Debate Over Vietnam* (Baltimore: Johns Hopkins University Press, 1991)
Lewy, G., *America in Vietnam* (New York: Oxford University Press, USA, 1978)
Logevall, F., *Choosing War – The Lost Chance for Peace and the Escalation of War in Vietnam* (Berkeley: University of California Press, 1999)
Logevall, F., *The Origins of the Vietnam War* (New York: Longman, 2001)
Long, A., *On 'Other War': Lessons from Five Decades of RAND Counterinsurgency Research* (Santa Monica: Rand Corporation, 2006)
Lynn, J.A., *Battle: A History of Combat and Culture from Ancient Greece to Modern America* (Cambridge: Westview, 2004)
Mackay, A., & Tatham, S., *Behavioural Conflict – Why Understanding People and their Motivations will Provide Decisive in Future Conflict* (Saffron Walden: Military Studies Press, 2011)
Mackinlay, J., & Al-Baddawy, A., *Rethinking Counterinsurgency* (Santa Monica: Rand, 2007)
Manwaring, M.G., *Shadows of Things Past and Images of the Future: Lessons for the Insurgencies in our Midst* (Carlisle, PA: Strategic Studies Institute, 2004)
Martin, G., *Understanding Terrorism: Challenges, Perspectives and Issues* (Thousand Oaks: Sage Publications, 2006)
McCauley, M., *Russia, America and the Cold War* (Harlow: Pearson Education, 2004)
McCauley, M., *The Origins of the Cold War* (New York: Longman, 1983)
McDonough, F., *The British Empire* (Bedford: Hodder and Stoughton, 1994)
McMahon, R.J. (ed.), *Major Problems in the History of the Vietnam War* (Boston: Houghton Mifflin Company, 2003)
McMahon, R.J., & Paterson, T.G., *Problems in American Civilisation: The Origins of the Cold War* (Boston: Houghton Mifflin, 1999)
McMahon, R., *Major Problems in the History of the Vietnam War* (Lexington, Mass: DC Heath & Co, 2008)
McNamara, R.S., Blight, J.G., & Brigham, R.K., *Argument without End – in Search of Answers to the Vietnam Tragedy* (New York: Public Affairs, 1999)
Mead, W.R., *God and Gold: Britain, America and the Making of the Modern World* (New York: Random House, 2007)
Merom, G., *How Democracies Lose Small Wars: State, Society and the Failures of France in Algeria, Israel in Lebanon and the United States in Vietnam* (New York: Cambridge University Press, 2003)
Metz, S., & Millen, R., *Insurgency and Counterinsurgency in the 21st Century: Reconceptualising Threat and Response* (Washington: Strategic Studies Institute, 2004)
Metz, S., & Millen, R., *Insurgency in Iraq and Afghanistan: Change and Continuity* (Washington: Strategic Studies Institute, 2007)
Miller, E., *Misalliance: Ngo Dinh Diem, the United States, and the Fall of South Vietnam* (Cambridge: Harvard University Press, 2013)
Moore, H., & Galloway, J., *We Were Soldiers Once … and Young: Ia Drang – the Battle that Changed the War in Vietnam* (Novato: Presidio Press, 2004)
Moyar, M., *A Question of Command: Counterinsurgency from the Civil War to Iraq* (New Haven: Yale University Press, 2009)
Moyar, M., *Phoenix and the Birds of Prey: Counterinsurgency and Counterterrorism in Vietnam* (Lincoln: University of Nebraska, 1997)
Moyar, M., *Triumph Forsaken: The Vietnam War, 1954–1965* (Cambridge: Cambridge University Press, 2006)
Mumford, A., *Puncturing the Counterinsurgency Myth: Britain and Irregular Warfare in the Past, Present, and Future* (Carlisle: US Army War College, 2011)
Mumford, A., *The Counter-insurgency Myth: The British Experience of Irregular Warfare. Cass Military Studies.* (London: Routledge, 2012)
Murray, W., & Mansoor, P.R. (eds), *Hybrid Warfare: Fighting Complex Opponents from the Ancient World to the Present* (Cambridge: Cambridge University Press, 2012)
Nagl, J.A., *Learning to Eat Soup with a Knife: Counterinsurgency Lessons from Malaya and Vietnam* (Chicago: University of Chicago Press, 2002)
Nalty, B.C., *The Vietnam War. The History of America's Conflict in Southeast Asia* (New York: Salamander Books, 1996)
Neale, J., *The American War: Vietnam 1960–1975* (London: Bookmarks, 2001)
Newman, J.M., *JFK and Vietnam* (New York: Warner Books, 1993)
Newsinger, J., *British Counterinsurgency: From Palestine to Northern Ireland* (Chippenham: Palgrave, 2002)
Nielson, K., & Kennedy, G. (eds), *The British Way in Warfare: Power and the International System, 1856–1956* (Farnham: Ashgate, 2006)
Nighswonger, W.A., *Rural Pacification in Vietnam* (New York: Praeger, 1966)
Nye, J.S., *Understanding International Conflicts: An Introduction to Theory and History* (New York: Pearson / Longman, 2007)
O'Brien, T., *The Things they Carried* (London: Flamingo, 1991)
Osborne, M., *Strategic Hamlets in South Vietnam: A Survey and Comparison* (New York: Cornell University, 1965)
Phillips, S., *The Cold War* (Oxford: Heinemann, 2001)
Pillar, P.R., *Terrorism and U.S. Foreign Policy* (Washington: Brookings Institution, 2001)
Pike, D., *PAVN: People's Army of Vietnam* (Novato, California: Presidio Press, 1986)
Pike, D., *Viet Cong – The Organization and Techniques of the National Liberation Front of South Vietnam* (Cambridge, Massachusetts: MIT Press, 1966)
Porch, D., *Counterinsurgency: Exposing the Myths of the New Way of War* (Cambridge: Cambridge University Press, 2013)
Prados, J., & Pratt-Porter, M. (eds), *Inside the Pentagon Papers* (Lawrence, Kansas: University of Kansas Press, 2004)
Preston, A., *The War Council. McGeorge Bundy, The NSC and Vietnam* (Cambridge: Harvard University Press, 2006)
Rabasa, A., Warner, L.A., Chalk, P., Khilko, I., & Shukla, P., *Money in the Bank: Lessons Learned from Past Counterinsurgency (COIN) Operations* (Santa Monica: RAND, 2007)
Record, J., *The Wrong War: Why we lost in Vietnam* (Annapolis, Maryland: Naval Institute Press, 1998)
Rich, P.B., & Duyvesteyn, I. (eds), *The Routledge Handbook of Insurgency and Counterinsurgency* (London: Routledge, 2012)
Rid, T., & Keaney, T. (eds), *Understanding Counterinsurgency: Doctrine, Operations and Challenges* (Oxford: Routledge, 2010)
Rose, G.D., *Operational Analysis in Support of Recent Military Operations* (Farnborough: DSTL, 2004)
Rosenau, W., *Subversion and Insurgency* (Santa Monica: RAND, 2007)
Rosenau, W., & Long, A., *The Phoenix Program and Counterinsurgency* (Santa Monica: RAND, 2009)
Ruane, K. (ed.), *The Vietnam Wars* (Manchester: Manchester University Press, 2000)
Ruane, K., *War and Revolution in Vietnam, 1930–75* (London: UCL Press, 1998)
Sams, K., *Command and Control 1965* (Christiansburg: Dalley Book Services, 1966)
Samson, J. (ed.), *The British Empire – Oxford Readers* (Oxford: Oxford University Press, 2001)
Sanders, V., *The USA and Vietnam 1945–75* (Abingdon: Hodder Murray, 2007)
Sarkasian, S., *Unconventional Conflicts in a New Security Era: Lessons from Malaya and Vietnam* (Westport: Greenwood Press, 1993)
Sauvain, P., *Vietnam* (Cheltenham: Stanley Thornes, 1997)
Scanlon. P., *The Tree Wants to be still but the Wind won't let it* (Bloomington, IN: the 1st Books Library, 2000)
Schlesinger, A.M., *A Thousand Days: John F. Kennedy in the White House* (Greenwich: Fawcett Crest, 1965)
Schleisinger, A.M., *Robert Kennedy and his Times* (New York: Mariner Books, 1979)
Schulinzger, R.D., *A Time for War: The United States and Vietnam, 1941–1975* (New York: Oxford University Press, USA 1997)
Schwab, O., *Defending the Free World. John F. Kennedy, Lyndon Johnson, and the Vietnam War; 1961–1965* (West Port, Connecticut: Praeger, 1998)
Selverstone, M.J. (ed.), *A Companion to John F. Kennedy* (Chichester: Wiley Blackwell, 2014)
Sevy, G. (ed.), *The American Experience in Vietnam* (Norman: University of Oklahoma Press, 1989)
Shay, J., *Achilles in Vietnam. Combat Trauma and the Undoing of Character* (New York: Touchstone, 1994)
Shaw, G.D.T., *The Lost Mandate of Heaven: The American Betrayal of Ngo Dinh Diem, President of Vietnam* (San Francisco: Ignatius Press, 2013)
Short, A., *The Origins of the Vietnam War* (London: Longman, 1989)
Smith, E.D., *Counter-insurgency Operations 1: Malaya and Borneo* (London: Ian Allen Ltd, 1985)
Smith, M.L.R., & Martin Jones, D., *The Political Impossibility of Modern Counterinsurgency. Strategic Problems, Puzzles and Paradoxes* (New York: Columbia University Press, 2015)
Smith, R., *An International History of the Vietnam War: The Kennedy Strategy* (New York: Palgrave Macmillan, 1985)
Smith, R., *The Utility of Force: The Art of War in the Modern World* (New York: Penguin, 2006)
Solomon, Z., *Combat Stress Reaction: The Enduring Toll of War* (New York: Plenum Press, 1993)
Sorensen, T.C., *Kennedy* (London: Pan Books, 1965)
Spector, R.H., *After Tet: The Bloodiest Year in Vietnam* (New York: The Free Press, 1993)
Stewart, G., *Vietnam's Lost Revolution: Ngo Dinh Diem's Failure to Build An Independent Nation, 1955–1963* (Cambridge: Cambridge University Press, 2017)

Stewart, N., *The Changing Nature of Warfare 1700–1945* (Oxford: Hodder Murray, 2001)
Strachan, H., *The Direction of War: Contemporary Strategies in Historical Perspective* (Cambridge: Cambridge University Press, 2013)
Taber, R., *The War of the Flea: Guerrilla Warfare – Theory and Practice* (St. Albans: Paladin Press, 1970)
Tanham, G.K., *Communist Revolutionary Warfare: From the Vietminh to the Viet Cong,* 2nd edition (Westport: Praeger Security International, 2006)
Tatham, S., & Mackay, A., *Behavioural Conflict: Why Understanding People and Their Motives Will Prove Decisive in Future Conflict* (London: Military Studies Press, 2011)
Thayer, C.W., *Guerrilla* (London: Michael Joseph Ltd, 1964)
Thompson, L., *The Counter – Insurgency Handbook* (London: Greenhill Books, 2002)
Thornton, R., *Asymmetric Warfare* (Cambridge: Polity Press, 2007)
Trinquier, R., *Modern Warfare: A French View of Counterinsurgency,* 3rd edition (Westport: Praeger Security International, 2006)
Trullinger, J.W., *Village at War: An Account of the Conflict in Vietnam* (Stanford: Stanford University Press, 1994)
Tse-Tung, M., *On Guerrilla Warfare* (Chicago: University of Illinois Press, 1961)
Tzu, S., *The Art of War* (Ware: Wordsworth Edition, 1998)
Valentine, D., *The Phoenix Program* (Lincoln: William Morrow and Co, 1990)
Vien, N.K. (ed.), *Vietnam Studies N° 20 – 'American Failure'* (Xunhasaba, Hanoi: 1968)
Warren, J.A., *Giap.The General who defeated America in Vietnam* (New York: Palgrave Macmillan, 2013)
Wiest, A., & Doidge, M.J. (eds), *Triumph Revisited: Historians Battle for the Vietnam War* (New York: Routledge, 2010)
Williams, W.A. (ed.), *America in Vietnam – A Documentary History* (New York: W.W. Norton and Company, 1975)
Wolf, C., *Insurgency and Counterinsurgency: New Myths and Old Realities* (Santa Monica: RAND Corporation, 1965)
Wolf, E.R., *Peasant Wars of the Twentieth Century* (London: Faber and Faber, 1971)
Woodruff, M.W., *Unheralded Victory. Who Won the Vietnam War?* (London: Harper Collins, 1999)

JOURNALS AND ARTICLES

Adloff, V.T., 'Britain's Policy in Malaya', *Far Eastern Survey*, 16 (1947), p.112
Adloff, V.T., 'Opposition in Malaya', *Far Eastern Survey*, 16 (1947), pp.130–131
Ahmed, S., 'The United States and Terrorism in Southwest Asia: September 11 and Beyond', *International Security,* 26 (2001/02), pp.79–93
Alexander, J., & McGregor, J., 'War Stories: Guerrilla Narratives of Zimbabwe's Liberation War', *History Workshop Journal*, 57 (2004), pp.79–100
Ambert, A.M., Adler, P.A., Adler, P., & Detzner, D.F., 'Understanding and Evaluating Qualitative Research', *Journal of Marriage and Family*, 57 (1995), pp.879–893
Andrade, D., 'Westmoreland was right: learning the wrong lessons from the Vietnam War', *Small Wars & Insurgencies*, 19 (2008), pp.145–181
Anderson, D., et al, 'Interchange: Legacies of the Vietnam War', *The Journal of American History*, 93 (2006), pp.452–490
Anderson, D.M., 'British Abuse and Torture in Kenya's Counter-insurgency, 1952–1960', *Small Wars & Insurgencies*, 23 (2012), pp.700–719
Andrade, D. & Willbanks, J.H., 'CORDS / Phoenix: Counterinsurgency Lessons from Vietnam for the Future', *Military Review*, March–April (2006), pp.9 – 23
Anonymous, 'An Interview with Bernard Fall', *Marine Corps Gazette*, 51 (1964), pp.10–11
Arquilla, J., 'The end of war as we knew it? Insurgency, counterinsurgency and lessons from the forgotten history of early terror networks', *Third World Quarterly*, 28 (2007), pp.369–386
Arreguin-Toft, I., 'How the Weak Win Wars – A Theory of Asymmetric Conflict', *International Security*, 26 (2001), pp.93–12
Aylwin-Foster, N., 'Changing the Army for Counterinsurgency Operations', *Military Review*, November–December (2005), pp.2–15
Barnes, T., 'War by Numbers: Another Quantitative Revolution', *Geopolitics*, 00 (2015), pp.1–6
Bass, T.A., 'Counterinsurgency and Torture', *American Quarterly*, 60 (2008), pp.233–240
Beckett, I.F., 'British Counter-insurgency: a Historiographical Reflection', *Small Wars & Insurgencies*, 23 (2012), pp.781–798
Bell, M., 'In Afghanistan, Memories of Vietnam', *New Statesman*, 20/08 (2007)
Bender, G.J., 'The Limits of Counterinsurgency: An African Case', *Comparative Politics*, 4 (1972), pp.331–360
Bennett, H., 'A Very Salutary Effect': The Counter–Terror Strategy in the Early Malayan Emergency, June 1948 to December 1949', *Journal of Strategic Studies*, 32 (2009), pp.415–444
Bennett. H., 'Minimum Force in British Counterinsurgency', *Small Wars & Insurgencies*, 21 (2010), pp.459–475
Benvenuti, A., 'The British Military Withdrawal from Southeast Asia and its Impact on Australia's Cold War Strategic Interests', *Cold War History*, 5 (2005), pp.189–210
Berger, M.T., & Borer, D.A., 'The Long War: insurgency, counterinsurgency and collapsing states', *Third World Quarterly*, 28 (2007), pp.197–215
Berger, M.T., Burgess, K., Mauldin, J., & Sullivan, M.P., '"Déjà Vu All Over Again": Counterinsurgency and the 'American Way of War', *Intelligence and National Security*, 22 (2007), pp.910–931
Betts, R.K., 'Is Strategy an Illusion?', *International Security*, 25 (2000), pp.5–50
Blanken, L., & Overbaugh, J., 'Looking for Intel? … or Looking for Answers? Reforming Military Intelligence for a Counterinsurgency Environment', *Intelligence and National Security*, 27 (2012), pp.559–575
Blanken, L.J., & Lepore, J.J., 'Performance measurement in military operations: information versus incentives', *Defence and Peace Economics*, 26 (2015), pp.516–535
Bortree, J.R., 'IO During the Malayan Emergency', *IO Sphere*, Spring (2007), pp.24–32
Breede, Captain C.H., 'Intelligence Lessons and The Emerging Canadian Counter-insurgency Doctrine', *Canadian Army Journal*, 9 (2006), pp.24–40
Brown, A., 'Perestroika and the End of the Cold War', *Cold War History*, 7 (2007), pp.1–17
Bryant, G.J., 'Asymmetric Warfare: The British Experience in Eighteenth-Century India', *The Journal of Military History*, 68 (2004), pp.431–469
Bulloch, G., 'Military Doctrine and Counterinsurgency: A British Perspective', *Parameters*, Summer (1996), pp.4–16
Burleigh, M., 'Britain's Brutal Battles for Hearts and Minds', *BBC History,* 14 (2013) no page number
Busch, P., 'Killing the 'Vietcong: The British Advisory Mission and the Strategic Hamlet Programme', *Journal of Strategic Studies*, 25 (2002), pp.135–162
Busch, P., 'Supporting the War: Britain's Decision to send the Thompson Mission to Vietnam, 1960–61', *Cold War History*, 2 (2001), pp.69–94
Byman, D., 'Death Solves All Problems': The Authoritarian Model of Counterinsurgency', *Journal of Strategic Studies*, No Volume (2015), pp.1–36
Carland, J.M., 'Winning the Vietnam War: Westmoreland's Approach in Two Documents', *The Journal of Military History*, 68 (2004), pp.553–574
Casebeer, W.D., 'The Importance of Treating Culture as a System: Lessons on Counter-insurgency Strategy from the British Iraqi Mandate', *Strategic Insights*, IV (2005)
Cassidy, R.M., 'Back to the Street without Joy: Counterinsurgency Lessons from Vietnam and Other Small Wars', *Parameters*, Summer (2004), pp.73–83
Cassidy, R.M., 'The British Army and Counterinsurgency: The Salience of Military Culture', *Military Review*, May–June (2005), pp.53–59
Cassidy, R.M., 'The Long Small War: Indigenous Forces for Counterinsurgency', *Parameters*, Summer (2006), pp.47–62
Cassidy, R.M., 'Winning the War of the Flea – Lessons from Guerilla Warfare', *Military Review*, September–October (2004), pp.41–46
Catton, P.E., 'Counter-insurgency and Nation Building: The Strategic Hamlet Programme in South Vietnam, 1961–1963', *The International History Review*, 21 (1999), pp.918–940
Catton, P.E., 'Refighting Vietnam in the History Books: The Historiography of the War', *OAH Magazine of History,* 18 (2004), pp.7–11
Caverley, J.D., 'The Myth of Military Myopia: Democracy, Small Wars, and Vietnam', *International Security*, 34 (2009/2010), pp.119–157
Celeski, J.D., 'Strategic Aspects of Counterinsurgency', *Military Review*, March–April (2005), pp.35–41
Chen, K.C., 'Hanoi's Three Decisions and the Escalation of the Vietnam War', *Political Science Quarterly*, 90 (1975), pp.239–259
Chin, W., 'Examining the Application of British Counterinsurgency Doctrine by the American Army in Iraq', *Small Wars & Insurgencies*, 18 (2007), pp.1–26
Clemis, M.G., 'Crafting non-kinetic warfare: the academic–military nexus in US counterinsurgency doctrine', *Small Wars & Insurgencies*, 20 (2009), pp.160–184
Cohen, E., Crane, C., Horvath, J., & Nagl, J., 'Principles, Imperatives, and Paradoxes of Counterinsurgency', *Military Review*, March–April (2006), pp.49–53
Cohen, M.A., 'The Myth of a Kinder, Gentler War', *World Policy Journal*, 27 (2010), pp.75–86
Cohen, R.S., 'Just How Important Are 'Hearts and Minds' Anyway? Counterinsurgency Goes to the Polls', *Journal of Strategic Studies*, 37 (2014), pp.609–636
Comber, L., 'The Malayan Special Branch on the Malayan–Thai frontier during the Malayan Emergency (1948–60)', *Intelligence & National Security*, 21 (2006), pp.77–99
Connolly, C., 'The American Factor: Sino–American Rapprochement and Chinese Attitudes to the Vietnam War, 1968–72', *Cold War History*, 5 (2005), pp.501–527
Cornish, P., 'The United States and Counterinsurgency: 'Political First, Political Last, Political Always', *International Affairs*, 85 (2009), pp.61–79
Cull, N.J., 'The Man who Invented Truth: The Tenure of Edward R. Murrow as Director of the United States Information Agency during the Kennedy years', *Cold War History*, 4 (2003), pp.23–48

Darley, W.M. (ed.), 'Counterinsurgency Reader: Special Edition', *Military Review*, October (2006), pp.2–195
Deery, P., 'The Terminology of Terrorism: Malaya, 1948–52', *Journal of Southeast Asian Studies*, 34 (2003), pp.231–247
Desai, R., & Eckstein, H., 'Insurgency: The Transformation of Peasant Rebellion', *World Politics*, 42 (1990), pp.441–465
de Sola-Pool, I., 'Political Alternatives to the Viet Cong', *Asian Survey*, 7 (1967), pp.555–566
Dixon, P., (2009): 'Hearts and Minds'? British Counter-insurgency from Malaya to Iraq', *Journal of Strategic Studies*, 32 (2009), pp.353–381
Donnell, J.C., 'Pacification Reassessed', *Asian Survey*, 7 (1967), pp.567–576
Dorussen, H., 'Mixing Carrots with Sticks: Evaluating the Effectiveness of Positive Incentives', *Journal of Peace Research*, 38 (2001), pp.251–262
Downes, A.B., 'Draining the Sea by Filling the Graves: Investigating the Effectiveness of Indiscriminate Violence as a Counterinsurgency Strategy', *Civil Wars*, 9 (2007), pp.420–444
Doyle, M.W., & Sambanis, N., 'International Peacebuilding: A Theoretical and Quantitative Analysis', *The American Political Science Review*, 94 (2000), pp.779–801
Duncanson, D., '"Symbiotic Insurgency" in Vietnam Ten Years after', *International Affairs (Royal Institute of International Affairs 1944–)*, 54 (1978), pp.589–601
Egnell, R., 'Lessons from Helmand, Afghanistan: what now for British counterinsurgency?', *International Affairs*, 87 (2011), pp.297–315
Egnell, R., 'Winning "Hearts and Minds"? A Critical Analysis of Counter-insurgency Operations in Afghanistan', *Civil Wars*, 12 (2010), pp.282–303
Fahey, J.J., 'A Peace Pilgrimage: From Total War to World Community', *U.S. Catholic Historian*, 27 (2009), pp.45–60
Fall, B.B., 'The Theory and Practice of Insurgency and Counterinsurgency', *Military Review*, September–October (2015), pp.40–48
Fall, B.B., 'The Theory and Practice of Insurgency and Counterinsurgency', *Naval War College Review*, Winter (1998), pp.1–11
Fearon, J.D., & Laitin, D.D., 'Ethnicity, Insurgency, and Civil War', *The American Political Science Review*, 97 (2003), pp.75–90
Findley, M.G., & Young, J.K., 'Fighting Fire with Fire? How (Not) to Neutralize an Insurgency', *Civil Wars*, 9 (2007), pp.378–401
Fitzgerald, D., 'Sir Robert Thompson, Strategic Patience and Nixon's War in Vietnam', *Journal of Strategic Studies*, 37 (2014), pp.998–1026
Fitzgerald, D., 'Vietnam, Iraq and the Rebirth of Counter-insurgency', *Irish Studies in International Affairs*, 21 (2010), pp.149–159
Ford, C.M., 'Speak No Evil: Targeting a Population's Neutrality to Defeat an Insurgency', *Parameters*, Summer (2005), pp.51–66
Friedman, J.A., 'Manpower and Counterinsurgency: Empirical Foundations for Theory and Doctrine', *Security Studies*, 20 (2011), pp.556–591
Gates, J.M., 'Two American Wars in Asia: Successful Colonial Warfare in the Philippines and Cold War Failure in Vietnam', *War in History*, 8 (2001), pp.47–71
Gentile, G.P., 'The Selective Use of History in the Development of American Counterinsurgency Doctrine', *Army History*, Summer (2009), pp.21–35
Ginty, R.M., 'Social network analysis and counterinsurgency: a counterproductive strategy?', *Critical Studies on Terrorism*, 3 (2010), pp.209–226
Gonzalez, R.J., 'Human Terrain', *Anthropology Today*, 24 (2008), pp.21–26
Gortzak, Y., 'The prospects of combined action: Lessons from Vietnam', *Small Wars & Insurgencies*, 25 (2014), pp.137–160
Gortzak, Y., 'Using Indigenous Forces in Counterinsurgency Operations: The French in Algeria, 1954–1962', *Journal of Strategic Studies*, 32 (2009), pp.307–333
Greenhill, K.M., & Staniland, P., 'Ten Ways to Lose at Counterinsurgency', *Civil Wars*, 9 (2007), pp.402–419
Griffin, A.L., Hall, B., & Ross, A.T., 'The Australian counterinsurgency campaign in the Vietnam war: the ambush battle', *Journal of Maps*, 10 (2014), pp.61–64
Grinter, L.E., 'How They Lost: Doctrines, Strategies and Outcomes of the Vietnam War', *Asian Survey*, 15 (1975), pp.1114–1132
Grossheim, M., 'Revisionism in the Democratic Republic of Vietnam: New Evidence from the East German Archives', *Cold War History*, 5 (2005), pp.451–477
Grubbs, L.K., 'Is There a Deep Fight in a Counterinsurgency?', *Military Review*, July–August (2005), pp.28–31
Guan, A.C., 'Khe Sanh – from the Perspective of the North Vietnamese Communists', *War in History*, 8 (2001) pp.87–98
Guan, A.C., 'The Vietnam War, 1962–64: The Vietnamese Communist Perspective', *Journal of Contemporary History*, 35 (2000), pp.601–618
Gventer, C.W., 'Counterinsurgency and its Critics', *Journal of Strategic Studies*, 37 (2014), pp.637–663
Hack, K., 'Everyone Lived in Fear: Malaya and the British Way of Counterinsurgency', *Small Wars & Insurgencies*, 23 (2012) pp.671–699
Hack, K., 'The Malayan Emergency as Counter-insurgency Paradigm', *Journal of Strategic Studies*, 32 (2009), pp.383–414
Hall, B., & Ross, A., 'Kinetics in counterinsurgency: some influences on soldier combat performance in the 1st Australian Task Force in the Vietnam War', *Small Wars & Insurgencies*, 21 (2010), pp.498–518
Hammes, T.X., 'The Future of Counterinsurgency', *Foreign Policy Research Institute*, Fall (2012), pp.565–587
Hannah, M., 'Torture and the Ticking Bomb: The War on Terrorism as a Geographical Imagination of Power/Knowledge', *Annals of the Association of American Geographers*, 96 (2006), pp.622–640
Hasik, J., 'Learning in counterinsurgency: what do we really know?', *Defense & Security Analysis*, 29 (2013), pp.203–217
Hassan, M.H.B., 'Key Considerations in Counter-ideological Work against Terrorist Ideology', *Studies in Conflicts and Terrorism*, 29 (2006), pp.531–558
Hendry, J.B., 'Economic Development under Conditions of Guerrilla Warfare: The Case of Viet Nam', *Asian Survey*, 2 (1962), pp.1–12
Heuser, B., 'The Cultural Revolution in Counter-insurgency', *Journal of Strategic Studies*, 30 (2007), pp.153–171
Hochmüller, M., & Müller, M.M., 'Locating Guatemala in Global Counterinsurgency', *Globalizations*, (2015), pp.1–17
Hoffman, F.G., 'Neo-Classical Counterinsurgency?', *Parameters*, Summer (2007), pp.71–87
Hoffmann, S, Huntington, S.P., May, E.R., Neustadt, R.N., & Schelling, T.C., 'Vietnam Reappraised', *International Security*, 6 (1981), pp.3–26
Homan, R., 'The Ethics of Covert Methods', *The British Journal of Sociology*, 31 (1980), pp.46–59
Hooks, G., & Mosher, C., 'Outrages against Personal Dignity: Rationalizing Abuse and Torture in the War on Terror', *Social Forces*, 83 (2005), pp.1627–1645
Hopkins, B.D., 'The Problem with "Hearts and Minds" in Afghanistan', *Middle East Report*, 255 (2010), pp.24–29
Hughes, J., 'Frank Kitson in Northern Ireland and the British Way of Counterinsurgency', *History Ireland*, 22 (2014), pp.44–48
Hughes, M., 'Introduction: British Ways of Counter-insurgency', *Small Wars & Insurgencies*, 23 (2012), pp.580–590
Jackson, B.A., 'Counterinsurgency Intelligence in a Long War: The British Experience in Northern Ireland', *Military Review*, January–February (2007), pp.74–85
Jackson, A., 'British Counterinsurgency in History: A Useful Precedent?', *British Army Review*, 139 (2006) p.12
Jackson, M., General, 'British Counter-insurgency from Malaya to Iraq', *Journal of Strategic Studies*, 32 (2007), pp.347–351
Jardine, E., 'Population-centric counterinsurgency and the movement of peoples', *Small Wars & Insurgencies*, 23 (2012), pp.264–294
Johnson, L.K., & Caruson, K., 'The Seven Sins of American Foreign Policy', *Political Science and Politics*, 36 (2003), pp.5–10
Joiner, C.A., 'The Ubiquity of the Administrative Role in Counterinsurgency', *Asian Survey*, August (1967), pp.1–23
Jones, D.M., Smith, M.L.R., & Stone, J., 'Counter-COIN: Counterinsurgency and the Pre-emption of Strategy', *Studies in Conflict & Terrorism*, 35 (2012), pp.597–617
Jones, D.M., & Smith, M.L.R., 'Myth and the Small War Tradition: Reassessing the discourse of British counter-insurgency', *Small Wars & Insurgencies*, 24 (2013), pp.436–464
Jones, D.M., & Smith, M.L.R., 'Whose Hearts and Whose Minds? The Curious Case of Global Counter-insurgency', *Journal of Strategic Studies*, 33 (2010), pp.81–121
Jorgensen, J.G., 'On Ethics and Anthropology', *Current Anthropology*, 12 (1971), pp.321–334
Jumper, R., 'The Communist Challenge to South Viet Nam', *Far Eastern Survey*, 25 (1956), pp.161–168
Jundanian, B.F., 'Resettlement Programs: Counterinsurgency in Mozambique', *Comparative Politics*, 6 (1974), pp.519–540
Kane, P., 'Renewal and Transformation: The Historian as How-to Guide', *U.S. Catholic Historian*, 25 (2007), pp.69–78
Kanet, R.E., 'The Superpower Quest for Empire: The Cold War and Soviet Support for "Wars of National Liberation"', *Cold War History*, 6 (2006), pp.331–352
Kalyvas, S.N., & Kocher, M.A., 'The Dynamics of Violence in Vietnam: An Analysis of the Hamlet Evaluation System (HES)', *Journal of Peace Research*, 46 (2009), pp.335–355
Katagiri, N., 'Winning hearts and minds to lose control: exploring various consequences of popular support in counterinsurgency missions', *Small Wars & Insurgencies*, 22 (2011), pp.170–195
Kebede, M., 'The Rehabilitation of Violence and the Violence of Rehabilitation: Fanon and Colonialism', *Journal of Black Studies*, 31 (2001), pp.539–562
Kennedy, R., 'Malaya: Colony without Plan', *Far Eastern Survey*, 14 (1945), pp.225–26
Khalili, L., 'The New (and Old) Classics of Counterinsurgency', *Middle East Report*, 255 (2010), pp.14–23

Khalili, L., 'Thinking about Violence', *International Journal of Middle East Studies*, 45 (2013), pp.791–794

Kirk-Greene, A., 'Decolonization: The Ultimate Diaspora', *Journal of Contemporary History*, 36 (2001), pp.133–151

Kocher, M.A., Pepinsky, T.B., & Kalyvas, S.N., 'Aerial Bombing and Counterinsurgency in the Vietnam War', *American Journal of Political Science*, 55 (2011), pp.201–218

Kollars, N.A., 'War's Horizon: Soldier-Led Adaptation in Iraq and Vietnam', *Journal of Strategic Studies*, 38 (2015), pp.529–553

Kovats-Bernat, J.C., 'Negotiating Dangerous Fields: Pragmatic Strategies for Fieldwork Amid Violence and Terror', *American Anthropologist*, New Series, 104 (2002), pp.208–222

Kiszely, J., 'Learning About Counterinsurgency', *RUSI Journal*, December (2006), pp.17–21

Kramer, M., 'The Perils of Counterinsurgency: Russia's War in Chechnya', *International Security*, 29 (2004/2005), pp.5–63

Kuzmarov, J., 'From Counter-insurgency to Narco-Insurgency: Vietnam and the International War on Drugs', *The Journal of Policy History*, 20 (2008), pp.344–378

Kydd, A.H., & Straus, S., 'The Road to Hell? Third-Party Intervention to Prevent Atrocities', *American Journal of Political Science*, 57 (2013), pp.673–684

Ladwig, W.C., 'Managing Counterinsurgency: Lessons from Malaya', *Military Review*, May–June (2007), pp.56–66

Latham, M.E., 'Redirecting the revolution? The USA and the failure of nation-building in South Vietnam', *Third World Quarterly*, 27:1 (2006), pp.27–41

Levine, D.H., 'Care and Counterinsurgency', *Journal of Military Ethics*, 9 (2010), pp.139–159

Liên, T.T., (2005) 'The Catholic Question in North Vietnam: From Polish Sources, 1954–56', *Cold War History*, 5 (2005), pp.427–449

Lomperis, T.J., 'Giap's Dream, Westmoreland's Nightmare', *Parameters*, June (1988), pp.18–31

Lyall, J., 'Are Coethnics More Effective Counterinsurgents? Evidence from the Second Chechen War', *American Political Science Review*, 104 (2010), p.1–20

Lyall, J., 'Do Democracies Make Inferior Counterinsurgents? Reassessing Democracy's Impact on War Outcomes and Duration', *International Organization*, 64 (2010), pp.167–192

Lyall, J., & Wilson, I., 'Rage against the Machines: Explaining Outcomes in Counterinsurgency Wars', *International Organization*, 63 (2009), pp.67–106

Lynn, J.A., 'Patterns of Insurgency and Counterinsurgency', *Military Review*, July–August (2005), pp.22–27

Luttwak, E.N., 'Dead End: Counterinsurgency Warfare as Military Malpractice', *Harper's Magazine*, February (2007), pp.33–42

Long, A., 'The Quiet Americans: CIA, NSA, and Counterinsurgency', *Journal of Cold War Studies*, 13 (2011), pp.149–184

MacDonald, P.K., '"Retribution Must Succeed Rebellion": The Colonial Origins of Counterinsurgency Failure', *International Organization*, 67 (2013), pp.253–286

Magno, J.P.Jr., & Gregor, A.J., 'Insurgency and Counterinsurgency in the Philippines', *Asian Survey*, 26 (1986), pp.501–517

Major, P., & Mitter, R., 'East is East and West is West? Towards a comparative socio-cultural history of the Cold War', *Cold War History*, 4 (2003), pp.1–22

Malkasian, C., 'Toward a Better Understanding of Attrition: The Korean and Vietnam Wars', *The Journal of Military History*, 68 (2004), pp.911–942

Maranto, R., & Tuchman, P.S., 'Knowing the Rational Peasant: The Creation of Rival Incentive Structures in Vietnam', *Journal of Peace Research*, 29 (1992), pp.249–264

Mack, A., 'Counterinsurgency in the Third World: theory and practice', British *Journal of International Studies*, 1 (1975), pp.226–253

Markel, W., 'Draining the Swamp: The British Strategy of Population Control', *Parameters*, Spring (2006), pp.35–48

Marks, T.A., 'Evaluating insurgent/counterinsurgent Performance', *Small Wars & Insurgencies*, 11 (2000), pp.21–45

Marr, D., 'Political Attitudes and Activities of Young Urban Intellectuals in South Viet-Nam', *Asian Survey*, 6 (1966), pp.249–263

Marshall, A. 'Imperial Nostalgia, the Liberal Lie, and the Perils of Postmodern Counterinsurgency', *Small Wars & Insurgencies*, 21 (2010), pp.233–258

Matthews, W.C., 'The Kennedy Administration, Counterinsurgency, and Iraq's First Bathist Regime', *International Journal of Middle East Studies*, 43 (2011), pp.635–653

McAdam, D., 'Tactical Innovation and the Pace of Insurgency', *American Sociological Review*, 48 (1983), pp.735–754

McAllister, J., 'Who Lost Vietnam: Soldiers, Civilians, and U.S Military Strategy', *International Security*, 35 (Winter 2010/11), pp.95–123

McAllister, J., & Schulte, I., 'The Limits of Influence in Vietnam: Britain, the United States and the Diem Regime, 1959–63', *Small Wars & Insurgencies*, 17:1 (2006), pp.22–43

McFadden, E.M., 'Contemporary Counterinsurgency Operations: History as a Guide to Assist in the Development of the Joint Interagency Task Force', *Comparative Strategy*, 24 (2005), pp.361–378

McFate, M., 'Anthropology and Counterinsurgency: The Strange Story of their Curious Relationship', *Military Review*, March–April (2005), pp.24–38

McFate, M., 'The Military Utility of Understanding Adversary Culture', *Joint Force Quarterly*, 38 (2005), pp.42–48

McFate, M., & Jackson, A.V., 'The Object Beyond War: Counterinsurgency and the Four Tools of Political Competition', *Military Review*, January–February (2006), pp.13–26

Merom, G., 'Strong Powers in Small Wars: The Unnoticed Foundations of Success', *Small Wars & Insurgencies*, 9 (1998), pp.38–63

Metz, S., 'A Flame Kept Burning: Counterinsurgency Support after the Cold War', *Parameters*, Autumn (1995), pp.31–41

Metz, S., 'Insurgency and Counterinsurgency in Iraq', *The Washington Quarterly*, 27 (2003–04), pp.25–36

Miakinkov, E., 'The Agency of Force in Asymmetrical Warfare and Counterinsurgency: The Case of Chechnya', *Journal of Strategic Studies*, 34 (2011), pp.647–680

Michaels, J.H., 'Agents for Stability or Chaos: Conceptualizing Intelligence "Relevance" in Counterinsurgency', *Studies in Conflict & Terrorism*, 34 (2011), pp.212–227

Michaels, J.H., 'Managing Global Counterinsurgency: The Special Group (CI) 1962–1966', *Journal of Strategic Studies*, 35 (2012), pp.33–61

Michaels, J.H., & Gawthorpe, A.J., 'Spies, advisors, and grunts: Film portrayals of counterinsurgency in Vietnam', *Small Wars & Insurgencies*, 26 (2015), pp.668–687

Mockaitis, T.R., 'The Minimum Force Debate: Contemporary Sensibilities meet Imperial Practice', *Small Wars & Insurgencies*, 23 (2012), pp.762–780

Moore, R.M., 'Counterinsurgency force ratio: strategic utility or nominal necessity', *Small Wars & Insurgencies*, 24 (2013), pp.857–878

Morales, O.P., The Evolution of Counterinsurgency Warfare: A Historical Overview', *Revista de Relaciones Internacionales*, 6 (2011), pp.195–220

Mueller, J., 'Six Rather Unusual Propositions about Terrorism', *Terrorism and Political Violence*, 17 (2005), pp.487–505

Mumford, A., 'Minimum Force meets Brutality: Detention, Interrogation and Torture in British Counter-insurgency Campaigns', *Journal of Military Ethics*, 11 (2012), pp.10–25

Murshed, S.M., 'Conflict, Civil War and Underdevelopment: An Introduction', *Journal of Peace Research*, 39 (2002), pp.387–393

Nadzhafov, D.G., 'The Beginning of the Cold War between East and West: The aggravation of ideological confrontation', *Cold War History*, 4 (2004), pp.140–174

Nicole, L., 'Torture: The Need for a Dialogue with Its Victims and Its Perpetrators', *Journal of Peace Research*, 24 (1987), pp.315–322

North, J., 'General Hoche and Counterinsurgency', *The Journal of Military History*, 67 (2003), pp.529–540

O'Brien, S.P., 'Anticipating the Good, the Bad, and the Ugly: An Early Warning Approach to Conflict and Instability Analysis', *The Journal of Conflict Resolution*, 46 (2002), pp.791–811

O'Dowd, E.C., 'What Kind of War is This?', *Journal of Strategic Studies*, 37 (2014), pp.1027–1049

Odgaard, L., & Nielsen, T.G., 'China's Counterinsurgency Strategy in Tibet and Xinjiang', *Journal of Contemporary China*, 23 (2014), pp.535–555

Osornprasop, S., 'Amidst the Heat of the Cold War in Asia: Thailand and the American Secret War in Indochina (1960–74)', *Cold War History*, 7 (2007), pp.349–371

Ouellet, E., & Pahlavi, P.V., 'Institutional Analysis and Irregular Warfare: A Case Study of the French Army in Algeria 1954–1960', *Journal of Strategic Studies*, 34 (2011), pp.799–824

Painter, D., 'A Partial History of the Cold War', *Cold War History*, 6 (2006), pp.527–534

Parker, T., 'Fighting an Antaean Enemy: How Democratic States Unintentionally Sustain the Terrorist Movements they Oppose', *Terrorism and Political Violence*, 19 (2007), pp.155–179

Payne, K., 'Some Principles for Influence in Counterinsurgency', *The British Army Review*, 150 (2010/2011), pp.23–30

Peic, G., 'Civilian Defense Forces, State Capacity, and Government Victory in Counterinsurgency Wars', *Studies in Conflict & Terrorism*, 37 (2014), pp.162–184

Pieper, H., 'The German Approach to Counterinsurgency in the Second World War', *The International History Review*, 37 (2015), pp.631–642

Plakoudas, S., 'Strategy in Counterinsurgency: A Distilled Approach', *Studies in Conflict & Terrorism*, 38 (2015), pp.132–145

Porch, D., (2011) 'The Dangerous Myths and Dubious Promise of COIN', *Small Wars & Insurgencies*, 22 (2011), pp.239–257

Pottier, P., (2005) 'A French Experience in Counterinsurgency during the French Indochina War', *Small Wars & Insurgencies*, 16 (2005), pp.125–146

Protheroe, G.J., 'Limiting America's Engagement: Roger Hilsman's Vietnam War, 1961–1963', *Diplomacy & Statecraft*, 19 (2008), pp.263–288

Quackenbush, S.L., & Murdie, A., 'We Always Fight the Last War? Prior Experiences in Counterinsurgency and Conventional Warfare and War Outcomes', *International Interactions*, 41 (2015), pp.183–200

Quester. G.H., The Guerrilla Problem in Retrospect, *Military Affairs*, 39 (1975), pp.192–196
Ramakrishna, K., 'Bribing the Reds to Give Up': Rewards Policy in the Malayan Emergency', *War in History*, 9 (2002), pp.332–353
Ravlo, H., Gleditsch, N.P, & Dorussen, H., 'Colonial War and the Democratic Peace', *The Journal of Conflict Resolution*, 47 (2003), pp.520–548
Regan, J.M., 'The "O'Brien Ethic" as an Interpretative Problem', *Journal of British Studies*, 52 (2013), pp.908–939
Reis, B. C., 'The Myth of British Minimum Force in Counterinsurgency Campaigns during Decolonisation (1945–1970)', *Journal of Strategic Studies*, 34 (2011), pp.245–279
Rid, T., 'The Nineteenth Century Origins of Counterinsurgency Doctrine', *Journal of Strategic Studies*, 33 (2010), pp.727–758
Ridler, J.S., 'A lost work of El Lobo: Lieutenant-Colonel Charles T.R. Bohannan's unpublished study of guerrilla warfare and counterinsurgency in the Philippines, 1899–1955', *Small Wars & Insurgencies*, 26 (2015), pp.292–312
Rogers, B.L., 'Teaching and Social Reform in the 1960s: Lessons from National Teacher Corps Oral Histories', *Oral History Review*, 35 (2008), pp.39–67
Rosen, S.P., 'Vietnam and the American Theory of Limited War', *International Security*, 7 (1982), pp.83–113
Roxborough, I., 'Learning and Diffusing the Lessons of Counterinsurgency: The U.S. Military from Vietnam to Iraq', *Sociological Focus*, 39 (2006), pp.319–346
Ruane, K., 'Refusing to Pay the Price: British Foreign Policy and the Pursuit of Victory in Vietnam, 1952–4', *The English Historical Review*, 110 (1995), pp.70–92
Rubin, B., 'The October War and US Counter-insurgency Strategy', *MERIP Reports*, 22 (1973), pp.22–24
Russell, J.A., 'Counterinsurgency American style: Considering David Petraeus and twenty-first century irregular war', *Small Wars & Insurgencies*, 25 (2014), pp.69–90
Savage Brosman, C., 'Torture and Terrorism', *The French Review*, 59 (1986), pp.723–729
Scigliano, R.G., 'Political Parties in South Vietnam under the Republic', *Pacific Affairs*, 33, (1960), pp.327–346
Scigliano, R., 'Vietnam: A Country at War', *Asian Survey*, 3 (1963), pp.48–54
Scigliano, R., 'Vietnam: Politics and Religion', *Asian Survey*, 4 (1964), pp.666–673
Schaffer, M.B., 'A Model of 21st Century Counterinsurgency Warfare', *The Journal of Defense Modeling and Simulation: Applications, Methodology and Technology*, 4 (2007) p.380
Schaffer, R., 'The 1940 Small Wars Manual and the "Lessons of History"', *Military Affairs*, 36 (1972), pp.46–51
Scheipers, S., 'Counterinsurgency or irregular warfare? Historiography and the study of "small wars"', *Small Wars & Insurgencies*, 25 (2014), pp.879–899
Schroden, J., 'A best practice for assessment in counterinsurgency', *Small Wars & Insurgencies*, 25 (2014), pp.479–486
Schroden, J.J., 'Measures for Security in a Counterinsurgency', *Journal of Strategic Studies*, 32 (2009), pp.715–744
Sepp, K.I., 'Best Practices in Counterinsurgency', *Military Review*, May–June (2005), pp.8–12
Shafer, M.D., 'The Unlearned Lessons of Counterinsurgency', *Political Science Quarterly*, 103 (1988), pp.57–80
Shultz, R., 'Breaking the Will of the Enemy during the Vietnam War: The Operationalization of the Cost–Benefit Model of Counterinsurgency Warfare', *Journal of Peace Research*, 15 (1978), pp.109–129
Silcock, T.H., 'Policy for Malaya 1952', *International Affairs (Royal Institute of International Affairs 1944–)*, 28 (1952), pp.445–451
Simpson, J.G., 'Not by Bombs Alone: Lessons from Malaya', *JFQ*, Summer (1999), pp.91–98
Smith, S.C., (2001) 'General Templer and Counter-insurgency in Malaya: Hearts and Minds, Intelligence, and Propaganda', *Intelligence & National Security*, 16 (2001), pp.60–78
Soderlund, W.C., 'An Analysis of the Guerrilla Insurgency and Coup D'Etat as Techniques of Indirect Aggression', *International Studies Quarterly*, 14 (1970), pp.335–360
Statler, K., 'Triumph Imagined', *Diplomatic History*, January (2008), pp.153–157
Strachan, H., 'British Counter-insurgency from Malaya to Iraq', *The RUSI Journal*, 152 (2007), pp.8–11
Strachan, H., 'The British Way in Warfare Revisited', *The Historical Journal*, 26 (1983), pp.447–461
Strachan, H., 'The Lost Meaning of Strategy', *Survival: Global Politics and Strategy*, 47 (2005), pp.33–54
Strachan, H., 'Training, Morale and Modern War', *Journal of Contemporary History*, 41 (2006), pp.211–227
Strickland, Maj A., 'Reinventing the Counterinsurgency Wheel', *Small Wars Journal*, July (2005), pp.13–17
Stringer, K.D., 'Global counterinsurgency and US Army expansion: the case for recruiting foreign troops', *Small Wars & Insurgencies*, 22 (2011), pp.142–169
Sullivan, P.L., 'War Aims and War Outcomes: Why Powerful States Lose Limited Wars', *The Journal of Conflict Resolution*, 51 (2007), pp.496–524
Suri, J., 'The Cold War, Decolonization, and Global Social Awakenings: Historical Intersections', *Cold War History*, 6 (2006), pp.353–363
Szalontai, B., 'Political and Economic Crisis in North Vietnam, 1955–56', *Cold War History*, 5 (2005), pp.395–426
Thomas, M., 'Silent Partners: SOE's French Indo–China Section, 1943–1945', *Modern Asian Studies*, 34 (2000), pp.943–976
Tilman, R.O., 'The Non–Lessons of the Malayan Emergency', *Asian Survey*, 6 (1966), pp.407–419
Tomes, R., 'Relearning Counterinsurgency Warfare', *Parameters*, Spring (2004), pp.16–28
Tovy, T., 'Peasants and Revolutionary Movements: The Viet Cong as a Case Study', *War in History*, 17 (2010), pp.217–230
Tovy, T., 'The Theoretical Aspect of Targeted Killings: The Phoenix Program as a Case Study', *Journal of Military and Strategic Studies*, 11 (2009), pp.1–24
Ucko, D., 'Countering Insurgents through Distributed Operations: Insights from Malaya 1948–1960', *Journal of Strategic Studies*, 30 (2007), pp.47–72
Varsori, A., 'Britain and US Involvement in the Vietnam War during the Kennedy Administration, 1961–63', *Cold War History*, 3 (2003), pp.83–112
Weaver, E., 'Strategic Hamlets', *Fortnight*, 293 (1991), p.19
White, N.J., 'Capitalism and Counter-insurgency? Business and Government in the Malayan Emergency1948–57', *Modern Asian Studies*, 32 (1998), pp.149–177
Whittingham, D., 'Savage Warfare': C.E. Callwell, the Roots of Counter-insurgency, and the Nineteenth Century Context', *Small Wars & Insurgencies*, 23 (2012), pp.591–607
Wilson, Major, I., 'Strategy Revisited', *Military Review,* January–February (2003), pp.42–49
Witty, D.M., 'A Regular Army in Counterinsurgency Operations: Egypt in North Yemen, 1962– 1967', *The Journal of Military History*, 65 (2001), pp.401–439
Young, J. W., 'Britain and 'LBJ's War', 1964–68', *Cold War History*, 2 (2002), pp.63–92
Young, M.B., 'Two, Three, Many Vietnams', *Cold War History*, 6 (2006), pp.413–424
Zambernardi, L., 'Counterinsurgency's Impossible Trilemma', *The Washington Quarterly*, 33 (2010), pp.21–34
Zasloff, J., 'Rural Resettlement in South Viet Nam: The Agroville Program', *Pacific Affairs*, 35 (1962–1963), pp.327–340

UNPUBLISHED PAPERS, PRESENTATIONS AND THESES

Papers

Conover, G.B., 'The Impact of Operational Void: The Strategic Hamlet Program, 1961–1963', (Paper, School of Advanced Military Studies United States Army Command and General Staff College, Fort Leavenworth, Kansas, 1989)
Cordesman, A.H., 'The Long War: The United States as a Self-Inflicted Wound', (Paper, The Center for Strategic and International Studies, Washington, 2007)
Findley, M.G., & Young, J.K., 'Swatting Flies with Pile Drivers? Modeling Insurgency and Counterinsurgency', (Paper, University of Illinois, 2006)
Mumford, A., 'Rethinking the Malayan Emergency: Counter-insurgency Lessons for Iraq', (Conference Papers, University of Sheffield, 2006)
Young, J.K., 'Iron Fist or Velvet Glove?: Evaluating Competing Approaches to Counterinsurgency', (Meeting Paper, International Studies Association, Chicago, 2007)

Presentations

Cordesman, A.H., 'Rethinking the Challenge of Counterinsurgency Warfare', (Presentation, The Centre for Strategic and International Studies, Washington, 2005)
Farmer, J., 'Counter-insurgency: Principles and Practice in Vietnam', (Lecture, RAND Corporation, Santa Monica, 1964)
O'Donnell, J.B., 'The Strategic Hamlet Program in Kien Hoa Province, South Vietnam: A Case Study in Counter-insurgency', (Conference Presentation, Princeton University Center of International Studies, Princeton, New Jersey, May 11, 1965)
Phillips, R., 'Rufus Phillips on Why Vietnam Matters: An Eyewitness Account of Lessons Not Learned', (Lecture, Arlington Learning in Retirement Institute, Arlington, VA, May 23, 2012)
Senlis, Countering the Insurgency in Afghanistan: Losing Friends and Making Enemies (Conference, London, 2007)
Wells, S.F. & Braestrup, P., 'Some Lessons and Non–Lessons of Vietnam: Ten Years After the Paris Peace Accords', (Conference Report, Woodrow Wilson International Center for Scholars, 1983)

Theses

Chong, O.W., 'War as they knew it: Revolutionary War and Counterinsurgency', (Thesis,
S. Rajaratnam School of International Studies, Nanyang Technological University, Singapore, 2007)

Cushman, J.H., 'External Support of the Viet Cong: An Analysis and Proposal', (Thesis, National War College, Washington D.C., 1965)

Farmer, J., 'Counter-insurgency: Vietnam 1962–1963', (Thesis, RAND Corporation, Santa Monica, 1963)

Higgins, J.M., 'The Misapplication of the Malayan Counterinsurgency Model to the Strategic Hamlet Program', (M.A. Thesis, Faculty of the U.S. Army Command and General Staff College, Fort Leavenworth, Kansas, 2001)

Kilcullen, D.J., 'The Political Consequences of Military Operations in Indonesia 1945 – 99: A fieldwork Analysis of the Power Diffusion effects of Guerrilla Conflict', (PhD, University of New South Wales, 2000)

Leahy, P.F., 'Why Did the Strategic Hamlets Program Fail?', (Thesis, Fort Leavenworth, Kansas, 1990)

Lovering, R. S., 'Sir Robert Thompson's Better War: The British Advisory Mission and the South Vietnamese Strategic Hamlet Program, 1961–1963', (Thesis, The University of Southern Mississippi, 2017)

Pelli, F.D., 'Insurgency, Counterinsurgency and the Marines in Vietnam' (Thesis, USMC, 1990)

Sepp, K.I., 'Resettlement, Regroupment, Reconcentration: Deliberate Government Directed Population Relocation in Support of Counter-insurgency Operations', (M.A. Thesis, U.S. Army Command and General Staff College, Fort Leavenworth, Kansas, 1975)

Miscellaneous Documentation

Kilcullen, D.J., *'Countering Global Insurgency'*, (Australian Government Department of Defence, 2004)

Kilcullen, D.J., *'Three Pillars of Counterinsurgency'*, (Washington D.C.: U.S. Government Counterinsurgency Conference, 2006)

WORLDWIDE WEB SOURCES

Video Primary Sources

Moyar, M., *Triumph Forsaken: The Vietnam War, 1954–1965* (US Army Heritage and Education Centre – Perspectives: December 12, 2007). Available: https://www.youtube.com/watch?v=Am7a–R2EsUs (accessed March 20, 2008)

Online Articles

Anthony Cordesman & Arleigh Burke, 'The Long War: The United States as a Self–inflicted Wound', *The Centre for Strategic and International Studies*, (2007), [Online]. Available: <www.csis.org/burke>(accessed March 20, 2008). Please note that as of 12/12/2018 this article has been removed from the website.

Daivd Kilcullen, 'A6 – Counterinsurgency in Iraq: Theory and Practice 2007', *Small Wars Journal*, (2007), [Online]. Available: <www.smallwarsjournal.com/documents/kilcullencoinbrief 26sept07.ppt>(accessed March 20, 2008), Please note that as of 12/12/2018 this article has been removed from the website.

Mark Moyar, 'Vietnam: Historians at War', *US Army Research – Paper 33*, (2008), [Online]. Available: <http://digitalcommons.unl.edu/cgi/ viewcontent.cgi?article= 1042&context= usarmyresearch> (accessed March 20, 2008)

NOTES

Introduction

1 Lyndon B Johnson Presidential Library and Museum (hereafter referred to as LBJ), Transcript, Elbridge Durbrow Oral History Interview, Interview I, June 03, 1981, p. 60.

Chapter 1

1 LBJ, Transcript, Elbridge Durbrow Oral History Interview, Interview I (by Ted Gittinger), June 03, 1981, Internet Copy, p. 59.

2 *Foreign Relations of the United States* (hereafter referred to as *FRUS*) *1961–63, Volume II: No 228. Memorandum of Conversation between the Counselor for Political Affairs in Vietnam (Mendenhall) and the Chinese Ambassador in Vietnam (Yuen Tse Kien) Saigon, June 26, 1962.*

3 See for example, Thompson, *Defeating Communist Insurgency.*

4 See for example, Thompson, *Defeating Communist Insurgency.* Burleigh argues in *Small Wars, Far Away Places*, that the Japanese may have influenced this concept too. See *Small Wars, Far Away Places,* p. 16 for further details.

5 See, for example, Thompson's version of the Delta Plan which can be read in the John F Kennedy Library and Museum (hereafter referred to as JFK), RHPP-003-009, Roger Hilsman Personal Papers, Countries Files, 1961–1964, Series 1, Box 3, Folder 5.

6 Interestingly – and as an aside – it is necessary to point out that winning 'hearts and minds' was rarely made an explicit goal within documentation from the time. Despite Thompson's overt involvement in planning the counterinsurgency concepts underpinning much of the Strategic Hamlet Programme, the exact wording of the phrase 'hearts and minds' does not appear with any regularity in government documentation. For example, although Hilsman credited Thompson with influencing 'A Strategic Concept for South Vietnam', the phrase is only mentioned once and it appears as 'minds and hearts' in the text. Instead, it seems to have been replaced with phrases such as 'popular support' and 'support of the people.' In correspondence between various government bodies, the phrase popular support appears 82 times, and support of the people appears 22 times. However, despite 'hearts and minds' rarely being explicitly discussed in the sources, the theory being implemented remained essentially the same: the counterinsurgency strategy was (in addition to military force) based around measures that would be aimed at obtaining the loyalty of the local population. As a result, 'winning the people' would enable more effective killing of insurgents to take place.

7 Texas Tech University (hereafter referred to as TTU), 2321518004, Strategic Hamlets, 01 July 1963, Folder 18, Box 15, Douglas Pike Collection: Unit 06 – Democratic Republic of Vietnam, p. 1; TTU, 2321518004, Strategic Hamlets, 01 July 1963, Folder 18, Box 15, Douglas Pike Collection: Unit 06 – Democratic Republic of Vietnam, p. 1.

8 TTU, 2321518004, Strategic Hamlets, 01 July 1963, Folder 18, Box 15, Douglas Pike Collection: Unit 06 – Democratic Republic of Vietnam, p. 3.

9 *FRUS 1961–63, Volume II: No 305. Telegram From the Embassy in Vietnam to the Department of State Saigon, December 3, 1961, 9 p.m.*

10 *FRUS 1961–63, Volume III: No 41. Letter From the Commander, Military Assistance Command, Vietnam (Harkins) to President Diem Saigon, February 23, 1963.*

11 *FRUS 1961–63, Volume III: No 41. Letter From the Commander, Military Assistance Command, Vietnam (Harkins) to President Diem Saigon, February 23, 1963.*

12 JFK, JFKNSF–203–003, Letter From the President's Military Representative (Taylor) to the President Appendix B Memorandum From the Chairman of the Vietnam Task Force (Cottrell) to the President's Military Representative (Taylor) Washington, October 27, 1961. Vietnam: Subjects: Taylor Report, 3 November 1961, p. 2; JFK, JFKNSF–203–003, Letter From the President's Military Representative (Taylor) to the President Appendix B Memorandum From the Chairman of the Vietnam Task Force (Cottrell) to the President's Military Representative (Taylor) Washington, October 27, 1961. Vietnam: Subjects: Taylor Report, 3 November 1961, p. 2.

13 *FRUS 1961–63, Volume I: No 59. Paper Prepared by the Vice President, undated, 1961; FRUS 1961–63, Volume I: No 59. Paper Prepared by the Vice President, undated, 1961.*

14 CIA Telegram, *Strategic Hamlets*, 20 February 1962, p. 2.

15 CIA Telegram, *Strategic Hamlets*, 20 February 1962, p. 2.

16 CIA Telegram, *Strategic Hamlets*, 20 February 1962, p. 2.

17 CIA Telegram, *Strategic Hamlets*, 20 February 1962, p. 3.

18 *FRUS 1961–63, Volume III: No 26. Report by an Investigative Team Headed by the Chief of Staff, United States Army (Wheeler), to the Joint Chiefs of Staff, Washington, January 1963.*

19 JFK, RHPP-003-010, Memorandum for the Record by the Director of the Bureau of Intelligence and Research (Hilsman) Saigon, January 2, 1963. Conversation with Major General Edward L. Rowny. Vietnam: Hilsman trip, December 1962–January 1963: Basic report and "Eyes Only" annex. Roger Hilsman Personal Papers, Countries Files, 1961–1964, Series 1, Box 3, p. 6.

20 SNIE, *14.3 / 53–61 Prospects for North and South Vietnam*, 15 August 1961, p. 9.

21 SNIE, *14.3 / 53–61 Prospects for North and South Vietnam*, 15 August 1961, p. 9.

22 *FRUS 1961–63, Volume III: No 77. Memorandum of Conversation, White House Washington, April 4, 1963, 10 a.m.; FRUS 1961–63, Volume III: No 77. Memorandum of Conversation, White House Washington, April 4, 1963, 10 a.m*

23 JFK, RHPP-003-009, Memorandum From the Director of the Bureau of Intelligence and Research (Hilsman) and Michael V. Forrestal of the National Security Council Staff to the President, Washington, January 25, 1963, p. 3.

24 Pearce, *RM–4692–1–ARPA – Evolution of a Vietnamese Village – Part II: The Past, August 1945 to April 1965*, p. 44.

25 Pearce, *RM–4692–1–ARPA*, p. 44.

26 Pearce, *RM–4692–1–ARPA*, p. 44.

27 *FRUS 1961–63, Volume II: No 328. Report by the Deputy Director of the Vietnam Working Group (Heavner), Washington, December 11, 1962.*

28 *FRUS 1961–63, Volume II: No 328. Senator Mansfield's Visit to Vietnam and Subsequent Report; Visits and Reports by Johnson and Heavner December 1962. Report by the Deputy Director of the Vietnam Working Group (Heavner) Washington, December 11, 1962.*

29 CIA Telegram, *Strategic Hamlets*, 20 February 1962, p. 3.

30 CIA Telegram, *Strategic Hamlets*, 20 February 1962, p. 3.

31 CIA Telegram, *Strategic Hamlets*, 20 February 1962, p. 3.

32 *FRUS 1961–63, Volume II: No 328. Report by the Deputy Director of the Vietnam Working Group (Heavner), Washington, December 11, 1962.*

33 *FRUS 1961–63, Volume II: No 328. Report by the Deputy Director of the Vietnam Working Group (Heavner), Washington, December 11, 1962.*

34 TTU, 23970130054, Booklet – Vietnam's Strategic Hamlets, February 1963, p. 4.

35 TTU, 23970130054, Booklet – Vietnam's Strategic Hamlets, February 1963, p. 4.

36 TTU, 23970130054, Booklet – Vietnam's Strategic Hamlets, February 1963, p. 4.
37 CIA Documents, *Minutes of the Meeting of the Special Group (Counterinsurgency)* (Washington D.C.: Director of Central Intelligence, 21 August 1962), p. 4.
38 Pearce, RM-4692-1-ARPA – *Evolution of a Vietnamese Village – Part II: The Past, August 1945 to April 1965*, p. 45.
39 JFK, JFKPOF-069a-005, Speech by W.W. Rostow at Fort Bragg June 28, 1961, Papers of John F. Kennedy. Presidential Papers. President's Office Files. Departments and Agencies. Army, 1961, Box 069a, p. 12.
40 JFK, JFKNSF-203-003, Letter From the President's Military Representative (Taylor) to the President, [Attachment 2] Paper Prepared by the President's Military Representative, Vietnam: Subjects: Taylor Report, 3 November 1961: Rostow Working Copy. Papers of John F. Kennedy, Presidential Papers, National Security Files, Countries, Vietnam, Box 203, Tab C, p. 5.
41 JFK, JFKNSF-203-003, Letter From the President's Military Representative (Taylor) to the President, [Attachment 2] Paper Prepared by the President's Military Representative, Vietnam: Subjects: Taylor Report, 3 November 1961: Rostow Working Copy. Papers of John F. Kennedy, Presidential Papers, National Security Files, Countries, Vietnam, Box 203, Tab C, p. 5.
42 *FRUS 1961–63, Volume III: No 77. Memorandum of Conversation, White House Washington, April 4, 1963, 10 a.m.*
43 Pearce, *RM-4692-1-ARPA – Evolution of a Vietnamese Village – Part II: The Past, August 1945 to April 1965*, p. 25.
44 Pearce, *RM-4692-1-ARPA*, p. 25.
45 Pearce, *RM-4692-1-ARPA*, p. 25.
46 Pearce, *RM-4692-1-ARPA*, p. 25.
47 Pearce, *RM-4692-1-ARPA*, p. 25.
48 Pearce, *RM-4692-1-ARPA*, p.vii; Pearce, *RM-4692-1-ARPA*, p.viii.
49 Pearce, *RM-4692-1-ARPA*, p. 25.
50 TTU, 23970130054, Booklet – Vietnam's Strategic Hamlets, February 1963, p. 4.
51 TTU, 2310402003, Monograph prepared for United States Mission, Viet-Nam – The Viet-Cong Strategy of Terror, 01 February 1970, Folder 02, Box 04, Douglas Pike Collection: Unit 05 – National Liberation Front, p. 6.
52 TTU, 2310402003, Monograph prepared for United States Mission, Viet-Nam – The Viet-Cong Strategy of Terror, 01 February 1970, Folder 02, Box 04, Douglas Pike Collection: Unit 05 – National Liberation Front, p. 6.
53 TTU, 2310402003, Monograph prepared for United States Mission, Viet-Nam – The Viet-Cong Strategy of Terror, 01 February 1970, Folder 02, Box 04, Douglas Pike Collection: Unit 05 – National Liberation Front, p. 6.
54 TTU, 2310402003, Monograph prepared for United States Mission, Viet-Nam – The Viet-Cong Strategy of Terror, 01 February 1970, Folder 02, Box 04, Douglas Pike Collection: Unit 05 – National Liberation Front, p. 6.
55 JFK, JFKPOF-069a-005, Speech by W.W. Rostow at Fort Bragg June 28, 1961, p. 12.
56 TTU, 2390711005, A Threat to the Peace, p. 12.
57 TTU, 2293801019, A Study Viet Cong Use of Terror, March 1967, p. 19.
58 Miami University Library, Ohio, OCLC Number: 1658815, Interview 77 – Member of the Village Information Section, Microfilm – RAND Vietnam Interview Series V: Viet Cong Organizational Activities at Hamlet/Village Level (Santa Monica: RAND Corporation, 1968), p. 1.
59 Miami University Library, Ohio, OCLC Number: 1658815, Interview 77 – Member of the Village Information Section, Microfilm – RAND Vietnam Interview Series V: Viet Cong Organizational Activities at Hamlet/Village Level (Santa Monica: RAND Corporation, 1968), p. 1.
60 TTU, 0720804004, Studies of the National Liberation Front of South Vietnam, 03 April 1965, Folder 04, Box 08, John Donnell Collection, p. 10.
61 JFK, RHPP-003-009, Memorandum From the Director of the Bureau of Intelligence and Research (Hilsman) and Michael V. Forrestal of the National Security Council Staff to the President, Washington, January 25, 1963, p. 3.
62 JFK, RHPP-003-009, Memorandum From the Director of the Bureau of Intelligence and Research (Hilsman) and Michael V. Forrestal of the National Security Council Staff to the President, Washington, January 25, 1963, p. 3.
63 JFK, JFKPOF-128-009, English text of GVN Letter to ICC re North Vietnam Subversion and aggression Saigon October 24 1961, p. 12
64 JFK, JFKPOF-128-009, English text of GVN Letter to ICC re North Vietnam Subversion and aggression Saigon October 24 1961, p. 12.
65 TTU, 2390711005, A Threat to the Peace, p. 13.
66 TTU, 2390711005, A Threat to the Peace, p. 13.
67 TTU, 2390711005, A Threat to the Peace, p. 13.
68 JFK, JFKPOF-128-009, English text of GVN Letter to ICC re North Vietnam Subversion and aggression Saigon October 24 1961, Papers of John F. Kennedy, Presidential Papers, Country Files, Vietnam: General, 1960–1961, Box 128, p. 12.
69 JFK, JFKPOF-128-009, English text of GVN Letter to ICC re North Vietnam Subversion and aggression Saigon October 24 1961, Papers of John F. Kennedy, Presidential Papers, Country Files, Vietnam: General, 1960–1961, Box 128, p. 12; JFK, JFKPOF-128-009, English text of GVN Letter to ICC re North Vietnam Subversion and aggression Saigon October 24 1961, Papers of John F. Kennedy, Presidential Papers, Country Files, Vietnam: General, 1960–1961, Box 128, p. 12.
70 TTU, 2293801019, A Study. Viet Cong Use of Terror, March 1967.
71 TTU, 2293801019, A Study. Viet Cong Use of Terror, March 1967, p. 19; TTU, 2293801019, A Study. Viet Cong Use of Terror, March 1967, p. 19; TTU, 2293801019, A Study. Viet Cong Use of Terror, March 1967, p. 20.
72 TTU, 2293801019, A Study. Viet Cong Use of Terror, March 1967, p. 20.
73 TTU, 2293801019, A Study. Viet Cong Use of Terror, March 1967, p. 20.
74 TTU, 2293801019, A Study. Viet Cong Use of Terror, March 1967, p. 93.
75 TTU, 2293801019, A Study. Viet Cong Use of Terror, March 1967, p. 93.
76 TTU, 2293801019, A Study. Viet Cong Use of Terror, March 1967, p. 94.
77 TTU, 2293801019, A Study. Viet Cong Use of Terror, March 1967, p. 94.
78 TTU, 2293801019, A Study. Viet Cong Use of Terror, March 1967, p. 94.
79 TTU, 2293801019, A Study. Viet Cong Use of Terror, March 1967, pp. 95–98.
80 See the first volume of this series for Thompson's evaluation of Viet Cong strategy.
81 TTU, 2390711005, A Threat to the Peace, p. 12
82 TTU, 2390711005, A Threat to the Peace, p. 12.
83 Pearce, *RM-4692-1-ARPA – Evolution of a Vietnamese Village – Part II: The Past, August 1945 to April 1965*, p. 43.
84 Pearce, *RM-4692-1-ARPA*, p. 43.
85 Donnell, *14436-IBA/ARPA – Viet Cong Recruitment: Why and How Men Join*, p.x.
86 TTU, 2390711005, A Threat to the Peace, p. 9.
87 SNIE, *14.3 / 53-61 Prospects for North and South Vietnam*, p. 11; SNIE, *14.3 / 53-61 Prospects for North and South Vietnam*, p. 11.
88 TTU, 0720406007, Studies of the National Liberation Front of South Vietnam, 16 April 1965, p. 4.
89 Davison & Zasloff, *RM-4983-1-ISA/ARPA – A Profile of Viet Cong Cadres*, p. 39.
90 TTU, 2121506008c, Monograph prepared for United States Mission, Viet-Nam – The Viet-Cong Strategy of Terror, 01 February 1970, Folder 06, Box 15, Douglas Pike Collection: Unit 01 – Assessment and Strategy, p. 117. Acts of terror also included sabotage, property destruction, confiscation of food and other goods and the 'sale' of Viet Cong war bonds.
91 TTU, 2121506008c Monograph prepared for United States Mission, Viet-Nam – The Viet-Cong Strategy of Terror, p. 118.
92 TTU, 2293801019, A Study Viet Cong Use of Terror, March 1967, p. 84.
93 TTU, 2311109005, VCD 27 – Death notice found pinned on shirt of assassinated district chief. Declares he had been tried and found guilty of "crimes against the people," 1962, Folder 09, Box 11, Douglas Pike Collection: Unit 05 – National Liberation Front.
94 Pearce, *RM-4692-1-ARPA – Evolution of a Vietnamese Village – Part II: The Past, August 1945 to April 1965*, p. 43; TTU, 1490117001, Publication – My Thuan: A Mekong Delta Village in South Vietnam, 1963, p. 9.
95 TTU, 1490117001, Publication – My Thuan: A Mekong Delta Village in South Vietnam, 1963, p. 10.
96 TTU, 2390711005, A Threat to the Peace, p. 12.
97 TTU, 2390711005, A Threat to the Peace, p. 13.
98 TTU, 2391207004, WCOTP Commission of Inquiry Report: Impact on Education of Terrorist Activities in Viet-Nam, 18–26 May 1962, Folder 07, Box 12, Douglas Pike Collection: Unit 11 – Monographs, p. 19.
99 TTU, 2391207004, WCOTP Commission of Inquiry Report: Impact on Education of Terrorist Activities in Viet-Nam, 18–26 May 1962, Folder 07, Box 12, Douglas Pike Collection: Unit 11 – Monographs, p. 19.
100 TTU, 2391207004, WCOTP Commission of Inquiry Report: Impact on Education of Terrorist Activities in Viet-Nam, 18–26 May 1962, Folder 07, Box 12, Douglas Pike Collection: Unit 11 – Monographs, p. 6.
101 TTU, 2391207004, WCOTP Commission of Inquiry Report: Impact on Education of Terrorist Activities in Viet-Nam, 18–26 May 1962, Folder 07, Box 12, Douglas Pike Collection: Unit 11 – Monographs, p. 5.
102 TTU, 2391207004, WCOTP Commission of Inquiry Report: Impact on Education of Terrorist Activities in Viet-Nam, 18–26 May 1962, Folder 07, Box 12, Douglas Pike Collection: Unit 11 – Monographs, p. 5.
103 TTU, 2391207004, WCOTP Commission of Inquiry Report: Impact on Education of Terrorist Activities in Viet-Nam, 18–26 May 1962, Folder 07, Box 12, Douglas Pike Collection: Unit 11 – Monographs, p. 7.
104 TTU, 2391207004, WCOTP Commission of Inquiry Report: Impact on Education of Terrorist Activities in Viet-Nam, 18–26 May 1962, Folder 07, Box 12, Douglas Pike Collection: Unit 11 – Monographs, p. 6.
105 TTU, 2293801019, A Study Viet Cong Use of Terror, March 1967, p. 22
106 TTU, 2391207004, WCOTP Commission of Inquiry Report: Impact on Education of Terrorist Activities in Viet-Nam, 18–26 May 1962, p. 2.
107 TTU, 2391207004, WCOTP Commission of Inquiry Report: Impact on Education of Terrorist Activities in Viet-Nam, 18–26 May 1962, Folder 07, Box 12, Douglas Pike Collection: Unit 11 – Monographs, p. 6.
108 JFK, JFKNSF-203-003, Letter From the President's Military Representative (Taylor) to the President [Appendix G] Memorandum From the Secretary of Defence's Assistant for Special Operations (Lansdale) to the President's Military Representative (Taylor) Washington, November 3, 1961, Vietnam: Subjects: Taylor Report, 3 November 1961: Rostow Working Copy. Papers of John F. Kennedy, Presidential Papers, National Security Files, Countries, Vietnam, Box 203, Appendix G, p. 6; JFK, JFKNSF-203-003, Letter From the President's Military Representative (Taylor) to the President [Appendix G] Memorandum From the Secretary of Defence's Assistant for Special Operations (Lansdale) to the President's Military Representative (Taylor) Washington, November 3, 1961, Vietnam: Subjects: Taylor Report, 3 November 1961: Rostow Working Copy. Papers of John F. Kennedy, Presidential Papers, National Security Files, Countries, Vietnam, Box 203, Appendix G, p. 6.
109 *FRUS 1961–63, Volume I: No 182. Memorandum From the Secretary of Defence's Deputy Assistant for Special Operations (Lansdale) to the President's Military Representative (Taylor), Saigon, October 21, 1961.*
110 JFK, RHPP-003-011, Memorandum From the Assistant Secretary of State for Far Eastern Affairs (Hilsman) to the Secretary of State Washington, April 1963. Vietnam: Hilsman trip, December 1962–January 1963: Basic report and "Eyes Only" Annex: related Documents, Roger Hilsman Personal Papers, Countries Files, 1961–1964, Series 1, Box 3, p. 2.
111 JFK, RHPP-003-011, Memorandum From the Assistant Secretary of State for Far Eastern Affairs (Hilsman) to the Secretary of State Washington, April 1963. Vietnam: Hilsman trip, December 1962–January 1963: Basic report and "Eyes Only" Annex: related Documents, Roger Hilsman Personal Papers, Countries Files, 1961–1964, Series 1, Box 3, p. 2.
112 JFK, RHPP-003-006, A Strategic Concept for South Vietnam, p. 4; JFK, RHPP-003-006, A Strategic Concept for South Vietnam, p. 4.
113 JFK, RHPP-003-006, A Strategic Concept for South Vietnam, p. 4.

114 JFK, RHPP-003-006, A Strategic Concept for South Vietnam, p. 18.
115 TTU, 23130005003, Communist assessment of South Vietnam scene: 1/62–6/63, 01 January 1963, p. 14.
116 *FRUS 1961–63, Volume II: No 319. Memorandum From the Chairman of the Joint Chiefs of Staff (Taylor) to the Secretary of Defence (McNamara) CM–117–62 Washington, November 17, 1962.*
117 Donnell, *14436–IBA/ARPA – Viet Cong Recruitment: Why and How Men Join*, p. 93.
118 Pearce, *RM–4692–1–ARPA – Evolution of a Vietnamese Village – Part II: The Past, August 1945 to April 1965*, p. 43.
119 TTU, 2120301025, Department of State Research Memorandum: Statistics on the War Effort in South Vietnam Show Unfavorable Trends, 22 October 1963, p. 2.
120 TTU, 2321518004, Strategic Hamlets, 01 July 1963, p. 5.
121 TTU, 2321518004, Strategic Hamlets, 01 July 1963, p. 5.
122 TTU, 23970128002, Report, A Report on Counter-insurgency in Vietnam, 20 July 1962, p. 14.
123 TTU, 2120301025, Department of State Research Memorandum: Statistics on the War Effort in South Vietnam Show Unfavorable Trends, 22 October 1963, p. 2.
124 Pearce, *RM–4692–1–ARPA – Evolution of a Vietnamese Village – Part II: The Past, August 1945 to April 1965*, p. 33.
125 Pearce, *RM–4692–1–ARPA*, p. 43; Pearce, *RM–4692–1–ARPA*, p. 43.
126 Pearce, *RM–4692–1–ARPA*, p. 43.
127 Pearce, *RM–4692–1–ARPA*, p. 4.
128 Pearce, *RM–4692–1–ARPA*, p. 4.
129 Pearce, *RM–4692–1–ARPA*, p.xi.
130 TTU, 23970133013, Report – A Critical Analysis of the Strategic Hamlet Programme, p. 14.
131 TTU, 23970128002, Report, A Report on Counter-insurgency in Vietnam, 20 July 1962, p. 9.
132 Cochran, *16157–ISA/ARPA – Motivation and Morale: Some Questions – Some Answers*, p. 36; Cochran, *16157–ISA/ARPA – Motivation and Morale: Some Questions – Some Answers*, p. 36.
133 Cochran, *16157–ISA/ARPA – Motivation and Morale: Some Questions – Some Answers*, p. 36; Cochran, *16157–ISA/ARPA – Motivation and Morale: Some Questions – Some Answers*, p. 36.
134 Cochran, *16157–ISA/ARPA – Motivation and Morale: Some Questions – Some Answers*, p. 36; Cochran, *16157–ISA/ARPA – Motivation and Morale: Some Questions – Some Answers*, p. 36.
135 Cochran, *16157–ISA/ARPA – Motivation and Morale: Some Questions – Some Answers*, p. 36.
136 *FRUS 1961–63, Volume II: No 319. Memorandum From the Chairman of the Joint Chiefs of Staff (Taylor) to the Secretary of Defence (McNamara) CM–117–62 Washington, November 17, 1962.*
137 TTU, 0720406006, Studies of the National Liberation Front of South Vietnam, 16 April 1965, p. 3.
138 JFK, JFKPOF–098–006, Bin Hung: A Counter–Guerilla Case Study, Papers of John F. Kennedy. Presidential Papers. President's Office Files. Subjects: Counterinsurgency, Box 098, p. 7; JFK, JFKPOF–098–006, Bin Hung: A Counter–Guerilla Case Study, Papers of John F. Kennedy. Presidential Papers. President's Office Files. Subjects: Counterinsurgency, Box 098, p. 7.
139 JFK, JFKPOF–098–006, Bin Hung: A Counter–Guerilla Case Study, Papers of John F. Kennedy. Presidential Papers. President's Office Files. Subjects: Counterinsurgency, Box 098, p. 7.
140 JFK, JFKPOF–098–006, Bin Hung: A Counter–Guerilla Case Study, Papers of John F. Kennedy. Presidential Papers. President's Office Files. Subjects: Counterinsurgency, Box 098, p. 5.
141 JFK, JFKPOF–098–006, Bin Hung: A Counter–Guerilla Case Study, Papers of John F. Kennedy. Presidential Papers. President's Office Files. Subjects: Counterinsurgency, Box 098, p. 5.
142 JFK, JFKPOF–098–006, Bin Hung: A Counter–Guerilla Case Study, Papers of John F. Kennedy. Presidential Papers. President's Office Files. Subjects: Counterinsurgency, Box 098, p. 5.
143 JFK, JFKPOF–098–006, Bin Hung: A Counter–Guerilla Case Study, Papers of John F. Kennedy. Presidential Papers. President's Office Files. Subjects: Counterinsurgency, Box 098, p. 5.
144 JFK, JFKPOF–098–006, Bin Hung: A Counter–Guerilla Case Study, Papers of John F. Kennedy. Presidential Papers. President's Office Files. Subjects: Counterinsurgency, Box 098, p. 5.
145 JFK, JFKPOF–098–006, Bin Hung: A Counter–Guerilla Case Study, Papers of John F. Kennedy. Presidential Papers. President's Office Files. Subjects: Counterinsurgency, Box 098, p. 6.
146 JFK, JFKPOF–098–006, Bin Hung: A Counter–Guerilla Case Study, Papers of John F. Kennedy. Presidential Papers. President's Office Files. Subjects: Counterinsurgency, Box 098, p. 6.
147 TTU, 23970134023, Study – When the Communists Come, July 1962, Folder 34, Box 01, Rufus Phillips Collection, p. 48.
148 TTU, 2120207007, Report on Struggle Efforts to Destroy Strategic Hamlet in Bien Hoa Province, January 1962, p. 4.
149 TTU, 2120207007, Report on Struggle Efforts to Destroy Strategic Hamlet in Bien Hoa Province, January 1962, p. 4.
150 Tanham, *Communist Revolutionary Warfare: From the Vietminh to the Viet Cong*, p. 65.
151 JFK, JFKNSF–203–003, Letter From the President's Military Representative (Taylor) to the President, [Attachment 2] Paper Prepared by the Members of the Taylor Mission Washington, Vietnam: Subjects: Taylor Report, 3 November 1961, Tab C. p. 7.
152 Tanham, *Communist Revolutionary Warfare: From the Vietminh to the Viet Cong*, p. 89.
153 JFK, JFKPOF–098–006, Bin Hung: A Counter–Guerilla Case Study, p. 11.
154 JFK, JFKPOF–098–006, Bin Hung: A Counter–Guerilla Case Study, p. 11.
155 JFK, JFKNSF–203–003, Letter From the President's Military Representative (Taylor) to the President, [Attachment 2] Paper Prepared by the Members of the Taylor Mission Washington, Vietnam: Subjects: Taylor Report, 3 November 1961, Tab C, p. 2.
156 JFK, JFKNSF–203–003, Letter From the President's Military Representative (Taylor) to the President, [Attachment 2] Paper Prepared by the Members of the Taylor Mission Washington, Vietnam: Subjects: Taylor Report, 3 November 1961, Tab C, p. 7.

Chapter 2

1 Pearce, *RM–4692–1–ARPA – Evolution of a Vietnamese Village – Part II: The Past, August 1945 to April 1965*, p. 44.
2 TTU, 2321518004, Strategic Hamlets, 01 July 1963, p. 6.
3 Donnell & Hickey, *RM–3208–ARPA – The Vietnamese 'Strategic Hamlets': A Preliminary Report.*
4 TTU, 23970201051, Extract – Interministerial Committee for Strategic Hamlets Criteria for Completed Hamlets, 19 July 1962.
5 TTU, 23970201051, Extract – Interministerial Committee for Strategic Hamlets Criteria for Completed Hamlets, 19 July 1962.
6 TTU, 23970201051, Extract – Interministerial Committee for Strategic Hamlets Criteria for Completed Hamlets, 19 July 1962.
7 Donnell & Hickey, *RM–3208–ARPA – The Vietnamese 'Strategic Hamlets': A Preliminary Report*, p. 21.
8 Donnell & Hickey, *RM–3208–ARPA – The Vietnamese 'Strategic Hamlets': A Preliminary Report*, p. 21; Donnell & Hickey, *RM–3208–ARPA – The Vietnamese 'Strategic Hamlets': A Preliminary Report*, p. 21.
9 Donnell & Hickey, *RM–3208–ARPA – The Vietnamese 'Strategic Hamlets': A Preliminary Report*, p. 21; Donnell & Hickey, *RM–3208–ARPA – The Vietnamese 'Strategic Hamlets': A Preliminary Report*, p. 21.
10 Donnell & Hickey, *RM–3208–ARPA – The Vietnamese 'Strategic Hamlets': A Preliminary Report*, p. 7.
11 Nighswonger, *Rural Pacification in Vietnam*, p. 96.
12 TTU, 2321518004, Strategic Hamlets, 01 July 1963, p. 2.
13 TTU, 23970130032, Draft – Some Thoughts on Provincial Problems in Strategic Hamlet Consolidation, No Date, Folder 30, Box 01, Rufus Phillips Collection, p. 1.
14 TTU, 23970130032, Draft – Some Thoughts on Provincial Problems in Strategic Hamlet Consolidation, No Date, Folder 30, Box 01, Rufus Phillips Collection, p. 1; *FRUS 1961–63, Volume II: No 187. Paper Prepared in the Department of Defence Washington, undated.*
15 *FRUS 1961–63, Volume II: No 248. Record of the Sixth Secretary of Defence Conference Camp Smith, Hawaii, July 23, 1962;* Donnell & Hickey, *RM–3208–ARPA – The Vietnamese 'Strategic Hamlets': A Preliminary Report*, p. 21
16 Pearce, *RM–4692–1–ARPA – Evolution of a Vietnamese Village – Part II: The Past, August 1945 to April 1965*, p. 44.
17 Pearce, *RM–4692–1–ARPA*, p. 44.
18 Pearce, *RM–4692–1–ARPA*, p. 44; Pearce, *RM–4692–1–ARPA*, p. 43.
19 TTU, 23970129001, Summary, Second Informal Appreciation of The Status of The Strategic Hamlet Programme, 01 September 1963, p. 2; TTU, 23970129001, Summary, Second Informal Appreciation of The Status of The Strategic Hamlet Programme, 01 September 1963, p. 2.
20 Pearce, *RM–4692–1–ARPA – Evolution of a Vietnamese Village – Part II: The Past, August 1945 to April 1965*, p. 43.
21 TTU, 23970129001, Summary, Second Informal Appreciation of The Status of The Strategic Hamlet Programme, 01 September 1963, p. 47.
22 TTU, 23970129001, Summary, Second Informal Appreciation of The Status of The Strategic Hamlet Programme, 01 September 1963, p. 1.
23 TTU, OH0121, Interview with William Shelton, 15 July 2000, William Shelton Collection, p. 39.
24 TTU, OH0121, Interview with William Shelton, 15 July 2000, William Shelton Collection, p. 39.
25 JFK, RHPP-003-009, Memorandum From the Director of the Bureau of Intelligence and Research (Hilsman) and Michael V. Forrestal of the National Security Council Staff to the President, Washington, January 25, 1963, Annex, p. 2.
26 TTU, 23970128002, Report, A Report on Counter-insurgency in Vietnam, 20 July 1962, p. 9.
27 JFK, RHPP-003-009, Memorandum From the Director of the Bureau of Intelligence and Research (Hilsman) and Michael V. Forrestal of the National Security Council Staff to the President, Washington, January 25, 1963, Annex, p. 2.
28 *FRUS 1961–63, Volume II: No 149. Memorandum From the Director of the Vietnam Task Force (Cottrell) to the Assistant Secretary of State for Far Eastern Affairs (Harriman), Washington, April 6, 1962.*
29 *FRUS 1961–63, Volume II: No 149. Memorandum From the Director of the Vietnam Task Force (Cottrell) to the Assistant Secretary of State for Far Eastern Affairs (Harriman), Washington, April 6, 1962.*
30 TTU, 23970133013, Report – A Critical Analysis of the Strategic Hamlet Programme, p. 14.
31 TTU, 23970133013, Report – A Critical Analysis of the Strategic Hamlet Programme, p. 14.
32 LBJ, Transcript, Colonel Jonathan F. Ladd, Oral History, Interview I (by Ted Gittinger), July 24, 1984, Internet Copy, p. 15.
33 TTU, 23970134024, Booklet – Notes on Strategic Hamlets, 15 August 1963, p. 7; TTU, 23970134024, Booklet – Notes on Strategic Hamlets, 15 August 1963, p. 7.
34 TTU, 23970134024, Booklet – Notes on Strategic Hamlets, 15 August 1963, p. 7.
35 TTU, 23970134024, Booklet – Notes on Strategic Hamlets, 15 August 1963, p. 7.

36 TTU, 23970134024, Booklet – Notes on Strategic Hamlets, 15 August 1963, p. 7; TTU, 23970134024, Booklet – Notes on Strategic Hamlets, 15 August 1963, p. 7.
37 TTU, 23970134024, Booklet – Notes on Strategic Hamlets, 15 August 1963, p. 7; TTU, 23970134024, Booklet – Notes on Strategic Hamlets, 15 August 1963, p. 7.
38 LBJ, Transcript, Colonel Jonathan F. Ladd, Interview I (by Ted Gittinger), 24 July 1984, p. 13.
39 LBJ, Transcript, Colonel Jonathan F. Ladd, Interview I (by Ted Gittinger), 24 July 1984, p. 13.
40 LBJ, Transcript, Colonel Jonathan F. Ladd, Interview I (by Ted Gittinger), 24 July 1984, p. 14.
41 LBJ, Transcript, Colonel Jonathan F. Ladd, Interview I (by Ted Gittinger), 24 July 1984, p. 14.
42 LBJ, Transcript, Colonel Jonathan F. Ladd, Interview I (by Ted Gittinger), 24 July 1984, p. 14.
43 *FRUS 1961–63, Volume II: No 328. Report by the Deputy Director of the Vietnam Working Group (Heavner), Washington, December 11, 1962.*
44 Donnell & Hickey, *RM–3208–ARPA – The Vietnamese 'Strategic Hamlets': A Preliminary Report*, p. 6.
45 Donnell & Hickey, *RM–3208–ARPA – The Vietnamese 'Strategic Hamlets': A Preliminary Report*, p. 6.
46 *FRUS 1961–63, Volume II: No 328. Report by the Deputy Director of the Vietnam Working Group (Heavner), Washington, December 11, 1962.*
47 TTU, 23970129002, Summary, An Informal Appreciation of The Status of The Strategic Hamlet Programme, p. 1.
48 TTU, 23970129002, Summary, An Informal Appreciation of The Status of The Strategic Hamlet Programme, p. 1.
49 TTU, 23970129002, Summary, An Informal Appreciation of The Status of The Strategic Hamlet Programme, p. 1.
50 Pearce, *RM–4692–1–ARPA – Evolution of a Vietnamese Village – Part II: The Past, August 1945 to April 1965*, p. 44.
51 Pearce, *RM–4692–1–ARPA*, p. 42.
52 CIA Documents, *Minutes of the Meeting of the Special Group (Counterinsurgency)* (Washington D.C.: Director of Central Intelligence 23 May 1963), p. 2.
53 *FRUS 1961–63, Volume II: No 187. Paper Prepared in the Department of Defence Washington, undated.*
54 JFK, Oral History Programme, Transcript, Michael V. Forrestal, Interview (by Joseph Kraft), 14 August 1964, p. 121.
55 JFK, Oral History Programme, Transcript, Michael V. Forrestal, Interview (by Joseph Kraft), 14 August 1964, p. 121.
56 TTU, 2120208020, Policy Instructions from "Chin Nam" to the South, 27 September 1962, p. 6.
57 Miami University Library, Ohio, OCLC Number: 1658815, Interview 4 – Civilian Prisoner, Microfilm – RAND Vietnam Interview Series V: Viet Cong Organizational Activities at Hamlet/Village Level (Santa Monica: RAND Corporation, 1968), p. 9; Miami University Library, Ohio, OCLC Number: 1658815, Interview 4 – Civilian Prisoner, Microfilm – RAND Vietnam Interview Series V: Viet Cong Organizational Activities at Hamlet/Village Level (Santa Monica: RAND Corporation, 1968), p. 26.
58 Pearce, *RM–4692–1–ARPA – Evolution of a Vietnamese Village – Part II: The Past, August 1945 to April 1965*, p. 40.
59 TTU, 2193401002, Book: Letters from South Vietnam – Foreign Languages Publishing House, Hanoi (1963), 1963, Folder 01, Box 34, Douglas Pike Collection: Unit 03 – Literature of the War, p. 18; TTU, 2193401002, Book: Letters from South Vietnam – Foreign Languages Publishing House, Hanoi (1963), 1963, Folder 01, Box 34, Douglas Pike Collection: Unit 03 – Literature of the War, p. 18.
60 See Chapter Two for examples of this propaganda.
61 Pearce, *RM–4692–1–ARPA – Evolution of a Vietnamese Village – Part II: The Past, August 1945 to April 1965*, p. 41.
62 Pearce, *RM–4692–1–ARPA*, p. 41.
63 *FRUS 1961–63, Volume III: No 207. Report by the Joint Chiefs of Staff's Special Assistant for Counterinsurgency and Special Activities (Krulak), Washington, undated.*
64 TTU, 0720406007, Studies of the National Liberation Front of South Vietnam, 15–16 April 1965, p. 2.
65 TTU, *10-62 Communist Objectives, Capabilities, and Intentions in Southeast Asia*, 21 February 1962; TTU, 23970128002, Report, A Report on Counter-insurgency in Vietnam, 20 July 1962, p. 11.
66 Donnell & Hickey, *RM–3208–ARPA – The Vietnamese 'Strategic Hamlets': A Preliminary Report*, p.viii.
67 Donnell & Hickey, *RM–3208–ARPA*, p. 13.
68 Donnell & Hickey, *RM–3208–ARPA*, pp. 6–7.
69 TTU, 0720406007, Studies of the National Liberation Front of South Vietnam, 16 April 1965, p. 3.
70 *FRUS 1961–63, Volume III: No 207. Report by the Joint Chiefs of Staff's Special Assistant for Counterinsurgency and Special Activities (Krulak), Washington, undated.*
71 Donnell & Hickey, *RM–3208–ARPA – The Vietnamese 'Strategic Hamlets': A Preliminary Report*, p. 11.
72 Donnell & Hickey, *RM–3208–ARPA*, p. 11.
73 *FRUS 1961–63, Volume II: No 116. Letter From the Officer in Charge of Vietnam Affairs (Heavner) to the Deputy Director of the Vietnam Task Force (Wood) Saigon, March 19, 1962* (Washington D.C.: US Department of State, 1988), p. 10.
74 TTU, 0720406007, Studies of the National Liberation Front of South Vietnam, 15–16 April 1965, p. 2.
75 Donnell & Hickey, *RM–3208–ARPA – The Vietnamese 'Strategic Hamlets': A Preliminary Report*, p. 11.
76 Donnell & Hickey, *RM–3208–ARPA*, pp. 11–12.
77 TTU, 23970128002, Report, A Report on Counter-insurgency in Vietnam, 20 July 1962, p. 11.
78 Donnell & Hickey, *RM–3208–ARPA – The Vietnamese 'Strategic Hamlets': A Preliminary Report*, pp. 13–14.
79 Donnell & Hickey, *RM–3208–ARPA*, p. 14.
80 Donnell & Hickey, *RM–3208–ARPA*, p. 14.
81 Donnell & Hickey, *RM–3208–ARPA*, pp.vii–viii.
82 *FRUS 1961–63, Volume II: No 116. Letter From the Officer in Charge of Vietnam Affairs (Heavner) to the Deputy Director of the Vietnam Task Force (Wood) Saigon, March 19, 1962.*
83 TTU, 0720406007, Studies of the National Liberation Front of South Vietnam, 15–16 April 1965, p. 2.
84 Miami University Library, Ohio, OCLC Number: 1658815, Interview 31 – Refugee Farmer, Microfilm – RAND Vietnam Interview Series V: Viet Cong Organizational Activities at Hamlet/Village Level (Santa Monica: RAND Corporation, 1968), p. 5.
85 Donnell & Hickey, *RM–3208–ARPA – The Vietnamese 'Strategic Hamlets': A Preliminary Report*, p. 12.
86 Donnell & Hickey, *RM–3208–ARPA*, p. 22.
87 Miami University Library, Ohio, OCLC Number: 1658815, Interview 4 – Civilian Prisoner, Microfilm – RAND Vietnam Interview Series V: Viet Cong Organizational Activities at Hamlet/Village Level (Santa Monica: RAND Corporation, 1968), p. 25.
88 *FRUS 1961–63, Volume II: No 173. Memorandum From the Officer in Charge of Vietnam Affairs (Heavner) to the Ambassador in Vietnam (Nolting), Saigon, April 27, 1962.*
89 CIA Telegram, *Strategic Hamlet Situation in Central Vietnam* (Washington D.C.: Director of Central Intelligence 05 October 1962), p. 1.
90 CIA Telegram, *Strategic Hamlet Situation in Central Vietnam* (Washington D.C.: Director of Central Intelligence 05 October 1962), p. 1.
91 TTU, 0720406007, Studies of the National Liberation Front of South Vietnam, 15–16 April 1965, p. 2.
92 Donnell & Hickey, *RM–3208–ARPA – The Vietnamese 'Strategic Hamlets': A Preliminary Report*, pp. 12–13.
93 Donnell & Hickey, *RM–3208–ARPA*, p. 13.
94 *FRUS 1961–63, Volume II: No 116. Letter From the Officer in Charge of Vietnam Affairs (Heavner) to the Deputy Director of the Vietnam Task Force (Wood) Saigon, March 19, 1962.*
95 *FRUS 1961–63, Volume II: No 116. Letter From the Officer in Charge of Vietnam Affairs (Heavner) to the Deputy Director of the Vietnam Task Force (Wood) Saigon, March 19, 1962.*
96 LBJ, Transcript, Douglas Pike, Oral History Interview I (by Ted Gittinger), 4 June 1981, Internet Copy, p. 10.
97 LBJ, Transcript, Douglas Pike, Oral History Interview I (by Ted Gittinger), 4 June 1981, Internet Copy, p. 10.
98 *FRUS 1961–63, Volume II: No 328. Report by the Deputy Director of the Vietnam Working Group (Heavner), Washington, December 11, 1962.*
99 TTU, 23970128002, Report, A Report on Counter-insurgency in Vietnam, 20 July 1962, p. 8.
100 TTU, 23970128002, Report, A Report on Counter-insurgency in Vietnam, 20 July 1962, p. 8.
101 CIA Telegram, *Strategic Hamlet Situation in Central Vietnam* (Washington D.C.: Director of Central Intelligence 05 October 1962), p. 2.
102 CIA Telegram, *Strategic Hamlet Situation in Central Vietnam* (Washington D.C.: Director of Central Intelligence 05 October 1962), p. 2.
103 CIA Telegram, *Hamlet Programmes* (Washington D.C.: Director of Central Intelligence 03 July 1962), p. 3.
104 CIA Telegram, *Hamlet Programmes* (Washington D.C.: Director of Central Intelligence 03 July 1962), p. 3.
105 *FRUS 1961–63, Volume III: No 77. Memorandum of Conversation, White House Washington, April 4, 1963, 10 a.m.*
106 JFK, RHPP–003–006, A Strategic Concept for South Vietnam, p. 13.
107 JFK, RHPP–003–006, A Strategic Concept for South Vietnam, p. 13.
108 JFK, RHPP–003–006, A Strategic Concept for South Vietnam, p. 12; JFK, RHPP–003–006, A Strategic Concept for South Vietnam, p. 12.
109 *FRUS 1961–63, Volume II: No 149. Memorandum From the Director of the Vietnam Task Force (Cottrell) to the Assistant Secretary of State for Far Eastern Affairs (Harriman), Washington, April 6, 1962.*
110 *FRUS 1961–63, Volume II: No 149. Memorandum From the Director of the Vietnam Task Force (Cottrell) to the Assistant Secretary of State for Far Eastern Affairs (Harriman), Washington, April 6, 1962.*
111 JFK, RHPP–003–010, Memorandum for the Record by the Director of the Bureau of Intelligence and Research (Hilsman) Saigon, January 2, 1963. Vietnam: Hilsman trip, December 1962–January 1963: Basic report and "Eyes Only" annex. Roger Hilsman Personal Papers, Countries Files, 1961–1964, Series 1, Box 3, p. 14.
112 *FRUS 1961–63, Volume III: No 66. Airgram From the Department of State to the Embassy in Vietnam CA–10362 Washington, March 22, 1963, 5:13 p.m.*
113 *FRUS 1961–63, Volume III: No 66. Airgram From the Department of State to the Embassy in Vietnam CA–10362 Washington, March 22, 1963, 5:13 p.m.*
114 *FRUS 1961–63, Volume III: No 48. Memorandum From the Director of the Vietnam Working Group (Wood) to the Assistant Secretary of State for Far Eastern Affairs (Harriman) Washington, February 28, 1963.*
115 *FRUS 1961–63, Volume III: No 48. Memorandum From the Director of the Vietnam Working Group (Wood) to the Assistant Secretary of State for Far Eastern Affairs (Harriman) Washington, February 28, 1963.*
116 JFK, RHPP–003–010, Memorandum for the Record by the Director of the Bureau of Intelligence and Research (Hilsman) Saigon, January 2, 1963. Vietnam: Hilsman trip, December 1962–January 1963: Basic report and "Eyes Only" annex. Roger Hilsman Personal Papers, Countries Files, 1961–1964, Series 1, Box 3, p. 2; JFK, RHPP–003–010, Memorandum for the Record by the Director of the Bureau of Intelligence and Research (Hilsman) Saigon, January

2, 1963. Vietnam: Hilsman trip, December 1962–January 1963: Basic report and "Eyes Only" annex, p. 2.
117 *FRUS 1961–63, Volume III: No 100. Airgram From the Embassy in Vietnam to the Department of State A–661 Saigon, April 25, 1963.*
118 *FRUS 1961–63, Volume III: No 100. Airgram From the Embassy in Vietnam to the Department of State A–661 Saigon, April 25, 1963.*
119 *FRUS 1961–63, Volume III: No 100. Airgram From the Embassy in Vietnam to the Department of State A–661 Saigon, April 25, 1963.*
120 *FRUS 1961–63, Volume III: No 100. Airgram From the Embassy in Vietnam to the Department of State A–661 Saigon, April 25, 1963.*
121 *FRUS 1961–63, Volume III: No 100. Airgram From the Embassy in Vietnam to the Department of State A–661 Saigon, April 25, 1963.*
122 L. Goure, & C.A.H. Thomson, *RM–4699–1–ISA/ARPA – Some Impressions of Viet Cong Vulnerabilities: An Interim Report* (Santa Monica: RAND Corporation, 1965), p. 17.
123 *FRUS 1961–63, Volume II: No 329. Senator Mansfield's Visit to Vietnam and Subsequent Report; Visits and Reports by Johnson and Heavner December 1962. Telegram From the Embassy in Vietnam to the Department of State Saigon, December 15, 1962, 6 p.m.*
124 *FRUS 1961–63, Volume II: No 127. Airgram From the Embassy in Vietnam to the Department of State A–257 Saigon, March 23, 1962.*
125 *FRUS 1961–63, Volume II: No 127. Airgram From the Embassy in Vietnam to the Department of State A–257 Saigon, March 23, 1962.*
126 *FRUS 1961–63, Volume II: No 268. Memorandum From the Former Political Counselor of Embassy in Vietnam (Mendenhall) to the Deputy Assistant Secretary of State for Far Eastern Affairs (Rice) Washington, August 16, 1962.*
127 JFK, JFKNSF–203–003, Letter From the President's Military Representative (Taylor) to the President, [Attachment 2] Paper Prepared by the Members of the Taylor Mission Washington, Vietnam: Subjects: Taylor Report, 3 November 1961, Tab C, p. 6.
128 JFK, JFKNSF–203–003, Letter From the President's Military Representative (Taylor) to the President, [Attachment 2] Paper Prepared by the Members of the Taylor Mission Washington, Vietnam: Subjects: Taylor Report, 3 November 1961, Tab C, p. 6.
129 TTU, 23970133013, Report – A Critical Analysis of the Strategic Hamlet Programme, p. 15.
130 *FRUS 1961–63, Volume II: No 328. Report by the Deputy Director of the Vietnam Working Group (Heavner), Washington, December 11, 1962.*
131 *FRUS 1961–63, Volume II: No 173. Memorandum From the Officer in Charge of Vietnam Affairs (Heavner) to the Ambassador in Vietnam (Nolting), Saigon, April 27, 1962.*
132 *FRUS 1961–63, Volume II: No 173. Memorandum From the Officer in Charge of Vietnam Affairs (Heavner) to the Ambassador in Vietnam (Nolting), Saigon, April 27, 1962.*
133 CIA Telegram, *Hamlet Programmes* (Washington D.C.: Director of Central Intelligence 03 July 1962), p. 2.
134 JFK, JFKNSF–203–003, Letter From the President's Military Representative (Taylor) to the President, [Attachment 2] Paper Prepared by the Members of the Taylor Mission Washington, Vietnam: Subjects: Taylor Report, 3 November 1961, Tab C, p. 6.
135 TTU, 23970328001, Interview Transcript of Rufus Phillips by Charles Stuart Kennedy [Part I], No Date, Folder 28, Box 03, Rufus Phillips Collection, p. 42.
136 TTU, 23970328001, Interview Transcript of Rufus Phillips by Charles Stuart Kennedy [Part I], No Date, Folder 28, Box 03, Rufus Phillips Collection, p. 42.
137 TTU, 23970328001, Interview Transcript of Rufus Phillips by Charles Stuart Kennedy [Part I], No Date, Folder 28, Box 03, Rufus Phillips Collection, p. 42.
138 TTU, 23970328001, Interview Transcript of Rufus Phillips by Charles Stuart Kennedy [Part I], No Date, Folder 28, Box 03, Rufus Phillips Collection, p. 42.
139 TTU, 23970129001, Summary, Second Informal Appreciation of The Status of The Strategic Hamlet Programme, 01 September 1963, p. 1.
140 TTU, 23970129001, Summary, Second Informal Appreciation of The Status of The Strategic Hamlet Programme, 01 September 1963, p. 1.
141 Phillips, 'Rufus Phillips on Why Vietnam Matters: An Eyewitness Account of Lessons Not Learned'; TTU, 0440413001, Letter from Ted Gittinger to William E. Colby, with Attached Transcript of Lyndon Baines Johnson Library's Oral History with Colby on 2 June 1981, 27 May 1983, Folder 13, Box 04, William Colby Collection.
142 Phillips, 'Rufus Phillips on Why Vietnam Matters: An Eyewitness Account of Lessons Not Learned', Time: 32:50
143 Miami University Library, Ohio, OCLC Number: 1658815, Interview 9 – Village Party Committee Member, Microfilm – RAND Vietnam Interview Series V: Viet Cong Organizational Activities at Hamlet/Village Level (Santa Monica: RAND Corporation, 1968), p. 3.
144 Miami University Library, Ohio, OCLC Number: 1658815, Interview 9 – Village Party Committee Member, Microfilm – RAND Vietnam Interview Series V: Viet Cong Organizational Activities at Hamlet/Village Level (Santa Monica: RAND Corporation, 1968), p. 3.
145 Donnell, *14436–IBA/ARPA – Viet Cong Recruitment: Why and How Men Join*, p. 89.
146 Donnell, *14436–IBA/ARPA – Viet Cong Recruitment: Why and How Men Join*, p. 61.
147 Donnell, *14436–IBA/ARPA – Viet Cong Recruitment: Why and How Men Join*, p. 61.
148 Donnell, *14436–IBA/ARPA – Viet Cong Recruitment: Why and How Men Join*, p. 61.
149 Donnell, *14436–IBA/ARPA – Viet Cong Recruitment: Why and How Men Join*, p. 61.
150 Donnell, *14436–IBA/ARPA – Viet Cong Recruitment: Why and How Men Join*, p. 63.
151 Donnell, *14436–IBA/ARPA – Viet Cong Recruitment: Why and How Men Join*, p. 63.
152 TTU, 25590123001, Reference Manual, Support & Translation Office – POW Interrogation Booklet of Commonly Used Questions and Answers, No Date, Folder 23, Box 01, p. 4, Harry Wagner Collection.
153 TTU, 0720406008, Studies of the National Liberation Front of South Vietnam, 12–14 April 1965, p. 7.
154 Cochran, *16157–ISA/ARPA – Motivation and Morale: Some Questions – Some Answers*, p. 34.
155 J.W. Trullinger, *Village at War: An Account of the Conflict in Vietnam* (Stanford: Stanford University Press, 1994), p. 90.
156 Donnell, *14436–IBA/ARPA – Viet Cong Recruitment: Why and How Men Join*, p.viii.
157 TTU, 0720406007, Studies of the National Liberation Front of South Vietnam, 15–16 April 1965, p. 4.
158 TTU, 0720406007, Studies of the National Liberation Front of South Vietnam, 15–16 April 1965, p. 4.
159 TTU, 2120208019, Experiences in the Antistrategic Hamlet Programme, October–November 1962, p. 2.
160 SNIE, *14.3 / 53–61 Prospects for North and South Vietnam*, 15 August 1961, p. 16.
161 SNIE, *14.3 / 53–61 Prospects for North and South Vietnam*, 15 August 1961, p. 16; SNIE, *14.3 / 53–61 Prospects for North and South Vietnam*, 15 August 1961, p. 16.
162 JFK, JFKNSF–330–002, NSAM 52, re: Report of the Vietnam Task Force, p. 4; J. Farmer, 'Counter-insurgency: Principles and Practice in Vietnam: 1962–1963', (Lecture, RAND Corporation, Santa Monica, 1964), p. 1.
163 JFK, RHPP–003–009, Memorandum From the Director of the Bureau of Intelligence and Research (Hilsman) and Michael V. Forrestal of the National Security Council Staff to the President, Washington, January 25, 1963, p. 10.
164 JFK, RHPP–003–009, Memorandum From the Director of the Bureau of Intelligence and Research (Hilsman) and Michael V. Forrestal of the National Security Council Staff to the President, Washington, January 25, 1963, p. 10.
165 JFK, RHPP–003–009, Memorandum From the Director of the Bureau of Intelligence and Research (Hilsman) and Michael V. Forrestal of the National Security Council Staff to the President, Washington, January 25, 1963, p. 10.
166 *FRUS 1961–63, Volume II: No 328. Report by the Deputy Director of the Vietnam Working Group (Heavner), Washington, December 11, 1962.*
167 *FRUS 1961–63, Volume II: No 328. Report by the Deputy Director of the Vietnam Working Group (Heavner), Washington, December 11, 1962.*
168 *FRUS 1961–63, Volume III: No 64. Memorandum From the Under Secretary of State for Political Affairs' Special Assistant (Jorden) to the Assistant Secretary of State for Far Eastern Affairs (Harriman), Washington, March 20, 1963.*
169 *FRUS 1961–63, Volume III: No 64. Memorandum From the Under Secretary of State for Political Affairs' Special Assistant (Jorden) to the Assistant Secretary of State for Far Eastern Affairs (Harriman), Washington, March 20, 1963.*
170 *FRUS 1961–63, Volume III: No 64. Memorandum From the Under Secretary of State for Political Affairs' Special Assistant (Jorden) to the Assistant Secretary of State for Far Eastern Affairs (Harriman), Washington, March 20, 1963.*
171 JFK, JFKNSF–203–003, Letter From the President's Military Representative (Taylor) to the President, [Attachment 2] Paper Prepared by the Members of the Taylor Mission Washington, Vietnam: Subjects: Taylor Report, 3 November 1961, Tab C, p. 6.
172 Farmer, 'Counter-insurgency: Principles and Practice in Vietnam: 1962–1963', pp. 21–22.
173 Farmer, 'Counter-insurgency: Principles and Practice in Vietnam: 1962–1963', pp. 21–22.
174 Farmer, 'Counter-insurgency: Principles and Practice in Vietnam: 1962–1963', p. 22.
175 Farmer, 'Counter-insurgency: Principles and Practice in Vietnam: 1962–1963', p. 22.
176 Farmer, 'Counter-insurgency: Principles and Practice in Vietnam: 1962–1963', p. 1.
177 *FRUS 1961–63, Volume II: No 328. Mansfield Visit to Vietnam and Subsequent Report, Report by the Deputy Director of the Vietnam Working Group (Heavner) Washington, December 11, 1962;* CIA Documents, *Minutes of the Meeting of the Special Group (Counterinsurgency)*, p. 1.
178 CIA Documents, *Minutes of the Meeting of the Special Group (Counterinsurgency)*, p. 1.
179 CIA Documents, *Minutes of the Meeting of the Special Group (Counterinsurgency)*, p. 1.
180 JFK, RHPP–003–010, Memorandum for the Record by the Director of the Bureau of Intelligence and Research (Hilsman) Saigon, January 2, 1963. Conversation with Major General Edward L. Rowny. Vietnam: Hilsman trip, December 1962–January 1963: Basic report and "Eyes Only" annex. Roger Hilsman Personal Papers, Countries Files, 1961–1964, Series 1, Box 3, p. 3.
181 JFK, RHPP–003–010, Memorandum for the Record by the Director of the Bureau of Intelligence and Research (Hilsman) Saigon, January 2, 1963. Conversation with Major General Edward L. Rowny. Vietnam: Hilsman trip, December 1962–January 1963: Basic report and "Eyes Only" annex. Roger Hilsman Personal Papers, Countries Files, 1961–1964, Series 1, Box 3, p. 3.
182 JFK, RHPP–003–010, Memorandum for the Record by the Director of the Bureau of Intelligence and Research (Hilsman) Saigon, January 2, 1963. Conversation with Major General Edward L. Rowny. Vietnam: Hilsman trip, December 1962–January 1963: Basic report and "Eyes Only" annex. Roger Hilsman Personal Papers, Countries Files, 1961–1964, Series 1, Box 3, p. 4.
183 JFK, RHPP–003–010, Memorandum for the Record by the Director of the Bureau of Intelligence and Research (Hilsman) Saigon, January 2, 1963. Conversation with Major General Edward L. Rowny. Vietnam: Hilsman trip, December 1962–January 1963: Basic report and "Eyes Only" annex. Roger Hilsman Personal Papers, Countries Files, 1961–1964, Series 1, Box 3, p. 4.
184 JFK, RHPP–003–010, Memorandum for the Record by the Director of the Bureau of Intelligence and Research (Hilsman) Saigon, January 2, 1963. Conversation with Major General Edward L. Rowny. Vietnam: Hilsman trip,

December 1962–January 1963: Basic report and "Eyes Only" annex. Roger Hilsman Personal Papers, Countries Files, 1961–1964, Series 1, Box 3, p. 4.

185 JFK, RHPP–003–010, Memorandum for the Record by the Director of the Bureau of Intelligence and Research (Hilsman) Saigon, January 2, 1963. Conversation with Major General Edward L. Rowny. Vietnam: Hilsman trip, December 1962–January 1963: Basic report and "Eyes Only" annex. Roger Hilsman Personal Papers, Countries Files, 1961–1964, Series 1, Box 3, p. 3.

Chapter 3

1 *FRUS 1961–63, Volume II: No 330. Report by the Senate Majority Leader (Mansfield), Washington, December 18, 1962.*

2 *FRUS 1961–63, Volume II: No 330. Report by the Senate Majority Leader (Mansfield), Washington, December 18, 1962.*

3 *FRUS 1961–63, Volume II: No 330. Report by the Senate Majority Leader (Mansfield), Washington, December 18, 1962.*

4 JFK, JFKNSF–203–003, Letter From the President's Military Representative (Taylor) to the President, [Attachment 2] Paper Prepared by the Members of the Taylor Mission Washington, Vietnam: Subjects: Taylor Report, 3 November 1961, Tab C, p. 6.

5 JFK, JFKNSF–203–003, Letter From the President's Military Representative (Taylor) to the President, [Attachment 2] Paper Prepared by the Members of the Taylor Mission Washington, Vietnam: Subjects: Taylor Report, 3 November 1961, Tab C, p. 6.

6 JFK, JFKNSF–203–003, Letter From the President's Military Representative (Taylor) to the President, [Attachment 2] Paper Prepared by the Members of the Taylor Mission Washington, Vietnam: Subjects: Taylor Report, 3 November 1961, Tab C, p. 6.

7 JFK, JFKNSF–203–003, Letter From the President's Military Representative (Taylor) to the President, [Attachment 2] Paper Prepared by the Members of the Taylor Mission Washington, Vietnam: Subjects: Taylor Report, 3 November 1961, Tab C, p. 6.

8 JFK, JFKNSF–203–003, Letter From the President's Military Representative (Taylor) to the President, [Attachment 2] Paper Prepared by the Members of the Taylor Mission Washington, Vietnam: Subjects: Taylor Report, 3 November 1961, Tab C, p. 6.

9 JFK, JFKNSF–203–003, Letter From the President's Military Representative (Taylor) to the President, [Attachment 2] Paper Prepared by the Members of the Taylor Mission Washington, Vietnam: Subjects: Taylor Report, 3 November 1961, Tab C, p. 7.

10 *FRUS 1961–63, Volume IV: No 83. Memorandum of Conversation Washington, September 10, 1963, 10:30 a.m.;* This statement has been corroborated by various sources and by Krulak himself and can be found in his interview at the Kennedy Library in Boston. Reference: JFK, Oral History Programme, Transcript, Victor H. Krulak, Interview (by William W. Moss), November 19, 1970, p. 19.

11 D. J. Kilcullen, *'Three Pillars of Counterinsurgency',* (Washington D.C.: US Government Counterinsurgency Conference, 2006), p. 2.

12 D. J. Kilcullen, *'Three Pillars of Counterinsurgency',* (Washington D.C.: US Government Counterinsurgency Conference, 2006), p. 2.

13 R. Trinquier, *Modern Warfare: A French View of Counterinsurgency* (Westport: Praeger Security International, 2006), p. 5.

14 *The FRUS 1961–63, Volume III: No 26. Report by an Investigative Team Headed by the Chief of Staff, United States Army (Wheeler), to the Joint Chiefs of Staff Washington, January 1963.*

15 D. J. Kilcullen, *'Three Pillars of Counterinsurgency',* p. 5.

16 *FRUS 1961–63, Volume IV: No 83. Memorandum of Conversation Washington, September 10, 1963, 10:30 a.m.;* TTU, 23970328001, Interview Transcript of Rufus Phillips by Charles Stuart Kennedy [Part I].

17 *FRUS 1961–63, Volume I: No 1. Paper Prepared by the Country Team Staff Committee, Saigon, January 4, 1961*; JFK, RHPP–003–006, A Strategic Concept for South Vietnam, p. 9.

18 *FRUS 1961–63, Volume III: No 26. Report by an Investigative Team Headed by the Chief of Staff, United States Army (Wheeler), to the Joint Chiefs of Staff, Washington, January 1963.*

19 *FRUS 1961–63, Volume III: No 26. Report by an Investigative Team Headed by the Chief of Staff, United States Army (Wheeler), to the Joint Chiefs of Staff, Washington, January 1963.*

20 *FRUS 1961–63, Volume I: No 1. Paper Prepared by the Country Team Staff Committee, Saigon, January 4, 1961.*

21 JFK, RHPP–003–010, Memorandum for the Record by the Director of the Bureau of Intelligence and Research (Hilsman). Vietnam: Hilsman trip, December 1962–January 1963: Basic report and "Eyes Only" annex. Roger Hilsman Personal Papers, Countries Files, 1961–1964, Series 1, Box 3, p. 1; JFK, RHPP–003–010, Memorandum for the Record by the Director of the Bureau of Intelligence and Research (Hilsman). Vietnam: Hilsman trip, December 1962–January 1963: Basic report and "Eyes Only" annex. Roger Hilsman Personal Papers, Countries Files, 1961–1964, Series 1, Box 3, p. 1.

22 TTU, 23970329002, Interview Transcript of Rufus Phillips by Ted Gettinger [Part II], 27 May 1982, Folder 29, Box 03, Rufus Phillips Collection, p. 17.

23 Thompson, *Defeating Communist Insurgency,* p. 143.

24 Thompson, *Defeating Communist Insurgency,* p. 143.

25 Thompson, *Defeating Communist Insurgency,* p. 143.

26 Thompson, *Defeating Communist Insurgency,* p. 128.

27 TTU, 2120301025, Department of State Research Memorandum: Statistics on the War Effort in South Vietnam Show Unfavorable Trends, 22 October 1963.

28 TTU, 2120301025, Department of State Research Memorandum: Statistics on the War Effort in South Vietnam Show Unfavorable Trends, 22 October 1963, p. 579.

29 *FRUS 1961–63, Volume IV: No 306. Memorandum From the Director of the Bureau of Intelligence and Research (Hilsman) to the Secretary of State, Washington, November 8, 1963.*

30 Thompson, *Defeating Communist Insurgency,* p. 154.

31 Thompson, *Defeating Communist Insurgency,* p. 154.

32 TTU, 23970329002, Interview Transcript of Rufus Phillips [Part II], 27 May 1982, p. 18.

33 TTU, 23970329002, Interview Transcript of Rufus Phillips [Part II], 27 May 1982, p. 18.

34 See for example, *FRUS 1964–68, Volume I: No 50. Memorandum From the Deputy Director for Plans, Central Intelligence Agency (Helms), to the Secretary of State – Washington, February 18, 1964.*

35 TTU, 23970329002, Interview Transcript of Rufus Phillips [Part II], 27 May 1982, p. 18; TTU, 23970329002, Interview Transcript of Rufus Phillips [Part II], 27 May 1982, p. 18.

36 TTU, 23970130040, Draft – The Story of America's Counterinsurgency Efforts in Vietnam in the Early 1960's, January 1966, Folder 30, Box 01, Rufus Phillips Collection, p. 2.

37 TTU, 23970329002, Interview Transcript of Rufus Phillips [Part II], 27 May 1982, p. 18.

38 Darren Poole, *Hunting the Viet Cong – The Counterinsurgency Campaign In South Vietnam 1961–1963 Volume 1: The Strategic Hamlet Programme* (Warwick: Helion & Co, 2022), p. 7.

39 TTU, 23970328001, Interview Transcript of Rufus Phillips by Charles Stuart Kennedy [Part I], p. 42.

40 JFK, Oral History Programme, Transcript, Victor H. Krulak, Interview (by William W. Moss), November 19, 1970, p. 19.

41 JFK, Oral History Programme, Transcript, Victor H. Krulak, Interview (by William W. Moss), November 19, 1970, p. 19.

42 *FRUS 1961–63, Volume IV: No 83. Memorandum of Conversation Washington, September 10, 1963, 10:30 a.m.*

43 LBJ, Transcript, General John Michael Dunn Oral History Interview I (by Ted Gittinger), July 24, 1984, Internet Copy, p. 14.

44 TTU, 23970328001, Interview Transcript of Rufus Phillips by Charles Stuart Kennedy [Part I], p. 42.

45 Thompson, *Defeating Communist Insurgency,* p. 127.

46 JFK, JFKNSF–203–003, Letter From the President's Military Representative (Taylor) to the President, [Attachment 2] Paper Prepared by the Members of the Taylor Mission Washington, Vietnam: Subjects: Taylor Report, 3 November 1961, Tab C, p. 11.

47 LBJ, Transcript, Edward G. Lansdale Oral History Interview (by Ted Gittinger), September 15, 1981, Internet Copy, p. 33.

48 Phillips, 'Rufus Phillips on Why Vietnam Matters: An Eyewitness Account of Lessons Not Learned', Time 27:10.

49 TTU, 23970130055, Paper – Notes from the Underground: The Mystique of a Viet Cong, February 1962, Folder 30, Box 01, Rufus Phillips Collection, p.i.

50 *FRUS 1961–63, Volume II: No 330. Report by the Senate Majority Leader (Mansfield), Washington, December 18, 1962.*

51 *FRUS 1961–63, Volume II: No 328. Report by the Deputy Director of the Vietnam Working Group (Heavner), Washington, December 11, 1962.*

52 *FRUS 1961–63, Volume II: No 328. Report by the Deputy Director of the Vietnam Working Group (Heavner), Washington, December 11, 1962.*

53 *FRUS 1961–63, Volume II: No 328. Report by the Deputy Director of the Vietnam Working Group (Heavner), Washington, December 11, 1962.*

54 TTU, 23970329002, Interview Transcript of Rufus Phillips [Part II], 27 May 1982, p. 7.

55 *FRUS 1961–63, Volume II: No 237. Memorandum from the Secretary of Defence's Assistant for Special Operations (Lansdale) to the Secretary of Defence (McNamara) Washington, July 7, 1962.*

56 *FRUS 1961–63, Volume II: No 237. Memorandum from the Secretary of Defence's Assistant for Special Operations (Lansdale) to the Secretary of Defence (McNamara) Washington, July 7, 1962.*

57 *FRUS 1961–63, Volume II: No 237. Memorandum from the Secretary of Defence's Assistant for Special Operations (Lansdale) to the Secretary of Defence (McNamara) Washington, July 7, 1962.*

58 *FRUS 1961–63, Volume II: No 237. Memorandum from the Secretary of Defence's Assistant for Special Operations (Lansdale) to the Secretary of Defence (McNamara) Washington, July 7, 1962.*

59 *FRUS 1961–63, Volume II: No 237. Memorandum from the Secretary of Defence's Assistant for Special Operations (Lansdale) to the Secretary of Defence (McNamara) Washington, July 7, 1962.*

60 *FRUS 1961–63, Volume II: No 237. Memorandum from the Secretary of Defence's Assistant for Special Operations (Lansdale) to the Secretary of Defence (McNamara) Washington, July 7, 1962.*

61 JFK, RHPP–003–006, A Strategic Concept for South Vietnam, p. 7.

62 JFK, JFKNSF–333–016, National Security Action Memoranda [NSAM]: NSAM 124, Establishment of the Special Group (Counter-insurgency), Papers of John F. Kennedy, Presidential Papers, National Security Files, Meetings and Memoranda, Box 333.

63 JFK, JFKNSF–333–016, National Security Action Memoranda [NSAM]: NSAM 124, Establishment of the Special Group (Counter-insurgency), Papers of John F. Kennedy, Presidential Papers, National Security Files, Meetings and Memoranda, Box 333.

64 JFK, JFKNSF–333–016, National Security Action Memoranda [NSAM]: NSAM 124, Establishment of the Special Group (Counter-insurgency), Papers of John F. Kennedy, Presidential Papers, National Security Files, Meetings and Memoranda, Box 333.

65 JFK, JFKNSF–333–016, National Security Action Memoranda [NSAM]: NSAM 124, Establishment of the Special Group (Counter-insurgency), Papers of John F. Kennedy, Presidential Papers, National Security Files, Meetings and Memoranda, Box 333.

66 *Ibi* JFK, JFKNSF–333–016, National Security Action Memoranda [NSAM]: NSAM 124, Establishment of the Special Group (Counter-insurgency), Papers of John F. Kennedy, Presidential Papers, National Security Files, Meetings and Memoranda, Box 333.

67 *FRUS 1961–63, Volume II: No 132. Memorandum From the Joint Chiefs of Staff's Special Assistant for Counterinsurgency and Special Activities (Krulak) to the Deputy Secretary of Defence (Gilpatric), Washington, March 26, 1962.*
68 *FRUS 1961–63, Volume II: No 132. Memorandum From the Joint Chiefs of Staff's Special Assistant for Counterinsurgency and Special Activities (Krulak) to the Deputy Secretary of Defence (Gilpatric), Washington, March 26, 1962.*
69 *FRUS 1961–63, Volume II: No 132. Memorandum From the Joint Chiefs of Staff's Special Assistant for Counterinsurgency and Special Activities (Krulak) to the Deputy Secretary of Defence (Gilpatric), Washington, March 26, 1962.*
70 *FRUS 1961–63, Volume II: No 132. Memorandum From the Joint Chiefs of Staff's Special Assistant for Counterinsurgency and Special Activities (Krulak) to the Deputy Secretary of Defence (Gilpatric), Washington, March 26, 1962.*
71 *FRUS 1961–63, Volume II: No 132. Memorandum From the Joint Chiefs of Staff's Special Assistant for Counterinsurgency and Special Activities (Krulak) to the Deputy Secretary of Defence (Gilpatric), Washington, March 26, 1962.*
72 *FRUS 1961–63, Volume II: No 132. Memorandum From the Joint Chiefs of Staff's Special Assistant for Counterinsurgency and Special Activities (Krulak) to the Deputy Secretary of Defence (Gilpatric), Washington, March 26, 1962.*
73 JFK, RHPP-003-010, Memorandum for the Record by the Director of the Bureau of Intelligence and Research (Hilsman) Saigon, January 2, 1963. Conversation with Major General Edward L. Rowny. Vietnam: Hilsman trip, December 1962–January 1963, p. 6; JFK, RHPP-003-010, Memorandum for the Record by the Director of the Bureau of Intelligence and Research (Hilsman) Saigon, January 2, 1963. Conversation with Major General Edward L. Rowny. Vietnam: Hilsman trip, December 1962–January 1963, p. 6.
74 *FRUS 1961–63, Volume III: No 26. Report by an Investigative Team Headed by the Chief of Staff, United States Army (Wheeler), to the Joint Chiefs of Staff, Washington, January 1963.*
75 *FRUS 1961–63, Volume III: No 26. Report by an Investigative Team Headed by the Chief of Staff, United States Army (Wheeler), to the Joint Chiefs of Staff, Washington, January 1963.*
76 JFK, RHPP-003-010, Memorandum for the Record by the Director of the Bureau of Intelligence and Research (Hilsman) Saigon, January 2, 1963. Vietnam: Hilsman trip, December 1962–January 1963: Basic report and "Eyes Only" annex. Roger Hilsman Personal Papers, Countries Files, 1961–1964, Series 1, Box 3, p. 1; JFK, RHPP-003-010, Memorandum for the Record by the Director of the Bureau of Intelligence and Research (Hilsman) Saigon, January 2, 1963. Vietnam: Hilsman trip, December 1962–January 1963: Basic report and "Eyes Only" annex. Roger Hilsman Personal Papers, Countries Files, 1961–1964, Series 1, Box 3, p. 1.
77 Thompson, *Defeating Communist Insurgency,* p. 134.
78 JFK, Oral History Programme, Transcript, *Arleigh A. Burke*, Interview (*Joseph E. O'Connor*), January 20, 1967.
79 JFK, Oral History Programme, Transcript, *Arleigh A. Burke*, Interview (*Joseph E. O'Connor*), January 20, 1967, p. 6.
80 JFK, Oral History Programme, Transcript, *Arleigh A. Burke*, Interview (*Joseph E. O'Connor*), January 20, 1967, p. 7; JFK, Oral History Programme, Transcript, *Arleigh A. Burke*, Interview (*Joseph E. O'Connor*), January 20, 1967, p. 7.
81 JFK, RHPP-003-010, Memorandum for the Record by the Director of the Bureau of Intelligence and Research (Hilsman) Saigon, January 1963. Vietnam: Hilsman trip, December 1962–January 1963: Basic report and "Eyes Only" annex. Roger Hilsman Personal Papers, Countries Files, 1961–1964, Series 1, Box 3, p. 1.
82 JFK, RHPP-003-009, Memorandum From the Director of the Bureau of Intelligence and Research (Hilsman) and Michael V. Forrestal of the National Security Council Staff to the President, Washington, January 25, 1963, Annex, p. 2.
83 JFK, RHPP-003-009, Memorandum From the Director of the Bureau of Intelligence and Research (Hilsman) and Michael V. Forrestal of the National Security Council Staff to the President, Washington, January 25, 1963, Annex, p. 2.
84 JFK, RHPP-003-011, Memorandum From the Assistant Secretary of State for Far Eastern Affairs (Hilsman) to the Secretary of State Washington, April 1963. Vietnam: Hilsman trip, December 1962–January 1963: Basic report and "Eyes Only" annex. Roger Hilsman Personal Papers, Countries Files, 1961–1964, Series 1, Box 3, p. 2.
85 JFK, RHPP-003-011, Memorandum From the Assistant Secretary of State for Far Eastern Affairs (Hilsman) to the Secretary of State Washington, April 1963. Vietnam: Hilsman trip, December 1962–January 1963: Basic report and "Eyes Only" annex. Roger Hilsman Personal Papers, Countries Files, 1961–1964, Series 1, Box 3.
86 Phillips, 'Rufus Phillips on Why Vietnam Matters: An Eyewitness Account of Lessons Not Learned', Time 47:11.
87 JFK, RHPP-003-010, Memorandum from the Director of the Bureau of Intelligence and Research (Hilsman) and Michael V. Forrestal of the National Security Council Staff to the President (annex), Washington, January 25, 1963. Vietnam: Hilsman trip, December 1962–January 1963: Basic report and "Eyes Only" annex. Roger Hilsman Personal Papers, Countries Files, 1961–1964, Series 1, Box 3, Annex, p. 1.
88 JFK, RHPP-003-010, Memorandum from the Director of the Bureau of Intelligence and Research (Hilsman) and Michael V. Forrestal of the National Security Council Staff to the President (annex), Washington, January 25, 1963. Vietnam: Hilsman trip, December 1962–January 1963: Basic report and "Eyes Only" annex. Roger Hilsman Personal Papers, Countries Files, 1961–1964, Series 1, Box 3, Annex, p. 1.
89 LBJ, Transcript, William E. Colby Oral History, Interview I (by Ted Gittinger), June 06, 1981, Internet Copy, p. 11.
90 SNIE, *50-61 Outlook in Mainland Southeast Asia,* 28 March 1961, p. 8.
91 See the Literature Review for examples of this criticism.
92 JFK, JFKNSF-203-003, Letter From the President's Military Representative (Taylor) to the President, [Attachment 2] Paper Prepared by the Members of the Taylor Mission Washington, Vietnam: Subjects: Taylor Report, 3 November 1961, Tab C, p. 8; *FRUS 1961–63, Volume I: No 7. Remarks by the Chief of the Military Assistance Advisory Group in Vietnam (McGarr), January 30, 1961.*
93 JFK, JFKNSF-203-003, Letter From the President's Military Representative (Taylor) to the President, [Attachment 2] Paper Prepared by the Members of the Taylor Mission Washington, Vietnam: Subjects: Taylor Report, 3 November 1961,Tab C, p. 8; *FRUS 1961–63, Volume I: No 7. Remarks by the Chief of the Military Assistance Advisory Group in Vietnam (McGarr), January 30, 1961.*
94 JFK, JFKNSF-203-003, Letter From the President's Military Representative (Taylor) to the President, [Attachment 2] Paper Prepared by the Members of the Taylor Mission Washington, Vietnam: Subjects: Taylor Report, 3 November 1961, Tab C, p. 7.
95 JFK, JFKNSF-203-003, Letter From the President's Military Representative (Taylor) to the President, [Attachment 2] Paper Prepared by the Members of the Taylor Mission Washington, Vietnam: Subjects: Taylor Report, 3 November 1961, Tab C, p. 7.
96 JFK, JFKNSF-203-003, Letter From the President's Military Representative (Taylor) to the President, [Attachment 2] Paper Prepared by the Members of the Taylor Mission Washington, Vietnam: Subjects: Taylor Report, 3 November 1961, Tab C, p. 7.
97 LBJ, Transcript, Douglas Pike Oral History Interview I, June 04, 1981, p. 19.
98 *FRUS 1961–63, Volume III: No 211. Telegram From Malcolm Browne of the Associated Press, David Halberstam of The New York Times, Peter Kalischer of CBS News, and Neil Sheehan of United Press International to the President Saigon, July 7, 1963, 10:20 a.m.*
99 Catton, *Diem's Final Failure,* pp. 41–42.
100 Unknown Correspondent, Saigon, 'Vietnam Dilutes its Democracy', *The Times,* 1 July 1963.
101 Pearce, *RM-4692-1-ARPA – Evolution of a Vietnamese Village – Part II: The Past, August 1945 to April 1965,* p. 18; Pearce, *RM-4692-1-ARPA – Evolution of a Vietnamese Village – Part II: The Past, August 1945 to April 1965,* p. 19.
102 Phillips, 'Rufus Phillips on Why Vietnam Matters: An Eyewitness Account of Lessons Not Learned', Time: 45:23.
103 Pearce, *RM-4692-1-ARPA – Evolution of a Vietnamese Village – Part II: The Past, August 1945 to April 1965,* p. 19.
104 Pearce, *RM-4692-1-ARPA,* p. 18.
105 JFK, JFKNSF-193-004, Memorandum From the President's Deputy Special Assistant for National Security Affairs (Rostow) to the President's Special Assistant for National Security Affairs (Bundy), Washington, January 30, 1961, Papers of John F Kennedy. Presidential Papers, National Security Files, Country Files, Vietnam, General, 1961: January–March, Box 193.
106 LBJ, Transcript, Elbridge Durbrow Oral History Interview, Interview I (by Ted Gittinger), June 03, 1981, Internet Copy, p. 47.
107 JFK, JFKNSF-203-003, Letter From the President's Military Representative (Taylor) to the President Appendix B Memorandum From the Chairman of the Vietnam Task Force (Cottrell) to the President's Military Representative (Taylor) Washington, October 27, 1961. Vietnam: Subjects: Taylor Report, 3 November 1961, p. 3.
108 SNIE, *50-61 Outlook in Mainland Southeast Asia,* p. 8; SNIE, *50-61 Outlook in Mainland Southeast Asia,* p. 8.
109 LBJ, Transcript, Frederick Nolting Oral History Interview, Interview I (by Ted Gittinger), November 11, 1982, Internet Copy, p. 14.
110 Unknown Diplomatic Correspondent, 'British Mission to South Vietnam', *The Times,* 18 September 1961.
111 Moyar, *Triumph Forsaken: The Vietnam War, 1954–1965* (US Army Heritage and Education Centre – Perspectives: December 12, 2007), Time 23:34.
Available: http://www.carlisle.army.mil/ahec/media/video_archive.cfm; Nagl, *Learning to Eat Soup with a Knife,* p. 122.
112 Higgins, 'The Misapplication of the Malayan Counterinsurgency Model to the Strategic Hamlet Program', p. 59.
113 JFK, JFKNSF-203-003, Letter From the President's Military Representative (Taylor) to the President, [Attachment 2] Paper Prepared by the Members of the Taylor Mission Washington, Vietnam: Subjects: Taylor Report, 3 November 1961, Tab C, p. 7.
114 JFK, RHPP-003-011, Memorandum From the Assistant Secretary of State for Far Eastern Affairs (Hilsman) to the Secretary of State Washington, April 1963. Vietnam: Hilsman trip, December 1962–January 1963: Basic report and "Eyes Only" annex. Roger Hilsman Personal Papers, Countries Files, 1961–1964, Series 1, Box 3.
115 JFK, RHPP-003-011, Memorandum From the Assistant Secretary of State for Far Eastern Affairs (Hilsman) to the Secretary of State Washington, April 1963. Vietnam: Hilsman trip, December 1962–January 1963: Basic report and "Eyes Only" annex. Roger Hilsman Personal Papers, Countries Files, 1961–1964, Series 1, Box 3.
116 Thompson, *Defeating Communist Insurgency,* p. 141.
117 Thompson, *Defeating Communist Insurgency,* p. 141.
118 Department of Defence, US-Vietnam Relations 1945–1967, Volume IV. B. 2, Evolution of the War, Strategic Hamlet Programme 1961–1963, Box 3, 270/80/9/7 (Washington D.C.: National Archives and Records Administration, declassified 2011), p.ii.
119 TTU, 23970128002, Report, A Report on Counter-insurgency in Vietnam, 20 July 1962, Folder 28, Box 01, Rufus Phillips Collection; TTU, 23970129002, Summary, An Informal Appreciation of The Status of The Strategic Hamlet Programme – Prepared by USOM Rural Affairs, 01 June 1963, Folder 29, Box 01, Rufus Phillips Collection; TTU, 23970129001, Summary, Second Informal Appreciation of The Status of The Strategic Hamlet Programme, 01 September 1963.
120 *FRUS 1961–63, Volume III: No 8. Memorandum for the Record by the Director of the Bureau of Intelligence and Research (Hilsman) Saigon, January 1963; FRUS 1961–63, Volume III: No 36. Memorandum of Conversation Between the Assistant Secretary of State for Far Eastern Affairs (Harriman) and the Chief of Staff, United States Army (Wheeler), Department of State Washington, February 9, 1963, 11:30 a.m.; FRUS 1961–63, Volume III: No 4. Memorandum for the Record*

by the Director of the Bureau of Intelligence and Research (Hilsman) Saigon, January 2, 1963.
121 TTU, 23970130014, Memorandum from Rufus Phillips to Colonel Hoang Van Lac – re: Consolidation of The Strategic Hamlet Program in the Delta, 20 July 1962, 04 September 1963 Box 01, Folder 30. Rufus Phillips Collection.
122 TTU, 23970129002, Summary, An Informal Appreciation of The Status of The Strategic Hamlet Programme – Prepared by USOM Rural Affairs, 01 June 1963, Folder 29, Box 01, Rufus Phillips Collection; TTU, 23970129001, Summary, Second Informal Appreciation of The Status of The Strategic Hamlet Programme, 01 September 1963.
123 TTU, 23970128002, Report, A Report on Counter-insurgency in Vietnam, 20 July 1962, p. 1.
124 TTU, 23970128002, Report, A Report on Counter-insurgency in Vietnam, 20 July 1962, p. 1.
125 TTU, 23970129001, Summary, Second Informal Appreciation of The Status of The Strategic Hamlet Programme, 01 September 1963, p. 1.
126 TTU, 23970129001, Summary, Second Informal Appreciation of The Status of The Strategic Hamlet Programme, 01 September 1963, p. 4.
127 TTU, 23970129001, Summary, Second Informal Appreciation of The Status of The Strategic Hamlet Programme, 01 September 1963, p. 5.
128 TTU, 23970129001, Summary, Second Informal Appreciation of The Status of The Strategic Hamlet Programme, 01 September 1963, pp. 3–4.
129 TTU, 23970129001, Summary, Second Informal Appreciation of The Status of The Strategic Hamlet Programme, 01 September 1963, p. 6.
130 TTU, 23970129001, Summary, Second Informal Appreciation of The Status of The Strategic Hamlet Programme, 01 September 1963, p. 7.
131 TTU, 23970129001, Summary, Second Informal Appreciation of The Status of The Strategic Hamlet Programme, 01 September 1963, p. 8.
132 TTU, 23970129001, Summary, Second Informal Appreciation of The Status of The Strategic Hamlet Programme, 01 September 1963, p. 8; TTU, 23970129001, Summary, Second Informal Appreciation of The Status of The Strategic Hamlet Programme, 01 September 1963, p. 9.
133 TTU, 23970129001, Summary, Second Informal Appreciation of The Status of The Strategic Hamlet Programme, 01 September 1963, p. 21.
134 TTU, 23970129001, Summary, Second Informal Appreciation of The Status of The Strategic Hamlet Programme, 01 September 1963, p. 15.
135 TTU, 23970129001, Summary, Second Informal Appreciation of The Status of The Strategic Hamlet Programme, 01 September 1963, p. 27; TTU, 23970129001, Summary, Second Informal Appreciation of The Status of The Strategic Hamlet Programme, 01 September 1963, p. 26.
136 TTU, 0720613001, The Strategic Hamlet Programme in Kien Hoa Province, South Vietnam: A Case Study of Counter-insurgency, 11 May 1965, Folder 13, Box 06, John Donnell Collection, p. 26.
137 TTU, 23970130040, Draft – The Story of America's Counterinsurgency Efforts in Vietnam in the Early 1960's, January 1966, Folder 30, Box 01, Rufus Phillips Collection, p. 9.
138 TTU, 23970130040, Draft – The Story of America's Counterinsurgency Efforts in Vietnam in the Early 1960's, January 1966, Folder 30, Box 01, Rufus Phillips Collection, p. 9.
139 TTU, 23970130040, Draft – The Story of America's Counterinsurgency Efforts in Vietnam in the Early 1960's, January 1966, Folder 30, Box 01, Rufus Phillips Collection, p. 9.
140 *FRUS 1961–63, Volume II: No 183. Telegram From the Embassy in India to the Department of State New Delhi, May 5, 1962–4 p.m.*
141 TTU, 23970130040, Draft – The Story of America's Counterinsurgency Efforts in Vietnam in the Early 1960's, January 1966, Folder 30, Box 01, Rufus Phillips Collection, p. 2; JFK, RHPP–003–009, Memorandum From the Director of the Bureau of Intelligence and Research (Hilsman) and Michael V. Forrestal of the National Security Council Staff to the President, Washington, January 25, 1963. Vietnam: Hilsman trip, December 1962–January 1963: Basic report and "Eyes Only" annex. Roger Hilsman Personal Papers, Countries Files, 1961–1964, Series 1, Box 3, p. 17.
142 TTU, 23970130040, Draft – The Story of America's Counterinsurgency Efforts in Vietnam in the Early 1960's, p. 36.
143 TTU, 23970204013, Draft – re: Letter to President Diem, 12 September 1963, Folder 04, Box 02, Rufus Phillips Collection, p. 3; *FRUS 1961–63, Volume II: No 323. Senator Mansfield's Visit to Vietnam and Subsequent Report; Visits and Reports by Johnson and Heavner December 1962 Memorandum of Conversation Saigon, December 1, 1962, 11:30 a.m.*
144 *FRUS 1961–63, Volume II: No 323. Senator Mansfield's Visit to Vietnam and Subsequent Report; Visits and Reports by Johnson and Heavner December 1962 Memorandum of Conversation Saigon, December 1, 1962, 11:30 a.m.*
145 TTU, 23970204013, Draft – re: Letter to President Diem, 12 September 1963, Folder 04, Box 02, Rufus Phillips Collection, p. 3; *FRUS 1961–63, Volume II: No 323. Senator Mansfield's Visit to Vietnam and Subsequent Report; Visits and Reports by Johnson and Heavner December 1962 Memorandum of Conversation Saigon, December 1, 1962, 11:30 a.m.*
146 JFK, RHPP–003–006, A Strategic Concept for South Vietnam, p. 7.
147 JFK, RHPP–003–006, A Strategic Concept for South Vietnam, p. 7.
148 *FRUS 1961–63, Volume I: No 7. Remarks by the Chief of the Military Assistance Advisory Group in Vietnam (McGarr), January 30, 1961; FRUS 1961–63, Volume I: No 7. Remarks by the Chief of the Military Assistance Advisory Group in Vietnam (McGarr), January 30, 1961.*
149 TTU, 2262905006, Report: NLF Memo On Press In Saigon, 04 March 1962, Folder 05, Box 29, Douglas Pike Collection: Unit 03 – The Press and the War, p. 1.
150 *FRUS 1961–63, Volume I: No 7. Remarks by the Chief of the Military Assistance Advisory Group in Vietnam (McGarr), January 30, 1961; FRUS 1961–63, Volume I: No 7. Remarks by the Chief of the Military Assistance Advisory Group in Vietnam (McGarr), January 30, 1961.*
151 TTU, 2262905006, Report: NLF Memo On Press In Saigon, 04 March 1962, Folder 05, Box 29, Douglas Pike Collection: Unit 03 – The Press and the War, p. 1.
152 TTU, 2262905006, Report: NLF Memo On Press In Saigon, 04 March 1962, Folder 05, Box 29, Douglas Pike Collection: Unit 03 – The Press and the War, p. 1
153 JFK, RHPP–003–009, Memorandum From the Director of the Bureau of Intelligence and Research (Hilsman) and Michael V. Forrestal of the National Security Council Staff to the President, Washington, January 25, 1963, p. 17.
154 *FRUS 1961–63, Volume III: No 26. Report by an Investigative Team Headed by the Chief of Staff, United States Army (Wheeler), to the Joint Chiefs of Staff, Washington, January 1963.*
155 See Ruane, *War and Revolution in Vietnam*, p. 47.
156 Ruane, *War and Revolution in Vietnam*, p. 47.
157 Ruane, *War and Revolution in Vietnam*, pp. 48–50.
158 Pike, *Viet Cong – The Organization and Techniques*, p. 73; see also Ruane, *War and Revolution in Vietnam*, pp. 39–40, 45–47 for further details.
159 Pike, *Viet Cong –The Organization and Techniques*, p. 73.
160 French, *The British Way in Counter-insurgency*, p. 219; J.S. Corum, *Bad Strategies – How Major Powers Fail in Counterinsurgency* (Minneapolis: Zenith Press, 2008), p. 26; Corum, *Bad Strategies – How Major Powers Fail in Counterinsurgency* (Minneapolis: Zenith Press, 2008), p. 26.
161 TTU, 23970206004, Booklet – South Vietnam CPSVN Comprehensive Plan, Box 02, Folder 06, Rufus Phillips Collection, p. 2.
162 Phillips, 'Rufus Phillips on Why Vietnam Matters: An Eyewitness Account of Lessons Not Learned', Time 1:01:10.
163 Phillips, 'Rufus Phillips on Why Vietnam Matters: An Eyewitness Account of Lessons Not Learned', Time: 33:20.
164 *FRUS 1961–63, Volume IV: No 321. Memorandum of Discussion at the Special Meeting on Vietnam, Honolulu, November 20, 1963.*
165 *FRUS 1961–63, Volume IV: No 347. Memorandum From the Assistant Secretary of State for Far Eastern Affairs (Hilsman) to the Secretary of State, Washington, December 5, 1963.*
166 Thompson, *Make for the Hills*, p. 144; Thompson, *Make for the Hills*, p. 144.
167 *FRUS 1961–63, Volume IV: No 351. Telegram From the Department of State to the Embassy in Vietnam, Washington, December 6, 1963, 10:29 p.m.*
168 *FRUS 1961–63, Volume IV: No 351. Telegram From the Department of State to the Embassy in Vietnam, Washington, December 6, 1963, 10:29 p.m.*
169 *FRUS 1961–63, Volume IV: No 372. Report by the Joint Chiefs of Staff's Special Assistant for Counterinsurgency and Special Activities (Krulak), Washington, December 21, 1963.*
170 *FRUS 1961–63, Volume IV: 349. Memorandum From the Chairman of the Central Intelligence Agency's Working Group on Vietnam (Cooper) to the Director of Central Intelligence (McCone), Washington, December 6, 1963.*
171 *FRUS 1961–63, Volume IV: No 309. Telegram From the Embassy in Vietnam to the Department of State – Saigon, November 11, 1963, 6 p.m.*
172 *FRUS 1961–63, Volume IV: No 352. Telegram From the Embassy in Vietnam to the Department of State – Saigon, December 7, 1963, midnight.*
173 *FRUS 1961–63, Volume IV: No 352. Telegram From the Embassy in Vietnam to the Department of State – Saigon, December 7, 1963, midnight.*
174 *FRUS 1961–63, Volume IV: No 364. Minutes of Meeting of the Special Group for Counterinsurgency, Washington, December 12, 1963, 2 p.m.*
175 Thompson, *Make for the Hills*, p. 142; Thompson, *Make for the Hills*, p. 142; Moyar, *Triumph Forsaken*, p. 285.
176 *FRUS 1964–68, Volume I: No 84. Memorandum From the Secretary of Defence (McNamara) to the President – Washington, March 16, 1964.*
177 *FRUS 1964–68, Volume I: No 84. Memorandum From the Secretary of Defence (McNamara) to the President – Washington, March 16, 1964.*
178 *FRUS 1964–68, Volume I: No 84. Memorandum From the Secretary of Defence (McNamara) to the President – Washington, March 16, 1964.*
179 *FRUS 1964–68, Volume I: No 84. Memorandum From the Secretary of Defence (McNamara) to the President – Washington, March 16, 1964.*
180 *FRUS 1964–68, Volume I: No 84. Memorandum From the Secretary of Defence (McNamara) to the President – Washington, March 16, 1964.*
181 See Chapter One and JFK, JFKNSF–330–002, NSAM 52, re: Report of the Vietnam Task Force, Annex 1, p. 2 for further details.
182 TTU, 23970108003, Memo, Rural Affairs Memorandum – Concept, Principle and Program of New Rural Life Hamlets, Ap Tan – Sinh, Box 01, Folder 08, Rufus Phillips Collection.
183 TTU, 21470124001, Memorandum from Ogden Williams to All USOM Regional and Provincial Representatives and Attachment – re: New Rural Life Hamlet Policy, Vincent Puritano Collection, Box 01, Folder 24, p. 1.
184 TTU, 23970108003, Memo, Rural Affairs Memorandum – Concept, Principle and Program of New Rural Life Hamlets, Ap Tan – Sinh, pp. 2–3.
185 TTU, 21470124001, Memorandum from Ogden Williams to All USOM Regional and Provincial Representatives and Attachment – re: New Rural Life Hamlet Policy, p. 1; TTU, 21470124001, Memorandum from Ogden Williams to All USOM Regional and Provincial Representatives and Attachment – re: New Rural Life Hamlet Policy, p. 1.
186 TTU, 21470124001, Memorandum from Ogden Williams to All USOM Regional and Provincial Representatives and Attachment – re: New Rural Life Hamlet Policy, p. 1; TTU, 23970108003, Memo, Rural Affairs Memorandum – Concept, Principle and Program of New Rural Life Hamlets, Ap Tan – Sinh, p. 3.
187 TTU, 21470124001, Memorandum from Ogden Williams to All USOM Regional and Provincial Representatives and Attachment – re: New Rural Life Hamlet Policy, p. 1.
188 Department of Defence, US–Vietnam Relations 1945–1967, Volume IV. B. 2, Evolution of the War, Strategic Hamlet Programme 1961–1963, Box 3, 270/80/9/7 (Washington D.C.: National Archives and Records Administration, declassified 2011), p.ii.
189 Thompson, *Make for the Hills*, p. 143.

190 See for example, Halberstam, *The Making of a Quagmire* and Thompson, *Defeating Communist Insurgency* for the Orthodox view or Phillips, *Why Vietnam Matters* and Moyar, *Triumph Forsaken* for Revisionist perspectives.
191 For further details see Neese, & O'Donnell, *Prelude to Tragedy: Vietnam 1960–1965.*
192 See work by Leahy, 'Why Did the Strategic Hamlet Programme Fail?' or Higgins, 'The Misapplication of the Malayan Counterinsurgency Model to the Strategic Hamlet Program'.
193 Some examples of these reports include W.P.Davison, & J.J. Zasloff, *RM–4983–1–ISA/ARPA – A Profile of Viet Cong Cadres* (Santa Monica: RAND Corporation, 1966); J.C. Donnell, *14436–IBA/ARPA – Viet Cong Recruitment: Why and How Men Join* (Santa Monica: RAND Corporation, 1966); R.M. Pearce, *RM–4692–1–ARPA – Evolution of a Vietnamese Village – Part II: The Past, August 1945 to April 1965* (Santa Monica: RAND Corporation, 1966); J.C. Donnell, & G.C. Hickey, *RM–3208–ARPA – The Vietnamese 'Strategic Hamlets': A Preliminary Report* (Santa Monica: RAND Corporation, 1962).
194 See Donnell, & Hickey, *RM–3208–ARPA – The Vietnamese 'Strategic Hamlets': A Preliminary Report.*
195 See TTU, 23970129001, Summary, Second Informal Appreciation of The Status of The Strategic Hamlet Programme, 01 September 1963, pp. 24–27.
196 See Hilsman, *To Move a Nation* or Ives, *US Special Forces and Counterinsurgency in Vietnam.*
197 Thompson, *Defeating Communist Insurgency,* p. 71.
198 See Phillips, *Why Vietnam Matters,* p. 139 or TTU, 23970328001, Interview Transcript of Rufus Phillips by Charles Stuart Kennedy [Part I], p. 42.
199 JFK, RHPP–003–010, Memorandum for the Record by the Director of the Bureau of Intelligence and Research (Hilsman). Vietnam: Hilsman trip, December 1962–January 1963: Basic report and "Eyes Only" annex. Roger Hilsman Personal Papers, Countries Files, 1961–1964, Series 1, Box 3, p. 1.
200 See pp. 62–67 of this book for details.
201 See JFK, RHPP–003–010, Memorandum for the Record by the Director of the Bureau of Intelligence and Research (Hilsman). Vietnam: Hilsman trip, December 1962–January 1963: Basic report and "Eyes Only" annex. Roger Hilsman Personal Papers, Countries Files, 1961–1964, Series 1, Box 3, p. 1
202 See JFK, Oral History Programme, Transcript, *Arleigh A. Burke*, January 20, 1967 for further details.
203 See Thompson, *Defeating Communist Insurgency* or Asprey, *War in the Shadows.*
204 See TTU, 23970129001, Summary, Second Informal Appreciation of The Status of The Strategic Hamlet Programme.
205 TTU, 23970129001, Summary, Second Informal Appreciation of The Status of The Strategic Hamlet Programme, pp. 23–27.
206 Thompson, *Defeating Communist Insurgency.*
207 Thompson, *Defeating Communist Insurgency,* p. 29; Halberstam, *The Making of a Quagmire,* p. 36.
208 See Fraleigh, 'Counterinsurgency in South Vietnam – The Real Story', in Neese, & O'Donnell, (eds), *Prelude to Tragedy: Vietnam 1960–1965* for details.
209 See JFK, RHPP–003–009, Memorandum From the Director of the Bureau of Intelligence and Research (Hilsman) and Michael V. Forrestal of the National Security Council Staff to the President, Washington, January 25, 1963, p. 3 or TTU, 23130005003, Communist assessment of South Vietnam scene: 1/62–6/63, 01 January 1963, p. 13.
210 TTU, 2120208021, The Destruction of the Enemy's Strategic Hamlet Programme, p. 2.
211 See Halberstam, *The Making of a Quagmire.*
212 See TTU, 23970129001, Summary, Second Informal Appreciation of The Status of The Strategic Hamlet Programme.
213 See Halberstam, *The Making of a Quagmire,* p. 38 and pp. 107–108 for examples of this attitude.
214 See P.E. Catton, *Diem's Final Failure: Prelude to America's War in Vietnam* (Lawrence: University of Kansas, 2002); R. Phillips, *Why Vietnam Matters: An Eyewitness Account of Lessons not Learned* (Annapolis, Naval Institute Press, 2008) and E. Miller, *Misalliance: Ngo Dinh Diem, the United States, and the Fall of South Vietnam* (Cambridge: Harvard University Press, 2013).

ABOUT THE AUTHOR

Dr Darren Poole is a lecturer in Military History at the University of Chester and University Centre, Shrewsbury. He specialises in counterinsurgency, the Vietnam War and general American history. Dr Poole has degrees in History, Military History, Geography and Education and he has been teaching for over 25 years. His current research examines the 'unheard voices' of conflict. These include, for example, the peasants caught in a crossfire in South Vietnam and the views of the Viet Cong themselves. Dr Poole aims to present research that complements and challenges the accepted historical narrative; in many cases his work reveals the cruelty of the 'insurgents' towards their own people and provides a 'moral' imperative for Western intervention. Dr Poole is currently working on a further book that examines the violence and terror of the Viet Cong themselves.